Starmaking

Representation and Mind
Hilary Putnam and Ned Block, editors

Starmaking
Realism, Anti-Realism, and Irrealism

edited by Peter J. McCormick

A Bradford Book
The MIT Press
Cambridge, Massachusetts
London, England

© 1996 Massachusetts Institute of Technology

This book was set in Sabon by Graphic Composition, Inc., Athens, Georgia. Printed on recycled paper and bound in the United States of America.

Library of Congress Cataloging-in-Publication Data

Starmaking : realism, anti-realism, and irrealism / edited by Peter J. McCormick.
   p.   cm. — (Representation and mind)
   "A Bradford book."
   Includes bibliographical references and index.
   ISBN 0-262-13320-2 (hc : alk. paper)
   1. Realism. 2. Pluralism. 3. Knowledge, Theory of. 4. Ontology.
5. Goodman, Nelson. 6. Putnam, Hilary. 7. Scheffler, Israel. 8. Hempel, Carl
Gustav, 1905–   . I. McCormick, Peter (Peter J.) II. Series.
B835.S835   1996
149'.2—dc20   95-48929
                                                                    CIP

Contents

Preface

The purpose of this collection is to bring together important yet widely separated materials published over the last thirty-five years that provide a background for understanding ongoing philosophical discussion of central problems of metaphysics and epistemology. At issue are such contrasts as realism versus idealism, absolutism versus relativism, and monism versus pluralism. The focus is on the relation between world-versions and the world, or worlds, answering to them.

What distinguishes this collection is its very sharp focus on the evolution in the understanding of these difficult matters since 1960 among four of the most important participants in this continuing reflection—the initiator of the discussion, Nelson Goodman, his two Harvard colleagues, Hilary Putnam and Israel Scheffler, and his long-time friend and philosophical associate, Carl Hempel. Although others continue to write on the central issues here, this collection brings together the central figures in the debate since its beginnings and follows closely its still developing form and substance.

Part I, "Backgrounds," provides one of Goodman's early statements, from 1960, of his still developing reflection on pluralism: what he referred to as "the ways the world is." Putnam relates some contemporary reflections on these issues to the early modern period, and Scheffler provides a close look at the Neurath–Schlick debate about a dilemma between coherence and certainty.

In part II, "Worldmaking," two of Goodman's most important elaborations of his earlier views, both taken from his 1978 book, *Ways of Worldmaking*, are reprinted. A very detailed set of reactions to these formulations can then be found in part III, "Reactions," which brings together in one place the papers from an American Philosophical Association Symposium on *Ways of Worldmaking*. Included here as well is Goodman's set of replies to each of the papers by Putnam, Hempel, and Scheffler.

Part IV, "Elaborations," provides a sharper focus on just one of various issues left outstanding at the end of the symposium, specifically on the difference between what can properly be said to make worlds and what can properly be said to make versions of worlds right. Goodman provides here a short set of comments to which Scheffler replies. Goodman then offers a rejoinder to Scheffler.

This sharp focus is now opened up in part V, "Responses," where Scheffler contributes a previously unpublished paper with a view to highlighting his continuing concerns not so much with pluralism or relativism as with what he calls a certain "voluntarism" with respect to the making of worlds. Next Putnam, in a wide-ranging recent paper taken from his Gifford Lectures contrasts several of the key issues in these ongoing debates with some work in recent continental philosophy. Goodman closes the collection in part VI, "Beyond Realism and Anti-Realism," with a new set of replies and comments.

Acknowledgments

I thank each of the contributors and their publishers for permission to reprint here work originally published elsewhere.

In particular, I thank Nelson Goodman, Carl Hempel, Hilary Putnam, and Israel Scheffler for permission to reprint previously published pieces for which they hold copyright.

I thank the Hackett Publishing Company for permission to reprint Nelson Goodman's pieces, "The Way the World Is" from his *Problems and Projects* (1960), pp. 24–32; "Words, Works, Worlds" and "On Rightness of Rendering" from his *Ways of Worldmaking* (1978), pp. 1–22 and 109–140; and Israel Scheffler's pieces, "Epistemology of Objectivity" from his *Science and Subjectivity*, 2d ed. (1982), pp. 91–124; and his "Reply to Goodman," as I have called it, from his *Inquiries* (1986), pp. 82–86.

I thank Harvard University Press for permission to reprint Nelson Goodman's pieces, "On Starmaking" and "Notes on the Well-Made World" from his *Of Mind and Other Matters* (1984), pp. 30–39 and 39–44; and Hilary Putnam's "Irrealism and Deconstruction" from his *Renewing Philosophy* (1992), pp. 108–133, 215–219.

I thank *The Journal of Philosophy* for permission to reprint Hilary Putnam's "Reflections on Goodman's *Ways of Worldmaking*," 76 (1980), 603–618.

I thank *Synthese* for permission to reprint Carl G. Hempel's "Comments on Goodman's *Ways of Worldmaking*," 45 (1980), 193–199; and Israel Scheffler's "The Wonderful Worlds of Goodman," 45 (1980), 201–209.

I thank Open Court Publishing Company for permission to reprint Hilary Putnam's "Is There Still Anything to Say about Reality and Truth" from his *The Many Faces of Realism* (1987), pp. 3–22.

I am especially grateful to Nelson Goodman, Hilary Putnam, and Israel Scheffler for their good advice and many kindnesses during my two-year stay at Harvard as a Visiting Scholar in Philosophy, and to the Killam Foundation of the Canada Council for its award of a two-year Research Fellowship that helped make my stay possible.

Introduction

Peter McCormick

Two Situations

One way to get an initial sense of the key issues that cluster around the title of this collection, the unusual expression, "starmaking," is to high-light several recurring examples in these chapters. To begin, consider two statements. The first goes: "The earth is at rest." And the second goes: "The earth is in motion."

These two statements clearly conflict. We want to say that both cannot be right in the same respect. And yet we also want to say that each captures rather well certain familiar experiences, whether of the earth under our feet in our gardens or of the earth when viewed from a satellite on our TVs. Each statement, that is, has strong intuitive appeal. How then to reconcile their apparent conflict?

Various options, as Nelson Goodman points out in several of his works included here, are on hand. In the interests of reconciliation we may, for instance, try to explicate the respective theoretical standpoints from which such statements are made. Thus, we may say that, with respect to a geocentric standpoint, the earth indeed is at rest. But, with respect to a heliocentric standpoint, the earth is indeed in motion. The problem is that the relativizations of these conflicting statements are weaker than the originals, which assert that the earth, respectively, either moves or does not move.

Despite the care and thoroughness of further investigations, the two conflicting statements we started with turn out to be reconcilable neither by simple relativization to a particular system, nor by restriction of their range of application, nor even by confinement of scope. Confronted with the persistent difficulty of reconciling such statements, Goodman suggests that they are true in different worlds. He writes: "The realist will resist the conclusion that there is no world; the idealist will resist the conclusion that all conflicting versions describe different worlds. As for me, I find these views equally delightful and equally deplorable." Goodman adds a remark that Carl G. Hempel will challenge: "For, after all, the difference between them is purely conventional."

We can, however, already see more generally that reconciling not just conflicting statements but conflicting truths seems to require further reflection on some of the central interconnections between certain conceptions we have of the way the world is and those we have about the truth or falsity of whatever we may say about the way the world is. Perhaps we can further narrow our focus.

Two Countings

Another recurring example in this collection takes up some of the issues about the world and truth in terms of the respective ways in which we talk about each.

Consider two additional situations. We walk into a Polish colleague's small home study and notice that, despite the study's very modest size, our friend has managed to furnish it comfortably with three pieces—a desk, a chair, and a large couch. In a moment of philosophical distraction, however, we may, with Hilary Putnam (see chapter 2), wonder as to just how many objects (never mind how much furniture) our colleague's home study contains. The question can, when we think twice, be surprisingly difficult to answer.

We may of course answer immediately that the study contains, quite simply, three objects just as it contains, quite simply, three pieces of furniture. But then we remember our Polish colleague's preoccupations with the calculus of parts and wholes. For, when viewed from his professional perspective, while the study indeed contains just three pieces of furniture, it may just as properly although not so simply be said to contain seven objects as three. How so?

We may count the three individual pieces of furniture as three objects—x1, x2, and x3. But, on adopting our colleague's habitual assumption of a simplified mereological perspective (that is, a perspective comprising the Polish logician S. Lezniewski's calculus of parts and whole), we may count the three individual pieces of furniture as seven objects—x1, x2, x3, x1 + x2, x1 + x3, x2 + x3, x1 + x2 + x3.

We may then properly say that either the study contains three objects or seven objects. We may say three objects in light of our ordinary everyday commonsense version of things. Alternately, we may say seven objects in the light of our Polish colleague's not-so-ordinary mereological version of things.

Are we to understand then that there may be as many worlds as there are versions, that just as there are heliocentric and geocentric versions so too there are heliocentric and geocentric worlds, that just as there are commonsense and mereological versions so too there are commonsense and mereological worlds?

But what about truth? Can we say—and, if so, on what warrant?—that, just as the heliocentric and geocentric versions cannot both be true in the same world, so too the commonsense and mereological versions cannot both be true in the same world either?

Constellations and Stars

Consider a third and final recurring example in these chapters. The initial question here is whether what makes stars is the same thing as what makes constellations.

Suppose your six-year-old daughter asks, "What's that in the sky?" and you answer without any hesitation, "That's the Big Dipper." Your daughter goes on, as children often do, to ask more questions, for example, "Who made the Big Dipper?"

When we try to answer this second question, we may find ourselves hesitating. Are we to answer, "Nature made the Big Dipper"? Or are we to answer, "We made the Big Dipper"? Our hesitation comes from the fact that we already anticipate more questions, for example, either something like "Well, what is Nature?" or "How did we make the Big

Dipper?" And trying to answer these questions may keep us up past our bedtime.

Nelson Goodman argues that we make the Big Dipper when we pick out certain configurations of stars by constructing some version of how things are. What makes these configurations the Big Dipper then is not Nature at all but some version we make of things. It is we, and not Nature, who make the Big Dipper.

The question then arises as to just what makes not the configurations of stars we call in some version of things "the Big Dipper" but the stars themselves. We want to say of course that, whereas we make the Big Dipper, Nature makes the stars that comprise the Big Dipper. But here Goodman claims that what makes them "stars" is not Nature at all but some version of Nature.

This may seem confusing. Here is the way Goodman puts the matter as recently as 1987, that is, after some of his most recent reformulations published in *Reconceptions in Philosophy* (Hackett: Indianapolis, 1988): "Indeed, according to any of our trusted familiar world-versions, a star came much earlier than any version. Such a version, call it W, politely puts its own origin much later than the origin of the star—that is, much earlier *in this version's own time-ordering.* Yet according to a quite different version, call it V, . . . the star and everything else come into being only *via* a version. . . . there is no ready-made world waiting to be labeled. There is no absolute time. In the time of W, the star comes first; in the time of V, the version comes first. Which is right? The answer is 'both'" (see chapter 12).

There are two issues here, two questions to be answered. The first goes, "What makes the stars 'stars'?" The answer here is: "a particular version of things." And the second question goes, "What then makes a particular version 'right'?" The answer to that question is, as this collection shows, still very much in dispute.

Israel Scheffler has pressed this second question repeatedly. In an earlier paper reprinted here (see chapter 8), Scheffler has pointed out a certain ambiguity in Goodman's use of the key expression "worlds." In some uses Goodman thinks of worlds in terms of objects—an "objectual" use, says Scheffler, with "objectual reference." But elsewhere Goodman uses the expression "worlds" to mean "versions"—a "versional" use with "versional reference."

The key issue however does not consist in the ambiguity in the use of "worlds" but in a misleading suggestion that may arise in connection with this ambiguity. The suggestion is that, if words make worlds in the sense of versions, they also make worlds in the sense of the objects of those versions. But, of course, we are not warranted to conclude from the fact that we make true descriptions of the world that we make the world. As Scheffler summarizes his objection, in a chapter written especially for this volume, "I can understand the making of words but not the making thereby of the worlds they refer to" (see chapter 13).

What makes versions right for Nelson Goodman is, presumably, some version of rightness we ourselves make. But, for Israel Scheffler, while it is indeed we who make versions, it is not we who make versions right.

In other words, what makes the concept "Big Dipper' is the fact that a particular version of the world we have adopted contains this term. Yet, as Goodman himself has pointed out, not all terms in a particular version denote. Some terms, for example "Don Quixote," are null in the sense that they do not denote any existing objects. So versions may contain both null and non-null terms. And the non-null character of a particular term is not version dependent.

As Scheffler writes, "The non-null character of 'Big Dipper' (i.e., the truth of its containing version) is not determined by the fact that our version contains the term." Moreover, the Big Dipper itself, the object that the non-null term "Big Dipper" may be said to denote, is also not version dependent. "Then," Scheffler concludes, "our Big Dipper version did not make it happen that the Big Dipper in fact exists—that it is *there* to be denoted. Our version did not, after all, make the Big Dipper" (chapter 13).

Some Backgrounds

Several of the issues here—notably the plurality of worlds, the relations between worlds and versions, and the difficulty of accounting for the truth of conflicting versions—have a remarkable consistency over the course of modern philosophy. Although in very different guises, these issues continue to recur in the modern period from Descartes's philosophical reflections down to the very different philosophical reflection of our own times.

Nelson Goodman's own preoccupations with pluralism, relativism, and the conceptual puzzles involved in the rejection of both metaphysical and epistemological forms of realism and anti-realism, as this collection shows, go far back in his very extensive work. One of the key figures in his own reflections has been the neo-Kantian philosopher, Ernst Cassirer.

Cassirer's three-volume treatment of what for Goodman would become the variety of versions, *The Philosophy of Symbolic Forms* (English translation, Yale University Press, 1953–57), had already devoted considerable space to looking carefully into some of the questions surrounding the idea of alternative conceptual frameworks. Goodman himself went on to draw on Cassirer's *Language and Myth* (English translation, Harper, 1946) in formulating still further questions for his own investigations.

Thus, at the very beginning of his 1978 *Ways of Worldmaking* Goodman writes: "My aim . . . is less to defend certain theses that Cassirer and I share than to take a hard look at some crucial questions they raise. In just what sense are there many worlds? What distinguishes genuine from spurious worlds? What are worlds made of? How are they made? What role do symbols play in the making? And how is worldmaking related to knowing? These questions must be faced even if full and final answers are far off" (see chapter 4).

Cassirer's own positions on the variety of symbol systems followed from a double rather than a single lineage. For not only did Cassirer elaborate his views across a wide-ranging series of both historical and philosophical investigations into the development of the sciences in the eighteenth century and the consequences of Kant's own struggles with articulating the conceptual and not just metaphysical foundations of those sciences. Cassirer also deliberately defined his own views against those other prominent post-Kantian philosophers of science, namely, some of the very differently focused members of the Vienna Circle. Several of their concerns can be found today behind our contemporary preoccupations with dissolving, if possible, the conceptual tensions between various forms of both realism and anti-realism.

Part of the interest in Carl Hempel's piece (see chapter 7) consists in drawing out not just the similarities but especially the differences between one of the Vienna Circle philosophers, Otto Neurath, and Nelson Goodman. These precisions Hempel uses to articulate a crucial question about Goodman's earlier claim that the difference between the realist and the idealist is "purely conventional." "But how can this verdict," Hempel asks, "be reconciled with Goodman's view [in *Ways of Worldmaking*, pp. 124–125] that there is no clear distinction between truth by convention and truth by content any more than between analytic and synthetic truth?" Several of the persistent difficulties here go back to a debate within the Vienna Circle itself.

In an important and carefully researched piece first published in 1967, Israel Scheffler explored some of the pertinent backgrounds here, the demanding and sustained debate between Otto Neurath and Moritz Schlick about what kinds of constraints, if any, must be acknowledged beyond the constraints of consistency (see chapter 3). The basic issue here comes to a dilemma between coherence and certainty. As Scheffler summarized the matter: "Either some of our beliefs must be transparently true of reality and beyond the scope of error and revision, or else we are free to choose any consistent set of beliefs whatever as our own, and to define 'correctness' or 'truth' accordingly. Either we suppose our beliefs to reflect the facts, in which case we beg the very question of truth and project our language gratuitously upon the world, or else we abandon altogether the intent to describe reality, in which case our scientific efforts reduce to nothing more than a word game. We can, in sum, neither relate our beliefs to a reality beyond them, nor fail so to relate them." Today this dilemma sounds to us, of course, very much like some of the problems involved in describing the relations between both version and world.

Scheffler's own position on the dilemma separating Neurath and Schlick lies behind his persistent criticisms, in the discussion of the Big Dipper example, of Goodman's reflections on what makes versions true or right. Thus, with respect to the dilemma, Scheffler looks for an alternative to either coherence or certainty, arguing that certainty is not only untenable; it is excessive. He concludes that just because no statement "can be *guaranteed* to be an absolutely reliable link to reality does not mean that we are free to assert any statements at will, provided that they cohere." As we have seen in the Big Dipper example much later, Scheffler concludes similarly that, although it is we who make versions, it is not we who make versions right.

The development of post-Kantian philosophies of science, however, in such different directions as those represented in some of the technical debates of the Vienna Circle about the appropriate conceptual constraints on confirmation statements and in some of the constructive theorizings of Ernst Cassirer's philosophy of symbolic forms owes something as well to much earlier concerns in early modern philosophies. For here, especially in the very different philosophies of René Descartes and John Locke, are the lineaments of two strongly opposed attitudes toward doing philosophy. Yet each would claim for itself, exclusively, the title of a "realist" attitude, a "realist" program for philosophy.

The early opposition here is between those who think of realism in terms of some scientific version of the world, say in terms of the Galilean version of the world as something that can be properly described in mathematical formulas only, and those who think of realism in terms of some nonscientific version of the world, say in terms of some commonsense version of the world as something properly describable with reference to the ordinary, middle-sized things that make up our workaday lives.

Drawing on work both in contemporary mathematical physics as well as on the historical and philosophical reflections of Edmund Husserl's *The Crisis of the European Sciences and Transcendental Phenomenology* (English translation, Northwestern, 1970), Hilary Putnam points out that what is "real" according to the first program, what things are "in themselves," is what some "finished science" will eventually say is real. But what is "real" according to the second program is what our "manifest image" of things suggests is real, what our so-called folk physics holds to be real. And very early on in the history of modern philosophy these two quite different attitudes to what is really real come to focus on the nature of disparate properties—primary and secondary, intrinsic and extrinsic, occurrent and dispositional—and on the opposition between primary qualities and the physical world on the one hand and sense data and the mind on the other (see chapter 2).

Whatever the fate of these two different attitudes and the different philosophical programs that they have generated throughout the course of modern philosophy, a pervasive problem lies close to the origin of the differences here. That problem is the operative assumption behind a certain objectivist picture of the world in which we most often can situate even today many strains of "scientific realisms." In Putnam's diagnosis, "the deep systematic root of the disease . . . lies in the notion of an 'intrinsic' property, a property something has 'in itself,' apart from any contribution made by language or the mind." For Putnam, there is no such thing as an "intrinsic property" in this sense, just as for Goodman there is no such thing as "the" world.

Putnam goes on to detail the particular elements of this fundamental objectivist assumption that animates modern materialism as twofold. He writes: "By the 'fundamental Objectivist assumptions,' I mean (1) the assumption that there is a clear distinction to be drawn between the properties things have 'in themselves' and the properties which are 'projected by us' and (2) the assumption that the fundamental science—in the singular, since only physics has that status today—tells us what properties things have 'in themselves.'" But the question here, for Goodman and for Scheffler as well as for Putnam, just as for Husserl and Wittgenstein before them and for a number of younger philosophers today, is whether the whole picture such fundamental assumptions generate is not just a deep-seated and long-standing mistake.

I

Backgrounds

1

The Way the World Is

Nelson Goodman

1.1 Introduction

Philosophers sometimes mistake features of discourse for features of the subject of discourse. We seldom conclude that the world consists of words just because a true description of it does, but we sometimes suppose that the structure of the world is the same as the structure of the description. This tendency may even reach the point of linguomorphism when we conceive the world as comprised of atomic objects corresponding to certain proper names, and of atomic facts corresponding to atomic sentences. A *reductio ad absurdum* blossoms when an occasional philosopher maintains that a simple description can be appropriate only if the world is simple; or asserts (and I have heard this said in all seriousness) that a coherent description will be a distortion unless the world happens to be coherent. According to this line of thinking, I suppose that before describing the world in English we ought to determine whether it is written in English, and that we ought to examine very carefully how the world is spelled.

Obviously enough the tongue, the spelling, the typography, the verbosity of a description reflect no parallel features in the world. Coherence is a characteristic of descriptions, not of the world: the significant question is not whether the world is coherent, but whether our account of it is. And what we call the simplicity of the world is merely the simplicity we are able to achieve in describing it.

But confusion of the sort I am speaking of is relatively transparent at the level of isolated sentences, and so relatively less dangerous than the error of supposing that the structure of a veridical systematic description mirrors forth the structure of the world. Since a system has basic or primitive terms or elements and a graded hierarchy built out of these, we easily come to suppose that the world must consist of corresponding atomic elements put together in similar fashion. No theory advocated in recent years by first-rate philosophers seems more obviously wrong than the picture theory of language. Yet we still find acute philosophers resorting under pressure to a notion of absolutely simple qualities or particles. And most of those who avoid thinking of the world as uniquely divisible into absolute elements still commonly suppose that *meanings* do resolve thus uniquely, and so accept the concealed absolutism involved in maintaining the distinction between analytic and synthetic propositions.

In this paper, however, I am not concerned with any of the more specific issues I have just touched upon, but with a more general question. I have been stressing the dangers of mistaking certain features of discourse for features of the world. This is a recurrent theme with me, but even this is not my main concern here. What I want to discuss is an uncomfortable feeling that comes upon me whenever I warn against the confusion in question. I can hear the anti-intellectualistic, the mystic—my arch enemy—saying something like this: "Yes, that's just what I've been telling you all along. All our descriptions are a sorry travesty. Science, language, perception, philosophy—none of these can ever be utterly faithful to the world as it is. All make abstractions or conventionalizations of one kind or another, all filter the world through the mind, through concepts, through the senses, through language; and all these filtering media in some way distort the world. It is not just that each gives only a partial truth, but that each introduces distortion of its own. We never achieve even in part a really faithful portrayal of the way the world is."

Here speaks the Bergsonian, the obscurantist, seemingly repeating my own words and asking, in effect, "What's the difference between us? Can't we be friends?" Before I am willing to admit that philosophy must make alliances that strange, I shall make a determined effort to formulate the difference between us. But I shall begin by discussing some preliminary, related questions.

1.2 The Way the World Is Given

Perhaps we can gain some light on the way the world is by examining the way it is given to us in experience. The question of the given has a slightly musty sound these days. Even hardened philosophers have become a little self-conscious about the futility of their debates over the given, and have the grace to rephrase the issue in terms of "ground-elements" or "protocol-sentences." But in one way or another we hear a good deal about getting down to the original, basic, bare elements from which all knowledge is manufactured. Knowing is tacitly conceived as a processing of raw material into a finished product; and an understanding of knowledge is thus supposed to require that we discover just what the raw material is.

Offhand, this seems easy enough. Carnap wanted the ground elements of his system in the *Aufbau* to be as nearly as possible epistemologically primary. In order to arrive at these, he says, we must leave out of ordinary experience all the results of any analysis to which we subject what we initially receive. This means leaving out all divisions along spatial or qualitative boundaries, so that our elements are big lumps, each containing everything in our experience at a given moment. But to say this is to make artificial temporal divisions; and the actual given, Carnap implies, consists not of these big lumps, but of one single stream.

But this way of arriving at the given assumes that the processes of knowing are all processes of analysis. Other philosophers have supposed rather that the processes are all processes of synthesis, and that the given therefore consists of minimal particles that have to be combined with one another in knowing. Still other thinkers hold that both these views are too extreme, and that the world is given in more familiar medium-size pieces, to which both analysis and synthesis are applied. Thus in views of the given we find duplicated the monism, atomism, and the intermediate pluralisms of metaphysics. But which view of the given is right?

Let's look at the question more closely. The several views do not differ about what is contained in the given, or what can be found there. A certain visual presentation, all agree, contains certain colors, places, designs, etc.; it contains the least perceptible particles and it is a whole. The question is not whether the given *is* a single undifferentiated lump or contains many tiny parts; it is a whole comprised of such parts. The issue is not *what* is given but *how* it is *given*. Is it *given* as a single whole or is it *given* as many small particles? This captures the precise issue—and at the same time discloses its emptiness. For I do not think any sense can be made of the phrase *"given as."* That an experience is given as several parts surely does not mean that these parts are presented torn asunder; nor can it mean that these parts are partitioned off from one another by perceptible lines of demarcation. For if such lines of demarcation are there at all, they are there within the given, for any view of the given. The nearest we could come to finding any meaning to the question what the world is *given as* would be to say that this turns on whether the material in question is apprehended with a kind of feeling of wholeness or a feeling of broken-upness. To come that near to finding a meaning for *"given as"* is not to come near enough to count.

So I am afraid we can get no light on the way the world is by asking about the way it is given. For the question about the way it is given evaporates into thin air.

1.3   The Way the World Is to Be Seen

Perhaps we shall get further by asking how the world is best seen. If we can with some confidence grade ways of seeing or picturing the world according to their degrees of realism, of absence of distortion, of faithfulness in representing the way the world is, then surely by reading back from this we can learn a good deal about the way the world is.

We need consider our everyday ideas about pictures for only a moment to recognize this as an encouraging approach. For we rate pictures quite easily according to their approximate degree of realism. The most realistic picture is the one most like a color-photograph; and pictures become progressively less realistic, and more conventionalized or abstract, as they depart from this standard. The way we see the world best, the nearest pictorial approach to the way the world is, is the way the camera sees it. This version of the whole matter is simple, straightforward, and quite generally held. But in philosophy as everywhere else, every silver lining has a big black cloud—and the view described has everything in its favor except that it is, I think, quite wrong.

If I take a photograph of a man with his feet towards me, the feet may come out as large as his torso. Is this the way I normally or properly see the man? If so, then why do we call such a photograph distorted? If not, then I can no longer claim to be taking the photographic view of the world as my standard of faithfulness.

The fact of the matter is that this "distorted" photograph calls our attention to something about seeing that we had ignored. Just in the way that it differs from an ordinary "realistic" picture, it reveals new facts and possibilities in visual experience. But the "distorted" photograph is a rather trivial example of something much more general and important. The "distortion" of the photograph is comparable to the distortion of new or unfamiliar styles of painting. Which is the more faithful portrait of a man—the one by Holbein or the one by Manet or the one by Sharaku or the one by Dürer or the one by Cézanne or the one by Picasso? Each different way of painting represents a different way of seeing; each makes its selection, its emphasis; each uses its own vocabulary of conventionalization. And we need only look hard at the pictures by any such artist to come to see the world in somewhat the same way. For seeing is an activity and the way we perform it depends in large part upon our training. I remember J. B. Neumann saying that once when he happened to see the faces of a movie audience in the reflected glare of the screen he first realized how an African sculptor saw faces. What we regard as the most realistic pictures are merely pictures of the sort that most of us, unfortunately, are brought up on. An African or a Japanese would make a quite different choice when asked to select the pictures that most closely depict what he sees. Indeed our resistance to new or exotic ways of painting stems from our normal lethargic resistance to retraining; and on the other hand the excitement lies in the acquisition of new skill. Thus the discovery of African art thrilled French painters and they learned from it new ways to see and paint. What is less often realized is that the discovery of European art is exciting to the African sculptor for the same reason; it shows him a new way of seeing, and he, too, modifies his work accordingly. Unfortunately, while European absorption of African style often results in an artistic advance, African adoption of European style almost always leads to artistic deterioration. But this is for incidental reasons. The first is that social deterioration of the African is usually simultaneous with the introduction of European art. The second reason is rather more intriguing: that while the French artist was influenced by the best of African art, the African was fed no doubt on calendar art and pin-up girls. Had he seen Greek and Mediaeval sculpture instead, the results might have been radically different. But I am digressing.

The upshot of all this is that we cannot find out much about the way the world is by asking about the best or most faithful or most realistic way of seeing or picturing it. For the ways of seeing and picturing are many and various; some are strong, effective, useful, intriguing, or sensitive; others are weak, foolish, dull, banal, or blurred. But even if all the latter are excluded, still none of the rest can lay any good claim to be the way of seeing or picturing the world the way it is.

1.4   The Way the World Is to Be Described

We come now to a more familiar version of the question of the way the world is. How is the world to be described? Does what we call a true description faithfully depict the world?

Most of us have ringing in our ears Tarski's statement that "it is raining" is true if and only if it is raining, as well as his remark (I think erroneous, but that is beside the point here) that acceptance of this formula constitutes acceptance of a correspondence theory of truth. This way of putting the matter encourages a natural tendency to think of truth in terms of mirroring or faithful reproduction; and we have a slight shock whenever we happen to notice the obvious fact that the sentence "it is raining" is about as different as possible from the rainstorm. This disparity is of the same sort for a true as for a false description. Luckily, therefore, we need not here concern ourselves with the difficult technical matter of the nature of truth; we can confine our attention to admittedly true descriptions. What we must face is the fact that even the truest description comes nowhere near faithfully reproducing the way the world is.

A systematic description of the world, as I noted earlier, is even more vulnerable to this charge; for it has explicit primitives, routes of construction, etc., none of them features of the world described. Some philosophers contend, therefore, that if systematic descriptions introduce an arbitrary artificial order, then we should make our descriptions unsystematic to bring them more into accord with the world. Now the tacit assumption here is that the respects in which a description is unsatisfactory are *just those respects in which it falls short of being a faithful picture;* and the tacit *goal* is to achieve a description that as nearly as possible gives a living likeness. But the goal is a delusive one. For we have seen that even the most realistic way of picturing amounts merely to one kind of conventionalization. In painting, the selection, the emphasis, the conventions are different from but no less peculiar to the vehicle, and no less variable, than those of language. The idea of making verbal descriptions approximate pictorial depiction loses its point when we understand that to turn a description into the most faithful possible picture would amount to nothing more than exchanging some conventions for others.

Thus neither the way the world is given nor any way of seeing or picturing or describing it conveys to us the way the world is.

1.5 The Way the World Is

We come now to the question: what, then, is the way the world is? Am I still threatened with the friendship of my enemies? It looks very much that way, for I have just reached the mystic's conclusion that there is no representation of the way the world is. But if our accord seems on the surface to have been reinforced, a second look will show how it has been undermined, by what we have been saying.

The complaint that a given true description distorts or is unfaithful to the world has significance in terms of some grading of descriptions according to faithfulness, or in terms of a difference in degree of faithfulness between true descriptions and good pictures. But if we say that all true descriptions and good pictures are equally unfaithful, then in terms of what sample or standard of relative faithfulness are we speaking? We have no longer before us any clear notion of what faithfulness would be. Thus I reject the idea that there is some test of realism or faithfulness in addition to the tests of pictorial goodness and descriptive truth. There are very many different equally true descriptions of the world, and their truth is the only standard of their faithfulness. And when we say of them that they all involve conventionalizations, we are saying that no one of these different descriptions is *exclusively* true, since the others are also true.

None of them tells us *the* way the world is, but each of them tells us *a* way the world is.

If I were asked what is *the food* for men, I should have to answer "none." For there are many foods. And if I am asked what is the way the world is, I must likewise answer, "none." For the world is many ways. The mystic holds that there is some way the world is and that this way is not captured by any description. For me, there is no way that is the way the world is; and so of course no description can capture it. But there are many ways the world is, and every true description captures one of them. The difference between my friend and me is, in sum, the enormous difference between absolutism and relativism.

Since the mystic is concerned with the way the world is and finds that the way cannot be expressed, his ultimate response to the question of the way the world is must be, as he recognizes, silence. Since I am concerned rather with the ways the world is, my response must be to construct one or many descriptions. The answer to the question "What is the way the world is? What are the ways the world is?" is not a shush, but a chatter.

1.6   Postscript

Near the beginning of this chapter, I spoke of the obvious falsity of the picture theory of language. I declared rather smugly that a description does not picture what it describes, or even represent the structure of what it describes. The devastating charge against the picture theory of language was that a description cannot represent or mirror forth the world as it is. But we have since observed that a picture doesn't do this either. I began by dropping the picture theory of language and ended by adopting the language theory of pictures. I rejected the picture theory of language on the ground that the structure of a description does not conform to the structure of the world. But I then concluded that there is no such thing as the structure of the world for anything to conform or fail to conform to. You might say that the picture theory of language is as false and as true as the picture theory of pictures; or in other words, that what is false is not the picture theory of language but a certain absolutistic notion concerning both pictures and language. Perhaps eventually I shall learn that what seems most obviously false sometimes isn't.

2

Is There Still Anything to Say about Reality and Truth?

Hilary Putnam

The man on the street, Eddington reminded us, visualizes a table as "solid"—that is, as *mostly* solid matter. But physics has discovered that the table is mostly empty space: that the distance between the particles is immense in relation to the radius of the electron or the nucleus of one of the atoms of which the table consists. One reaction to this state of affairs, the reaction of Wilfrid Sellars,[1] is to deny that there are tables at all as we ordinarily conceive them (although he chooses an ice cube rather than a table as his example). The commonsense conception of ordinary middle-sized material objects such as tables and ice cubes (the "manifest image") is simply *false* in Sellars's view (although not without at least some cognitive value—there are real objects that the "tables" and "ice cubes" of the manifest image "picture," according to Sellars, even if these real objects are not the layman's tables and ice cubes). I don't agree with this view of Sellars's, but I hope he will forgive me if I use it, or the phenomenon of its appearance on the philosophical scene, to highlight certain features of the philosophical debate about "realism."

First of all, this view illustrates the fact that Realism with a capital "R" doesn't always deliver what the innocent expect of it. If there is any appeal of Realism which is wholly legitimate it is the appeal to the commonsense feeling that *of course* there are tables and chairs, and any philosophy that tells us that there really aren't—that there are really only sense data, or only "texts," or whatever, is more than slightly crazy. In appealing to this commonsense feeling, Realism reminds me of the Seducer in the old-fashioned melodrama. In the melodramas of the 1890s the Seducer always promised various things to the Innocent Maiden which he failed to deliver when the time came. In this case the Realist (the evil Seducer) promises common sense (the Innocent Maiden) that he will rescue her from her enemies (Idealists, Kantians and Neo-Kantians, Pragmatists, and the fearsome self-described "Irrealist" Nelson Goodman) who (the Realist says) want to deprive her of her good old ice cubes and chairs. Faced with this dreadful prospect, the fair Maiden naturally opts for the company of the commonsensical Realist. But when they have travelled together for a little while the "Scientific Realist" breaks the news that what the Maiden is going to get *isn't* her ice cubes and tables and chairs. In fact, all there *really* is—the Scientific Realist tells her over breakfast— is what "finished science" will say there is—whatever that may be. She is left with a promissory note for She Knows Not What, and the assurance that even if there *aren't* tables and chairs, still there are some *Dinge an sich* that her "manifest image" (or her "folk physics," as some Scientific Realists put it) "pictures." Some will say that the lady has been had.

Thus, it is clear that the name "Realism" can be claimed by or given to at least two very different philosophical attitudes (and, in fact, to many). The philosopher who claims that only scientific objects "really exist" and that much, if not all, of the commonsense world is mere "projection" claims to be a "realist," but so does the philosopher who insists that there *really are* chairs and ice cubes (and some of these ice cubes really are *pink*), and these two attitudes, these two images of the world, can lead to and have led to many different programs for philosophy.

Husserl[2] traces the first line of thought, the line that denies that there "really are" commonsense objects, back to Galileo, and with good reason. The present Western worldview depends, according to Husserl, on a new way of conceiving "external objects"—the way of mathematical physics. An external thing is conceived of as a congeries of particles (by atomists) or as some kind of extended disturbance (in the seventeenth century, a "vortex," and later a collection of "fields"). Either way, the table in front of me (or the object that I "picture as" a table) is described by "mathematical formulas," as Husserl says. And this, he points out, is what above all came into Western thinking with the Galilean revolution: the idea of the "external world" as something whose true description, whose description "in itself," consists of mathematical formulas.

It is important to this way of thinking that certain familiar properties of the table—its size and shape and location—are "real" properties, describable, for example, in the language of Descartes's analytic geometry. Other properties, however, the so-called secondary properties, of which *color* is a chief example, are *not* treated as real properties in the same sense. No "occurrent" (non-dispositional) property of that swarm of molecules (or that space-time region) recognized in mathematical physics can be said to be what we all along called its *color*.

What about dispositional properties? It is often claimed that color is simply a function of *reflectancy*, that is, of the disposition of an object (or of the surface of an object) to selectively absorb certain wavelengths of incident light and reflect others. But this doesn't really do much for the reality of colors. Not only has recent research shown that this account is much too simple (because changes of reflectancy across edges turn out to play an important role in determining the colors we see), but reflectancy itself does not have one uniform physical explanation. A red star and a red apple and a reddish glass of colored water are red for quite different physical reasons. In fact, there may well be an infinite number of different physical conditions which could result in the disposition to reflect (or emit) red light and absorb light or other wavelengths. A dispositional property whose underlying non-dispositional "explanation" is so very non-uniform is simply incapable of being represented as a mathematical function of the dynamical variables. And these—the dynamical variables—are the parameters that this way of thinking treats as the "characteristics" of "external" objects.

Another problem[3] is that *hues* turn out to be much more subjective than we thought. In fact, any shade on the color chart in the green part of the spectrum will be classed as "standard green" by some subject—even if it lies at the extreme "yellow-green" end or the extreme "blue-green" end.

In sum, no "characteristic" recognized by this way of thinking—no "well-behaved function of the dynamical variables"—corresponds to such a familiar property of objects as *red* or *green*. The idea that there is a property all red objects have in common—the same in all cases—and another property all green objects have in common—the same in all cases—is a kind of illusion, on the view we have come more and more to take for granted since the age of Descartes and Locke.

However, Locke and Descartes did give us a sophisticated substitute for our pre-scientific notion of color; a substitute that has, perhaps, come to seem mere "post-scientific common sense" to most people. This substitute involves the idea of a sense datum (except that, in the seventeenth- and eighteenth-century vocabulary, sense data were referred to as "ideas" or "impressions"). The red sweater I see is not red in the way I thought it was (there is no "physical magnitude" which is its redness), but it does have a disposition (a Power, in the seventeenth- and eighteenth-century idiom) to affect me in a certain way—to cause me to have sense data. And these, the sense data, do truly have a simple, uniform, non-dispositional sort of redness."

This is the famous picture, the dualistic picture of the physical world and its primary qualities, on the one hand, and the mind and its sense data, on the other, that philosophers have been wrangling over since the time of Galileo, as Husserl says. And it is Husserl's idea—as it was the idea of William James, who influenced Husserl—that this picture is disastrous.

But why should we regard it as disastrous? It was once shocking, to be sure, but as I have already said it is by now widely accepted as "post-scientific common sense." What is *really* wrong with this picture?

For one thing, *solidity* is in much the same boat as color. If objects do not have color as they "naively" seem to, no more do they have solidity as they "naively" seem to.[4] It is this that leads Sellars to say that such commonsense objects as ice cubes do not really exist at all. What *is* our conception of a typical commonsense object if not of something solid (or liquid) which exhibits certain colors? What there really are, in Sellars's scientific metaphysics, are objects of mathematical physics, on the one hand, and "raw feels," on the other. This is precisely the picture I have just described as "disastrous"; it is the picture that denies precisely the common man's kind of realism, his realism about tables and chairs.

The reply to me (the reply a philosopher who accepts the post-Galilean picture will make) is obvious: "You are just nostalgic for an older and simpler world. This picture works; our acceptance of it is an 'inference to

the best explanation.' We cannot regard it as an objection to a view that
it does not preserve everything that laymen once falsely believed."

If it is an inference to the best explanation, it is a strange one, however.
How does the familiar explanation of what happens when I "see something red" go? The light strikes the object (say, a sweater), and is reflected
to my eye. There is an image on the retina (Berkeley knew about images
on the retina, and so did Descartes, even if the wave aspect of light was
not well understood until much later). There are resultant nerve impulses
(Descartes knew there was some kind of transmission along the nerves,
even if he was wrong about its nature—and it is not clear we know its
nature either, since there is again debate about the significance of chemi-
cal, as opposed to electrical, transmissions from neuron to neuron.) There
are events in the brain, some of which we understand thanks to the work
of Hubel and Wiesel, David Marr, and others. And then—this is the mysterious part—there is somehow a "sense datum" or a "raw feel." *This* is
an *explanation?*

An "explanation" that involves connections of a kind we do not understand at all ("nomological danglers," Herbert Feigl called them[5]) and concerning which we have not even the sketch of a theory is an explanation
through something more obscure than the phenomenon to be explained.
As has been pointed out by thinkers as different from one another as
William James, Husserl, and John Austin, every single part of the sense
datum story is supposition—theory—and theory of a most peculiar kind.
Yet the epistemological role "sense data" are supposed to play by traditional philosophy required them to be what is "given," to be *what we are
absolutely sure of independently of scientific theory.* The kind of scientific
realism we have inherited from the seventeenth century has not lost all its
prestige even yet, but it has saddled us with a disastrous picture of the
world. It is high time we looked for a different picture.

2.1 Intrinsic Properties: Dispositions

I want to suggest that the problem with the "Objectivist" picture of the
world (to use Husserl's term for this kind of scientific realism) lies deeper
than the postulation of "sense data"; sense data are, so to speak, the

visible symptoms of a systemic disease, like the pock marks in the case of smallpox. The deep systemic root of the disease, I want to suggest, lies in the notion of an "intrinsic" property, a property something has "in itself," apart from any contribution made by language or the mind.

This notion, and the correlative notion of a property that is merely "appearance," or merely something we "project" onto the object, has proved extremely robust, judging by its appeal to different kinds of philosophers. In spite of their deep disagreements, all the strains of philosophy that accepted the seventeenth-century circle of problems—subjective idealists as well as dualists and materialists—accepted the distinction, even if they disagreed over its application. A subjective idealist would say that there are only sense data (or minds and sense data, in some versions), and that "red" is an intrinsic property of these objects, while persistence (being there even when we don't look) is something we "project"; a dualist or a materialist would say the "external" objects have persistence as an intrinsic property, but red is, in their case, something we "project." But all of these philosophers *have* the distinction. Even Kant, who expresses serious doubts about it in the first Critique (to the point of saying that the notion of a "Ding an sich" *may* be "empty"), makes heavy use of it in the second Critique.

Putting aside the Berkeleyan view (that there aren't really any external objects at all) as an aberrant form of the seventeenth-century view, we may say that the remaining philosophers all accept the account of "redness" and "solidity" that I have been describing; these are not "intrinsic properties" of the external things we ascribe them to, but rather (in the case of external things) dispositions to affect us in certain ways—to produce certain sense data in us, or, the materialist philosophers would say, to produce certain sorts of "states" in our brains and nervous systems. The idea that these properties are "in" the things themselves, an intrinsic properties, is a spontaneous "projection."

The Achilles' heel of this story is the notion of a disposition. To indicate the problems that arise—they have preoccupied many first-rate philosophical minds, starting with Charles Peirce's—let me introduce a technical term (I shall not introduce much terminology in this lecture, I promise!). A disposition that something has to do something *no matter what*, I shall call a *strict disposition*. A disposition to do something under "normal conditions," I shall call an *"other things being equal" disposition*. Perhaps it would be wise to give examples.

The disposition of bodies with non-zero rest mass to travel at sub-light speeds is a *strict* disposition; it is physically impossible for a body with non-zero rest mass to travel at the speed of light. Of course, the notion of a "strict disposition" presupposes the notion of "physical necessity," as this example illustrates, but this is a notion I am allowing the "scientific realist," at least for the sake of argument. What of the disposition of sugar to dissolve in water?

This is not a strict disposition, since sugar which is placed in water which is already saturated with sugar (or even with other appropriate chemicals) will not dissolve. Is the disposition of sugar to dissolve in *chemically pure water*, then, a strict disposition?

This is also not a strict disposition; the first counterexample I shall mention comes from thermodynamics. Suppose I drop a sugar cube in water and the sugar cube dissolves. Consider sugar which is in water, but in such a way that while the situation is identical with the situation I just produced (the sugar is dissolved in the water) with respect to the position of each particle, and also with respect to the numerical value of the momentum of each particle, all the momentum vectors have the exactly opposite directions from the ones they now have. This is a famous example: what happens in the example is that the sugar, instead of staying dissolved, simply forms a sugar cube which spontaneously leaps out of the water! Since every normal state (every state in which sugar dissolves) can be paired with a state in which it "undissolves," we see that there are infinitely many physically possible conditions in which sugar "undissolves" instead of staying in solution. Of course, these are all states in which entropy decreases; but that is not impossible, only extremely improbable!

Shall we say, then, that sugar has a strict disposition to dissolve unless the condition is one in which an entropy decrease takes place? No, because if sugar is put in water and there is immediately a flash freeze, the sugar will not dissolve if the freezing takes place fast enough. . . .

The fact is that what we can say is that under *normal* conditions sugar will dissolve if placed in water. And there is no reason to think that all the various abnormal conditions (including bizarre quantum mechanical states, bizarre local fluctuations in the space-time, etc.) under which sugar would not dissolve if placed in water could be summed up in a closed formula in the language of fundamental physics.

This is exactly the problem we previously observed in connection with redness and solidity! If the "intrinsic" properties of "external" things are the ones that we can represent by formulas in the language of fundamental physics, by "suitable functions of the dynamical variables," then *solubility* is also not an "intrinsic" property of any external thing. And, similarly, neither is any "other things being equal" disposition. The Powers, to use the seventeenth-century language, have to be set over against, and carefully distinguished from, the properties the things have "in themselves."

2.2   Intrinsic Properties: Intentionality

Well, what of it? Why should we not say that dispositions (or at least "other things being equal" dispositions, such as solubility) are also not "in the things themselves" but rather something we "project" onto those things? Philosophers who talk this way rarely if ever stop to say what *projection* itself is supposed to be. Where in the scheme does the ability of the mind to "project" anything onto anything come in?

Projection is thinking of something as having properties it does not have, but that we can imagine (perhaps because something else we are acquainted with really does have them), without being conscious that this is what we are doing. It is thus a species of *thought*—thought about something. Does the familiar "Objectivist" picture have anything to tell us about thought (or, as philosophers say, about "intentionality," that is, about *aboutness*)?

Descartes certainly intended that it should. His view was that there are two fundamental substances—mind and matter—not one, and, correspondingly there should be two fundamental sciences: physics and psychology. But we have ceased to think of mind as a separate "substance" at all. And a "fundamental science" of psychology which explains the nature of thought (including how thoughts can be true or false, warranted or unwarranted, about something or not about something) never did come into existence, contrary to Descartes's hopes. So to explain the features of the commonsense world, including color, solidity, causality—I include causality because the commonsense notion of "the cause" of something is a "projection" if dispositions are "projections"; it depends on the notion of "normal conditions" in exactly the same way—in terms of a mental operation called "projection" is to explain just about every feature of the commonsense world in terms of *thought*.

But wasn't that what idealists were accused of doing? This is the paradox that I pointed out at the beginning of this lecture. So far as the commonsense world is concerned (the world we experience ourselves as *living* in, which is why Husserl called it the *Lebenswelt*), the effect of what is called 'realism' in philosophy is to deny objective reality, to make it all simply *thought*. It is the philosophers who in one way or another stand in the Neo-Kantian tradition—James, Husserl, Wittgenstein—who claim that commonsense tables and chairs and sensations and electrons are *equally real,* and not the metaphysical realists.

Today, some metaphysical realists would say that we don't need a perfected science of psychology to account for thought and intentionality, because the problem is solved by some philosophical theory; while others claim that a perfected "cognitive science" based on the "computer model" will solve the problem for us in near or distant future. I obviously do not have time to examine these suggestions closely today, but I shall indicate briefly why I believe that none of them will withstand close inspection.

2.3   Why Intentionality Is So Intractable

The problem, in a nutshell, is that thought itself has come to be treated more and more as a "projection" by the philosophy that traces its pedigree to the seventeenth century. The reason is clear: we have not succeeded in giving the theory that thought is just a primitive property of a mysterious "substance," mind, any content. As Kant pointed out in the first Critique, we have no theory of this substance or its powers and no prospect of having one. If *unlike* the Kant of the first Critique (as I read the *Critique of Pure Reason*), we insist on sticking to the fundamental "Objectivist" assumptions, the only line we can then take is that *mental phenomena must be highly derived physical phenomena in some way,* as

Diderot and Hobbes had already proposed. By the "fundamental Objectivist assumptions," I mean (1) the assumption that there is a clear distinction to be drawn between the properties things have "in themselves" and the properties which are "projected by us" and (2) the assumption that the fundamental science—in the singular, since only physics has that status today—tells us what properties things have "in themselves." (Even if we were to assume, with Wilfrid Sellars, that "raw feels"—fundamental sensuous qualities of experience—are not going to be reduced to physics, but are in some way going to be added to fundamental science in some future century, it would not affect the situation much; Sellars does not anticipate that *intentionality* will turn out to be something we have to add to physics in the same way, but rather supposes that a theory of the "use of words" is all that is needed to account for it.)

Modern Objectivism has simply become Materialism. And the central problem for Materialism is 'explaining the emergence of mind'. But if "explaining the emergence of mind" means solving Brentano's problem, that is, saying in *reductive* terms what 'thinking there are a lot of cats in the neighborhood' *is,* and what 'remembering where Paris is' *is,* etc., why should we now think *that*'s possible? If reducing color or solidity or solubility to fundamental physics has proved impossible, why should this vastly more ambitious reduction program prove tractable?

Starting in the late 1950s, I myself proposed a program in the philosophy of mind that has become widely known under the name "Functionalism." The claim of my "Functionalism" was that thinking beings are *compositionally plastic*—that is, that there is no one physical state or event (i.e., no necessary and sufficient condition expressible by a finite formula in the language of first-order fundamental physics) for being even a *physically possible* (let alone "logically possible" or "metaphysically possible") occurrence of a thought with a given propositional content, or of a feeling of anger, or of a pain, etc. *A fortiori,* propositional attitudes, emotions, feelings, are not *identical* with brain states, or even with more broadly characterized physical states. When I advanced this claim, I pointed out that thinking of a being's mentality, affectivity, etc., as aspects of its *organization to function* allows one to recognize that all sorts of logically possible "systems" or beings could be conscious, exhibit mentality and affect, etc., in exactly the same sense without having the same matter (without even consisting of "matter" in the sense of elementary particles and electromagnetic fields at all). For beings of many different physical (and even "non-physical") constitutions could have the same functional organization. The thing we want insight into is the nature of human (and animal) functional organization, not the nature of a mysterious "substance," on the one hand, or merely additional physiological information on the other.

I also proposed a theory as to what our organization to function is, one I have now given up—this was the theory that our functional organization is that of a Turing machine. I have given this up because I believe that there are good arguments to show that mental states are not only compositionally plastic but also *computationally plastic.* What I mean by this is that physically possible creatures who believe that there are a lot of cats in the neighborhood, or whatever, may have an *indefinite number of different "programs."* The hypothesis that there is a necessary and sufficient condition for the presence of a given belief in computational (or computational *cum* physical) terms is unrealistic in just the way that the theory that there is a necessary and sufficient condition for the presence of a table in phenomenalistic terms is unrealistic. Such a condition would have to be infinitely long, and not constructed according to any effective rule, or even according to a non-effective prescription that we could state without using the very terms to be reduced. I do not believe that even all *humans* who have the same belief (in different cultures, or with the different bodies of knowledge and different conceptual resources) have in common a physical *cum* computational feature which could be "identified with" that belief. The "intentional level" is simply not reducible to the "computational level" any more than it is to the "physical level."[6]

If this is right, then the Objectivist will have to conclude that intentionality *too* must be a mere "projection." But how can any philosopher think this suggestion has even the semblance of making sense? As we saw, the very notion of "projection" *presupposes* intentionality!

Strange to say, the idea that thought *is* a mere projection is being defended by a number of philosophers in the United States and England, in spite of its absurdity. The strength of the "Objectivist" tradition is so strong that some philosophers will abandon the deepest intuitions we have about ourselves-in-the-world, rather than ask (as Husserl and

Wittgenstein did) whether the whole picture is not a mistake. Thus it is that in the closing decades of the twentieth century we have intelligent philosophers[7] claiming that intentionality itself is something we project by taking a "stance" to some parts of the world (as if "taking a stance" were not itself an intentional notion!), intelligent philosophers claiming that no one really has propositional attitudes (beliefs and desires), that 'belief' and 'desire' are just notions from a false theory called "folk psychology," and intelligent philosophers claiming there is no such property as 'truth' and no such relation as reference, that "is true" is just a phrase we use to "raise the level of language." One of these—Richard Rorty—a thinker of great depth—sees that he is committed to rejecting the intuitions that underly every kind of realism[8] (and not just metaphysical realism), but most of these thinkers write as if they were *saving* realism (in its Materialist version) by abandoning intentionality! It's as if it were all right to say "I don't deny that there is an external world; I just deny that we *think* about it"! Come to think of it, this is the way Foucault wrote, too. The line between relativism *à la française* and Analytic Philosophy seems to be thinner than anglophone philosophers think! Amusingly enough, the dust-jacket of one of the latest attacks on "folk psychology"[9] bears an enthusiastic blurb in which a reviewer explains the importance of the book inside the dust-jacket by saying that most people *believe* that there are such things as beliefs!

2.4   "The Trail of the Human Serpent Is Over All"

If seventeenth-century Objectivism has led twentieth-century philosophy into a blind alley, the solution is neither to fall into extreme relativism, as French philosophy has been doing, nor to deny our commonsense realism. There *are* tables and chairs and ice cubes. There are also electrons and space-time regions and prime numbers and people who are a menace to world peace and moments of beauty and transcendence and many other things. My old-fashioned story of the Seducer and the Innocent Maiden was meant as a double warning; a warning against giving up commonsense realism and, simultaneously, a warning against supposing that the seventeenth-century talk of "external world" and "sense impressions," "intrinsic properties," and "projections," etc., was in any way a Rescuer of our commonsense realism. Realism with a capital "R" is, sad to say, the foe, not the defender, of realism with a small "r."

If this is hard to see, it is because the task of overcoming the seventeenth-century world picture is only begun. I asked—as the title of this lecture—whether there is still anything to say, anything really new to say, about reality and truth. If "new" means "absolutely unprecedented," I suspect the answer is "no." But if we allow that William James might have had something "new" to say—something new to *us,* not just new to his own time—or, at least, might have had a program for philosophy that is, in part, the right program, even if it has not been properly worked out yet (and may never be completely "worked out"); if we allow that Husserl and Wittgenstein and Austin may have shared something of the same program, even if they too, in their different ways, failed to state it properly; then there is still something new, something *unfinished and important* to say about reality and truth. And that is what I believe.

The key to working out the program of preserving commonsense realism while avoiding the absurdities and antinomies of metaphysical realism in all its familiar varieties (Brand X: Materialism; Brand Y: Subjective Idealism; Brand Z: Dualism. . . . . . .) is something I have called *internal realism* (I should have called it pragmatic realism!) Internal realism is, at bottom, just the insistence that realism is *not* incompatible with conceptual relativity. One can be *both* a realist *and* a conceptual relativist. Realism (with a small "r") has already been introduced; as was said, it is a view that takes our familiar commonsense scheme, as well as our scientific and artistic and other schemes, at face value, without helping itself to the notion of the thing "in itself." But what is conceptual relativity?

Conceptual relativity sounds like 'relativism', but has none of the "there is no truth to be found . . . 'true' is just a name for what a bunch of people can agree on" implications of 'relativism'. A simple example will illustrate what I mean. Consider "a world with three individuals" (Carnap often used examples like this when we were doing inductive logic together in the early nineteen-fifties), x1, x2, x3. How many *objects* are there in this world?

Well, I *said* "consider a world with just three individuals," didn't I? So mustn't there be three objects? Can there by non-abstract entities which are not "individuals"?

One possible answer is "no." We can identify 'individual', 'object', 'particular', etc., and find no absurdity in a world with just three objects which are independent, unrelated 'logical atoms." But there are perfectly good logical doctrines which lead to different results.

Suppose, for example, that like some Polish logicians, I believe that for every two particulars there is an object which is their sum. (This is the basic assumption of "mereology," the calculus of parts and wholes invented by Lezniewski.) If I ignore, for the moment, the so-called null object, then I will find that the world of "three individuals" (as Carnap might have had it, at least when he was doing inductive logic) actually contains *seven* objects:

World 1	World 2
x1, x2, x3	x1, x2, x3, x1 + x2, x1 + x3, x2 + x3, x1 + x2 + x3
(A world à la Carnap)	("Same" world à la Polish logician)

Some Polish logicians would also say that there is a "null object" which they count as a part of every object. If we accepted this suggestion, and added this individual (call it O), then we would say that Carnap's world contains *eight* objects.

Now, the classic metaphysical realist way of dealing with such problems is well-known. It is to say that there is a single world (think of this as a piece of dough) which we can slice into pieces in different ways. But this "cookie cutter" metaphor founders on the question, "What are the 'parts' of this dough?" If the answer is that O, x1, x2, x3, x1 + x2, x1 + x3, x2 + x3, x1 + x2 + x3 are all the different 'pieces', then we have not a *neutral* description, but rather a *partisan* description—just the description of the Warsaw logician! And it is no accident that metaphysical realism cannot really recognize the phenomenon of conceptual relativity—for that phenomenon turns on the fact that *the logical primitives themselves, and in particular the notions of object and existence, have a multitude of different uses rather than one absolute 'meaning'.*

An example which is historically important, if more complex than the one just given, is the ancient dispute about the ontological status of the Euclidean plane. Imagine a Euclidean plane. Think of the points in the plane. Are these parts of the plane, as Leibniz thought? Or are they "mere limits," as Kant said?

If you say, in *this* case, that these are "two ways of slicing the same dough," then you must admit that what is a *part* of space, in one version of the facts, is an abstract entity (say, a set of convergent spheres—although there is not, of course, a *unique* way of construing points as limits) in the other version. But then you will have conceded that which entities are "abstract entities" and which are "concrete objects," at least, is version-relative. Metaphysical realists to this day continue to argue about whether points (space-time points, nowadays, rather than points in the plane or in three-dimensional space) are individuals or properties, particulars or mere limits, etc. My view is that God himself, if he consented to answer the question, 'Do points really exist or are they mere limits?', would say 'I don't know'; not because His omniscience is limited, but because there is a limit to how far questions make sense.

One last point before I leave these examples: *given* a version, the question, 'How many objects are there?' has an answer, namely 'three' in the case of the first version ("Carnap's World") and 'seven' (or 'eight') in the case of the second version ("The Polish Logician's World"). Once we make clear how we are using 'object' (or 'exist'), the question 'How many objects exist?' has an answer that is not at all a matter of "convention." That is why I say that this sort of example does not support *radical* cultural relativism. Our concepts may be culturally relative, but it does not follow that the truth or falsity of everything we say using those concepts is simply "decided" by the culture. But the idea that there is an Archimedean point, or a use of 'exist' inherent in the world itself, from which the question 'How many objects *really* exist?' makes sense, is an illusion.

If this is right, then it may be possible to see how it can be that what is in one sense the "same" world (the two versions are deeply related) can be described as consisting of "tables and chairs" (and these described as colored, possessing dispositional properties, etc.) in one version *and* as consisting of space-time regions, particles and fields, etc., in other versions. To require that all of these *must* be reducible to a single version is to make the mistake of supposing that "Which are the real objects?" is a question that makes sense *independently of our choice of concepts.*

What I am saying is frankly programmatic. Let me close by briefly indicating where the program leads, and what I hope from it.

Many thinkers have argued that the traditional dichotomy between the world "in itself" and the concepts we use to think and talk about it must be given up. To mention only the most recent examples, Davidson has argued that the distinction between 'scheme' and 'content' cannot be drawn; Goodman has argued that the distinction between 'world' and 'versions' is untenable; and Quine has defended 'ontological relativity'. Like the great pragmatists, these thinkers have urged us to reject the spectator point of view in metaphysics and epistemology. Quine has urged us to accept the existence of abstract entities on the ground that these are indispensible in mathematics,[10] and of microparticles and space-time points on the ground that these are indispensible in physics; and what better justification is there for accepting an ontology than its indispensibility in our scientific practice? he asks. Goodman has urged us to take seriously the metaphors that artists use to restructure our worlds, on the ground that these are an indispensible way of understanding our experience. Davidson has rejected the idea that talk of propositional attitudes is "second class," on similar grounds. These thinkers have been somewhat hesitant to forthrightly extend the same approach to our moral images of ourselves and the world. Yet what can giving up the spectator view in philosophy mean if we don't extend the pragmatic approach to the most indispensible "versions" of ourselves and our world that we possess?

Notes

1. *Science, Perception, and Reality,* Atlantic Highlands, NJ: Humanities Press, 1963.

2. *The Crisis of the European Sciences and Transcendental Phenomenology,* translated by David Carr, Evanston: Northwestern University Press, 1970.

3. See C. L. Hardin's "Are 'Scientific' Objects Colored?," in *Mind,* XCIII, No. 22 (October 1964), 491–500.

4. The commonsense notion of 'solidity' should not be confused with the physicist's notion of being in 'the solid state'. For example, a sand dune is in the 'solid state' but is not solid in the ordinary sense of the term, while a bottle of milk may be solid, but most of its contents are not in the solid state.

5. "The 'Mental' and the 'Physical,'" in *Minnesota Studies in the Philosophy of*

Science, vol. II, *Concepts, Theories and the Mind-Body Problem,* ed. by Feigl, Scriven, and Maxwell, Minneapolis: University of Minnesota Press, 1958, 370–497.

6. This is argued in my *Representation and Reality,* Cambridge, MA: MIT Press, 1988.

7. D. C. Dennett, *Content and Consciousness,* Atlantic Highlands, NJ: Humanities Press, 1969.

8. *Philosophy and the Mirror of Nature,* Princeton: Princeton University Press, 1979.

9. Stephen Stich, *From Folk Psychology to Cognitive Science: The Case Against Belief,* Cambridge, MA: MIT Press, 1983.

10. "On What There Is," reprinted in *From a Logical Point of View,* Cambridge, MA: Harvard, 1953.

3

Epistemology of Objectivity

Israel Scheffler

The so-called certainty of the given cannot protect its purported descriptions from mistake; the given can therefore not provide a fixed control over conceptualization. If we attempt to picture all our beliefs as somehow controlled by our reports of the given, we shall have to concede that these reports are themselves not rigidly constrained by what is given in fact, since they are themselves subject to error. It does no good, then, to suppose that they constitute points of direct and self-evident contact between our belief systems and reality—firm touchstones by which all our other beliefs are to be judged but which are themselves beyond criticism. Observation reports, in short, cannot be construed as isolated certainties. They must survive a continuous process of accommodation with our other beliefs, a process in the course of which they may themselves be overridden. The control they exercise lies not in an *infallibility* which is beyond their reach; it consists rather in an *independence* of other beliefs, an ability to clash with the rest in such a way as to force a systematic review threatening to all.

But can such a conception of independence be sufficient for a theory of objective control over belief? Does it provide an adequate restriction of arbitrariness in the choice of hypotheses? Conflict provides at best, after all, a motivation for restoring consistency. However, if this is the only motivation I am bound to honor, I am free to choose at will among equally coherent bodies of belief at variance with one another; I need not prefer the consistent factual account to the consistent distortion nor, indeed, to the coherent fairy tale. Faced with a conflict between my observation reports and my theory, I may freely alter or discard the former or the latter or both, so long as I replace my initial inconsistent set of beliefs with one that is coherent. Clearly, this much freedom is too much freedom. Constraints beyond that of consistency must be acknowledged.

Yet, in denying the doctrine of certainty, have we not made it impossible to do just that? If all our beliefs are infected with the possibility of error, if none of our descriptions is guaranteed to be true, none can provide us with an absolutely reliable link to reality. None can serve, through an immediately transparent correspondence with fact, as an additional, referential constraint upon our choices of belief. Our beliefs float free of fact, and the best we can do is to ensure consistency among them. The dilemma is severe and uncomfortable: swallow the myth of certainty or concede that we cannot tell fact from fancy.

This dilemma lies at the root of much controversy among scientifically minded philosophers in recent decades. A review of certain elements of the controversy will enrich our grasp of the problem and help to elucidate the approach of these lectures. We take as the primary object of such review the debate within the Vienna Circle in the 1930s concerning the status of so-called protocol sentences in science. Two chief protagonists in this debate were Otto Neurath and Moritz Schlick, the former rejecting the doctrine of certainty and insisting "that science keeps within the domain of propositions, that propositions are its starting point and terminus," [1] and the latter urging rather that science is "a means of finding one's way among the facts," its confirmation-statements constituting "absolutely fixed points of contact" between "knowledge and reality." [2]

Let us turn first to Neurath who, in his anti-metaphysical zeal, proposes not only that science be purged of phenomenalism and unified through expression in physicalistic language, but also that scientific operations be understood as wholly confined to the realm of statements:

It is always science as a system of statements which is at issue. *Statements are compared with statements,* not with "experiences," "the world," or anything else. All these meaningless *duplications* belong to a more or less refined metaphysics and are, for that reason, to be rejected. Each new statement is compared with the totality of existing statements previously coordinated. To say that a statement is correct, therefore, means that it can be incorporated in this totality. What cannot be incorporated is rejected as incorrect. The alternative to rejection of the new statement is, in general, one accepted only with great reluctance: the whole previous system of statements can be modified up to the point where it becomes possible to incorporate the new statement. . . . The definition of "correct" and "incorrect" proposed here departs from that customary among the "Vienna Circle," which appeals to "meaning" and "verification." In our presentation we confine ourselves always to the sphere of linguistic thought [SP, 291].

Against the notion of a primitive and incorrigible set of so-called protocol statements as the basis of science, Neurath is adamant. "There is no way of taking conclusively established pure protocol sentences as the starting point of the sciences," he writes.[3] Aside from tautologies, the protocol as well as the non-protocol sentences of unified science share the same physicalistic form and are subject to the same treatment. The protocol statements are distinguished by the fact that "in them, a personal noun always occurs several times in a specific association with other terms. A complete protocol sentence might, for instance, read: 'Otto's protocol at 3:17 o'clock: [At 3:16 o'clock Otto said to himself: (at 3:15 o'clock there was a table in the room perceived by Otto)]'" (PS, 202). However, the main point to be stressed is not that protocol sentences are distinct but rather that *"Every law and every physicalistic sentence of unified-science or of one of its sub-sciences is subject to . . . change. And the same holds for protocol sentences"* (PS, 203).

The motivation for change is the wish to maintain consistency, for "In unified science we try to construct a non-contradictory system of protocol sentences and non-protocol sentences (including laws)" (PS, 203). Thus it is that a new sentence in conflict with the accepted system may dislodge a systematic sentence or may itself be rejected, and "The fate of being discarded may befall even a protocol sentence" (PS, 203).

The notion that protocol sentences are primitive and beyond criticism because they are free of interpretation must be abandoned, for "The above formulation of a complete protocol sentence shows that, insofar as personal nouns occur in a protocol, interpretation must *always* already have taken place" (PS, 205). Furthermore, there is, within the innermost brackets, an inescapable reference to some person's "act of perception" (PS, 205). The conclusion is that no sentence of science is to be regarded as more primitive than any other:

All are of equal primitiveness. Personal nouns, words denoting perceptions, and other words of little primitiveness occur in all factual sentences, or, at least, in the hypotheses from which they derive. All of which means that *there are neither primitive protocol sentences nor sentences which are not subject to verification* [PS, 205].

Further, since *"every* language *as such,* is inter-subjective"* (PS, 205), it is meaningless to talk of private languages, or to regard protocol languages as initially disparate, requiring ultimately to be brought together in some special manner. On the contrary, "The protocol languages of the Crusoe of yesterday and of the Crusoe of today are as close and as far apart from one another as are the protocol languages of Crusoe and of Friday" (PS, 206).

Basically, it makes no difference at all whether Kalon works with Kalon's or with Neurath's protocols, or whether Neurath occupies himself with Neurath's or with Kalon's protocols. In order to make this quite clear, we could conceive of a sorting-machine into which protocol sentences are thrown. The laws and other factual sentences (including protocol sentences) serving to mesh the machine's gears sort the protocol sentences which are thrown into the machine and cause a bell to ring if a contradiction ensues. At this point one must either replace the protocol sentence whose introduction into the machine has led to the contradiction by some other protocol sentence, or rebuild the entire machine. *Who* rebuilds the machine, or *whose* protocol sentences are thrown into the machine is of no consequence whatsoever. Anyone may test his own protocol sentences as well as those of others [PS, 207].

Neurath stresses the place of prediction in science. He argues against phenomenal language that it "does not even seem to be usable for 'prediction'—the essence of science . . ." (SP, 290), and urges in favor of physicalism that it enables us to "achieve successful predictions" (SP, 286). He hopes that the fruitfulness of social behaviorism will be shown by the "successful predictions" it will yield (SP, 317), and looks forward to the day when a physicalistic sociology will "formulate valid predictions on a large scale" (SP, 317). Yet, true to his self-imposed restriction to the realm of statements alone, he does not construe the success of a prediction as consisting in its agreement with fact. Rather, he declares: "A prediction is a statement which it is assumed will agree with a future statement" (SP, 317).

Despite his refusal, however, to contrast the "thinking personality" with "experience" (SP, 290), to compare statements with " 'experiences,' 'the world,' or anything else" (SP, 291), and to ask such " 'dangerous' questions . . . as how 'observation' and 'statement' are connected; or, further, how 'sense data' and 'mind,' the 'external world' and the 'internal world' are connected,"[4] he slips into what he ought surely to have regarded, in a more careful moment, as dangerous metaphysics:

Ignoring all meaningless statements, the unified science proper to a given historical period proceeds from proposition to proposition, blending them into a self-consistent system which is an instrument for successful prediction, and, consequently, for life [SP, 286].

To speak rashly in this way of the relation between science and life is clearly to leave the pure realm of statements and to admit, after all, that science cannot be adequately characterized in terms of consistency alone, that its very point, indeed, is to refer to what lies beyond itself.

Surely, not all self-consistent systems are "instruments for life," in the intended sense. The supposition that unified science issues in such practically useful instruments goes beyond the range of consistency in a manner that is not satisfactorily explained by Neurath's general account. He implies, of course, that practical usefulness accrues to science in virtue of its yielding successful predictions. This explanation is hardly adequate, however, for Neurath understands the success of a prediction to consist simply in its agreement with a later statement; on this criterion all predictions succeed which are followed by reiterations of themselves or by other statements coherent with them.

In the first of the passages by Neurath earlier quoted, he speaks of comparing each new statement with "the totality of existing statements previously coordinated" (SP, 291), to determine whether or not the statement can be incorporated in the totality. Perhaps the idea is that there is one presumably coherent totality which is to be singled out as a standard on each occasion of comparison, namely, that totality last ratified by acceptance and still in force on that occasion. The factor of *acceptance* may thus be thought to constitute a relevant selective consideration beyond consistency—a consideration that, moreover, escapes the dangers of metaphysics by avoiding appeal to a reality to which statements refer.

Now the *acceptance* of a statement is indeed relevantly independent of its *reference,* but acceptance also fails to differentiate between beliefs that are critically accepted on the basis of factual evidence and those that are not. The method of comparison recommended in the passage under consideration thus applies as well to entrenched myths and indoctrinated distortions as to scientific systems. What is of crucial significance, however, is that this method provides no incentive to *revise* the accepted totality of beliefs. For the assumed coherence of this totality can always be preserved by rejecting *all* new conflicting sentences. Neurath concedes, in fact, that the alternative to such rejection, consisting in revision of the accepted totality, is adopted "only with great reluctance" (SP, 291). The mystery, on his account, is why it should ever be adopted at all. Any coherent totality is, so far as his method is concerned, capable of being established as forever safe from revision, and thereby warranted as correct, to boot.

It is, moreover, pertinent to question the assumed interpretation of acceptance: acceptance by whom? The assumption that acceptance singles out one presumably coherent totality on each occasion of comparison is perhaps plausible if we consider just one individual. It is groundless if we take into account the acceptances of the whole "inter-subjective" community in line with Neurath's general attitude. For he deplores the "emphasis on the 'I' familiar to us from idealistic philosophy" (PS, 206), and considers it meaningless to talk of personal protocol languages. "One can," he writes, "distinguish an *Otto-protocol* from a *Karl-protocol*, but not a protocol of one's own from a protocol of others" (PS, 206). A general rather than an individual appeal to the factor of acceptance, however, yields a multiplicity of conflicting totalities of belief: Which of these is to serve as a standard?

There are passages, indeed, in which Neurath seems to be making no appeal to anything even approximating acceptance. He does not speak, in these passages, of "*the* totality of existing statements previously coordinated," but acknowledges rather a plurality of mutually conflicting totalities simply as abstract choices open to the investigator. To be consistent, the investigator may not choose more than one of these, but there is no further constraint on his choice beyond convenience. Thus, Neurath writes:

A social scientist who, after careful analysis, rejects certain reports and hypotheses, reaches a state, finally, in which he has to face comprehensive sets of statements which compete with other comprehensive sets of statements. All these sets may be composed of statements which seem to him plausible and acceptable. There is no place for an empiricist question: Which is the "true" set? but only whether the social scientist has sufficient time and energy to try more than one set or to decide that he, in regard to his lack of time and energy—and this is the important point—should work with one of these comprehensive sets only.[5]

We find here, to be sure, a passing reference to plausibility and acceptability, but it is wholly unexplained, and can, moreover, have no point
unless we move outside the "sphere of linguistic thought" (SP, 291) in a
manner for which Neurath has altogether failed to prepare us. As to the
choice among incompatible systems, any one is as good as any other;
within the limits of time and energy, the decision between them is arbitrary. The machine analogy earlier quoted does indeed, as Neurath says,
make the point "quite clear." The machine detects contradictions but,
aside from a general restriction to physicalistic language which may be
assumed, no principle of selection is supplied for determining its input.
Protocol sentences, distinguished solely by their form, may be chosen arbitrarily for insertion. Nor is there any restriction on the structure of the
machine beyond its requiring the inclusion of at least some laws, presumably also distinguished by their form alone. So long as no contradiction
has been detected among its virtually arbitrary elements, moreover, the
machine is to be taken as the very embodiment and standard of correctness. The picture is one of unrelieved coherence free of any taint of fact.
Since any consistent statement or system whatever can be accommodated
by some such machine, any such statement or system can be fastened
upon, held to be correct, and thenceforth protected forever from revision.
The dogmatism of certainty has given way to the dogmatism of coherence.
We have here not a picture of science but a desperate philosophical
caricature.

What impels Neurath to construct this caricature? To appreciate his
philosophical motivation is to gain a deeper understanding of the basic
dilemma we face between coherence and certainty. He is, as we have seen,
opposed to the idea that protocol sentences are above criticism because
totally free of interpretation, serving simply to register the raw facts as
given. On the contrary, he upholds the view that all statements in science
are subject to change, insisting that observation reports may themselves
be discarded under pressure of conflict with other scientific statements.
Accordingly he emphasizes the "unified" nature of science, that is to say,
the fact that no statement is an island—that each can survive only within
a systematically harmonious community of statements. In place of the
doctrine that selected statements provide an infallible contact with reality
and are thus privileged to exercise unilateral control over the rest,

Neurath urges a fluid and egalitarian conception: control is provisional, mutual, and diffused throughout the community of statements, resting in no case upon infallible access to fact.

Indeed, the very notion of such access seems to require the supposition that statement and reality might, through direct comparison, be determined to correspond with each other. But such a supposition is meaningless from Neurath's point of view. One can certainly compare statements with statements, but to imagine that statements can be literally compared with reality or with facts is to fall prey to an obfuscating metaphysics.

Now Neurath's remarks on this theme may appear, at first blush, to be simply a dogmatic denial of the obvious. His underlying thought may perhaps be interpreted more plausibly as a rejection of the philosophical tendency to read linguistic features into reality. The structure of language is not, after all, to be taken naively as a clue to the structure of reality. The correspondence suggested, for example, between atomic statements and atomic facts, and between molecular statements and molecular facts, is supported by nothing more than an anterior, and quite gratuitous hypostatization of objects to which certain elements of a language may be said to be directed. Facts, in general, understood as peculiar extralinguistic entities precisely parallel to true statements, belong, in Neurath's scheme, to the class of "meaningless duplications . . . to be rejected" (SP, 291).[6]

Not only are such duplications superfluous; they mislead us into supposing that, in locating them independently and finding them to share the same structure with certain statements, we have a genuine method of justifying the acceptance of these statements. But facts, as entities distinct from the true statements to which they are presumed to correspond, have no careers of their own capable of sustaining such a method. These ghostly copies of true statements cannot be independently specified, confronted, or analyzed; their reality is no easier to determine than the truth of their respective parent sentences. Faced with the problem whether to *judge* a given sentence *as* true, it therefore does us no good to be told simply to ascertain whether there exists a structurally corresponding fact. If I am undecided about the truth of the sentence "The car is in the garage," I am equally undecided as to whether or not it is a fact that the car is in the garage: there are not two issues here, but one. Nor do I see how to go about resolving the latter indecision in a way that differs from my attempt to resolve the former. Appeal to the facts, taken strictly, thus turns out question-begging as a general method for ascertaining truth. For it requires, in effect, that the truth be determined as a condition of its own ascertainment.

The import of this line of reasoning may be illustrated strikingly by a consideration of prediction. The prevalent view is that in science, at any rate, a set of beliefs is put to the test by deriving therefrom a prediction that can be checked observationally against actual experience. When such a prediction is borne out by experience, the set of beliefs in question has passed a critical test; when the prediction is violated by experience, the test has been failed and the set must thereupon be revised so as to eliminate the prediction in question. The question that needs to be faced, however, is the question of how we can tell whether or not a prediction has been borne out or violated by experience. It must be stressed to begin with that the relations of logical consistency and contradiction hold only between certain statements and others, and *not* between statements and experiences. It may well be granted, therefore, that if a system *S* yields a prediction *P* and if we independently require *S* to be logically consistent with *Not-P*, we shall have to revise *S*. So far the issue concerns only the consistency relations among statements. But what, it may be asked, is our initial basis for setting logical consistency with *Not-P* as a constraint upon *S*? What can lead us to adopt *Not-P* in the first place?

To appeal to the logical consistency of *Not-P* with experience is nonsense. To say that we accept *Not-P* if it in turn yields predictions that are borne out by experience is to take the fatal first step in an infinite regress. To suggest that *Not-P* be judged true if and only if the corresponding fact represented by *Not-P* is real begs the question, as we have seen. To suppose, finally, that we have an infallible intuition of the truth of *Not-P* as a description of reality, that somehow its truth is immediately and indubitably evident to us upon intellectual inspection, is to revert to the myth of certainty. The conclusion to which we thus appear driven is that the whole idea of checking beliefs against experience is misguided. We do not go outside the realm of statements at all. What figures in the control of our system of beliefs is not experience, but purported statements of experience; not observation, but observation reports. Such is Neurath's conclusion, as we have already seen—a conclusion that, however well motivated, must surely be judged unacceptable as an account of science.

Convinced of the unacceptability of Neurath's account, Schlick insists that there must be an "unshakeable point of contact between knowledge and reality" (p. 226). To give up "the good old expression 'agreement with reality'" (p. 215), and to espouse instead a coherence theory such as that propounded by Neurath yields intolerable consequences:

> If one is to take coherence seriously as a general criterion of truth, then one must consider arbitrary fairy stories to be as true as a historical report, or as statements in a textbook of chemistry, provided the story is constructed in such a way that no contradiction ever arises. I can depict by help of fantasy a grotesque world full of bizarre adventures: the coherence philosopher must believe in the truth of my account provided only I take care of the mutual compatibility of my statements, and also take the precaution of avoiding any collision with the usual description of the world, by placing the scene of my story on a distant star, where no observation is possible. Indeed, strictly speaking, I don't even require this precaution; I can just as well demand that the others have to adapt themselves to my description; and not the other way round. They cannot then object that, say, this happening runs counter to the observations, for according to the coherence theory there is no question of observations, but only of the compatibility of statements.
>
> Since no one dreams of holding the statements of a story book true and those of a text of physics false, the coherence view fails utterly. Something more, that is, must be added to coherence, namely, a principle in terms of which the compatibility is to be established, and this would alone then be the actual criterion [pp. 215–216].

Since, in the case of conflict within a given set of statements, the coherence theory allows us to eliminate such conflict in various ways, "on one occasion selecting certain statements and abandoning or altering them and on another occasion doing the same with the other statements that contradict the first," the theory fails to provide an unambiguous criterion, yielding "any number of consistent systems of statements which are incompatible with one another" (p. 216). Schlick concludes that "The only way to avoid this absurdity is not to allow any statements whatever to be abandoned or altered, but rather to specify those that are to be maintained, to which the remainder have to be accommodated" (p. 216).

One might suppose, on the basis of such a conclusion, that Schlick would proceed to a defense of the certainty of protocol statements. Not so, however. He grants that such statements, as exemplified by familiar recorded accounts of scientific observation, and associated with "empirical facts upon which the edifice of science is subsequently built," are indeed subject to error and revision. "They are anything but incontrovertible, and one can use them in the construction of the system of science only so long as they are supported by, or at least not contradicted by, other hypotheses" (pp. 212–213). Even our own previously enunciated protocol statements may be withdrawn. "We grant," writes Schlick,

that our mind at the moment the judgment was made may have been wholly confused, and that an experience which we now say we had two minutes ago may upon later examination be found to have been an hallucination, or even one that never took place at all.

Thus it is clear that on this view of protocol statements they do not provide one who is in search of a firm basis of knowledge with anything of the sort. On the contrary, the actual result is that one ends by abandoning the original distinction between protocol and other statements as meaningless [p. 213].

Schlick thus agrees with Neurath in denying a privileged role to protocol statements. Like Neurath, he insists that they "have in principle exactly the same character as all the other statements of science: they are hypotheses, nothing but hypotheses" (p. 212). Where, then, is the fixed point of contact between knowledge and reality? Schlick's view is that it is to be located in a special class of statements that are not themselves within science but are nevertheless essential to its function and, in particular, to its confirmation. His special term for these statements is *Konstatierungen*, though he sometimes calls them "observation statements"; I shall here refer to them uniformly as "confirmation statements."[7]

A confirmation statement is a momentary description of what is simultaneously perceived or experienced. It provides an *occasion* for the production of a protocol statement proper, which is preserved in writing or in memory; it must, however, be sharply distinguished from the protocol statement to which it may give rise. For this protocol statement can no longer describe what is simultaneous with itself; the critical experience has lapsed during the time taken to fix it in writing or memory. The protocol statement, moreover, unlike the confirmation statement, does not die as soon as it is born; its own life extends far beyond the initial point nearest the experience in question. Though it has, to be sure, the advantage of providing an enduring account, the protocol statement is, thus, never more than a hypothesis, subject to interpretation and revision. "For, when we have such a statement before us, it is a mere assumption that it is true, that it agrees with the observation statements [i.e., the confirmation statements] that give rise to it" (pp. 220–221).

Confirmation statements may serve to stimulate the development of genuine scientific hypotheses, but they are too elusive to be construed as the ultimate and certain *basis* of knowledge. Their contribution consists rather in providing an absolute and indubitable culmination to the process of testing hypotheses. When a predicted experience occurs, and we simultaneously pronounce it to have occurred, we derive "thereby a feeling of *fulfilment*, a quite characteristic satisfaction: we are *satisfied*" (p. 222). Confirmation statements perform their characteristic function when we obtain such satisfaction.

And it is obtained in the very moment in which the confirmation takes place, in which the observation statement [i.e., confirmation statement] is made. This is of the utmost importance. For thus the function of the statements about the immediately experienced itself lies in the immediate present. Indeed we saw that they have so to speak no duration, that the moment they are gone one has at one's disposal in their place inscriptions, or memory traces, that can play only the role of hypotheses and thereby lack ultimate certainty. One cannot build any logically tenable structure upon the confirmations, for they are gone the moment one begins to construct. If they stand at the beginning of the process of cognition they are logically of no use. Quite otherwise however if they stand at the end; they bring verification (or also falsification) to completion, and in the moment of their occurrence they have already fulfilled their duty. Logically nothing more depends on them, no conclusions are drawn from them. They constitute an absolute end [p. 222].

In bringing a cycle of testing to an absolute close, a confirmation statement helps to steer the further course of scientific investigation: a falsified hypothesis is rejected and the search for an adequate replacement ensues; a verified hypothesis is upheld and "the formulation of more general hypotheses is sought, the guessing and search for universal laws goes on" (p. 222). The cognitive culmination represented by confirmation statements had, originally, according to Schlick, a purely practical import: it indicated the reliability of underlying hypotheses as to the nature of man's environment, and thus aided man's adjustment to this environment. In science, the joy of confirmation is no longer tied to the "purposes of life" (p. 222), but is pursued for its own sake:

And it is this that the observation statements [confirmation statements] bring about. In them science as it were achieves its goal: it is for their sake that it exists. . . . That a new task begins with the pleasure in which they culminate, and with the hypotheses that they leave behind does not concern them. Science does not rest upon them but leads to them, and they indicate that it has led correctly. They are really the absolute fixed points; it gives us joy to reach them, even if we cannot stand upon them [p. 223].

What is it, however, that enables confirmation statements to constitute "absolute fixed points"? In what does their special claim to certainty consist? Schlick conceives these statements as always containing demonstrative terms. His examples are, "Here yellow borders on blue," "Here two black points coincide," "Here now pain." The constituent demonstratives function as gestures. "In order therefore to understand the meaning of such an observation statement [confirmation statement] one must simultaneously execute the gesture, one must somehow point to reality" (p. 225). Thus, he argues, one can understand a confirmation statement "only by, and when, comparing it with the facts, thus carrying out that process which is necessary for the verification of all synthetic statements" (p. 225). For to comprehend its meaning is simultaneously to apprehend the reality indicated by its demonstrative terms.

While in the case of all other synthetic statements determining the meaning is separate from, distinguishable from, determining the truth, in the case of observation statements [confirmation statements] they coincide. . . . the occasion of understanding them is at the same time that of verifying them: I grasp their meaning at the same time as I grasp their truth. In the case of a confirmation it makes as little sense to ask whether I might be deceived regarding its truth as in the case of a tautology. Both are absolutely valid. However, while the analytic, tautological, statement is empty of content, the observation statement [confirmation statement] supplies us with the satisfaction of genuine knowledge of reality [p. 225].

The distinctiveness of confirmation statements lies, then, in their immediacy, that is, their capacity to point to a simultaneous experience, in the manner of a gesture. To such immediacy they "owe their value and disvalue; the value of absolute validity, and the disvalue of uselessness as an abiding foundation" (p. 225). It is of the first importance, for Schlick's view, to recognize the distinctiveness of confirmation statements and, in particular, to separate them from protocol statements, for this separation is the key to the problem as he sees it. "Here now blue" is thus not to be confused with the protocol statement of Neurath's type: "M. S. perceived blue on the nth of April 1934 at such and such a time and such and such a place." The latter is an uncertain hypothesis, but it is distinct from the former: it must mention a perception and identify an observer. On the other hand, one cannot write down a confirmation statement without altering the meaning of its demonstratives, nor can one formulate an equivalent without demonstratives, for one then "unavoidably substitutes . . . a protocol statement which as such has a wholly different nature" (p. 226).

In sum, if we consider simply the body of scientific statements, they are all hypotheses, all uncertain. To take into account also the relation of this body of statements to reality requires, however, that we acknowledge the special role of confirmation statements as well. An understanding of these statements enables us to see science as "that which it really is, namely, a means of finding one's way among the facts; of arriving at the joy of confirmation, the feeling of finality" (p. 226). These statements do not "lie at the base of science; but like a flame, cognition, as it were, licks out to them, reaching each but for a moment and then at once consuming it. And newly fed and strengthened, it flames onward to the next" (p. 227).

We have already expressed our own agreement with the critical side of Schlick's doctrine, namely, his rejection of a coherence theory such as Neurath's. We, too, have stressed the importance of acknowledging constraints upon our belief beyond those imposed by consistency alone. We can therefore sympathize with Schlick's effort to propose an account of scientific systems that relates them to the reality to which they purport to refer. And it must indeed be admitted that the spirit of his general view of science is in closer accord than Neurath's with our familiar conceptions as well as with the understandings of scientists themselves as to the purport of their own activities.

Yet Schlick's positive theory suffers from a variety of fundamental difficulties that render it altogether unacceptable. Let us consider, first of all, whether his doctrine of confirmation statements is capable of meeting the problem as he has diagnosed it. He seeks, after all, a principle beyond coherence "in terms of which the compatibility is to be established," insisting that the only way to avoid the difficulties of the coherence theory is to avoid allowing "any statements whatever to be abandoned or altered, but rather to specify those that are to be maintained, to which the remainder have to be accommodated" (p. 216).

But if this is indeed the only way to avoid the difficulties of the coherence view, then it must be doubted that Schlick's positive doctrine in fact succeeds in avoiding them. For the coherence view purports to be a theory of science—of "science as a system of statements," as Neurath puts it. Any attempt to restrict the arbitrariness of coherence along the lines of Schlick's diagnosis must specify fixed points to which the statements of science are to be adjusted. It must, that is, specify a fixity to which *science* is responsive, by which *scientific* spontaneity is contained. In particular, it must not permit every scientific statement whatever to be subject to revision but must, on the contrary, place definite limits upon statement revision within science.

It is just here that Schlick's doctrine fails. For he identifies as "absolute fixed points" only *confirmation statements,* which fall outside science, and he insists, moreover, that these statements provide no barrier whatever to the revision of scientific statements proper. In particular, Schlick stresses that protocol statements, which are the closest counterparts of confirmation statements within science, "have in principle exactly the same character as all the other statements of science: they are hypotheses, nothing but hypotheses . . . one can use them in the construction of the system of science only so long as they are supported by, or at least not contradicted by, other hypotheses" (pp. 212–213). We have here, it seems, a clear admission that, within the realm of science, coherence continues to rule, despite the certainty attributed to confirmation statements. The latter have in effect been so sharply sundered from the body of science that they can yield it no advantage derived from their own presumed fixity. If reality alone provides no fixed control over scientific systems, the postulation of intermediate confirmation statements thus accomplishes nothing in the way of achieving such control.

Nor is it easy to make Schlick's general account of the scientific role of such statements intelligible. They are described as having an essential role in scientific functioning—in particular, in the testing and verification of hypotheses. They are not to be thought of as constituting a logical basis or origin of science. "If they stand at the beginning of the process of cognition they are logically of no use" (p. 222). Rather, "they bring verification (or also falsification) to completion. . . . Logically nothing more depends on them, no conclusions are drawn from them. They constitute an absolute end" (p. 222). In marking the fulfillment of scientific predictions, confirmation statements are, however, said not only to yield a characteristic satisfaction, but to influence the course of subsequent inquiry: "the hypotheses whose verification ends in them are considered to be upheld, and the formulation of more general hypotheses is sought, the guessing and search for universal laws goes on" (p. 222). The problem is whether these various features ascribed to confirmation statements can be reconciled with one another.

For, on the one hand, these statements constitute an absolute end, having no logical function when standing at the beginning of further cognitive processes, since "the moment they are gone one has at one's disposal in their place inscriptions, or memory traces, that can play only the role of hypotheses and thereby lack ultimate certainty" (p. 222). On the other hand, they enable us to uphold the hypotheses they serve to verify and to reject those they falsify, in either case leading us to conduct subsequent inquiry in a significantly different manner. If, however, a confirmation statement truly constitutes an absolute end, how can it serve thus to qualify our further treatment of relevant hypotheses? Why, indeed, should a hypothesis, supposedly verified by a confirmation statement a moment before the last, be considered *now* to have been clearly upheld, leading us to search for broader hypotheses rather than simply to continue testing the original one? We now have, after all, only the fallible record of an alleged earlier verification and, as Schlick remarks, "it is a mere assumption that it is true" (p. 220), that it agrees with its parent confirmation statement. Similarly, why should the present protocol statement recording an alleged past falsification be taken as the trace of an absolute falsification by its parent confirmation statement, since it is itself no more than a hypothesis, subject only to the weak demands of coherence? In short, if the door closed by a given confirmation statement is indeed immediately reopened, this statement can constitute no absolute end; if, on the other hand, the door remains shut, the statement clearly has a logical bearing, in fact, an unwarranted logical bearing, upon subsequent in investigation. Confirmation statements, it seems, cannot bring testing processes to absolute completion without qualifying further inquiry in a manner precluded by their momentary duration. However, unless they do bring such processes to absolute completion, they have, on Schlick's account, no function at all in the economy of science. The conclusion that Schlick's account of these statements is self-contradictory seems inescapable.

The notion that confirmation statements can have no logical function for subsequent cognitive processes rests on their radical immediacy, that is, on the idea that their function "lies in the immediate present" (p. 222). Schlick thus emphasizes their differentiation from the protocol statements to which they may give rise, statements which are "always characterized by uncertainty" (p. 226). To write down a confirmation statement or even to preserve it in memory is, strictly speaking, impossible, for the meaning of critical demonstratives is altered by preservation; replacement of these demonstratives "by an indication of time and place" moreover inevitably results in the creation of "a protocol statement which as such has a wholly different nature" (p. 226). But immediacy, one may feel, should cut both ways: if it eliminates logical bearing on subsequent processes, it must equally eliminate such bearing on earlier ones. Yet Schlick holds, as we have seen, that confirmation statements bring testing processes to an absolute completion.

> Have our predictions actually come true? In every single case of verification or falsification a "confirmation" [confirmation statement] answers unambiguously with a yes or a no, with joy of fulfilment or disappointment. The confirmations are final [p. 223].

How can this be? The prediction is, after all, a scientific hypothesis with "a wholly different nature" from that of the confirmation statement in question. How can it derive any benefit from the latter's certainty any more than a later protocol statement can?

Schlick gives, as an example of a prediction: "If at such and such a time you look through a telescope adjusted in such and such a manner you will see a point of light (a star) in coincidence with a black mark (cross wires)" (p. 221). Suppose we now have the confirmation statement, "Here now a point of light in coincidence with a black mark." For the sake of argument, let us grant that the latter statement is, at the critical moment, certain. Does it follow that it constitutes an unambiguous and final answer to the question of whether the prediction has in fact come true? Not at all. For the prediction stipulates, in its antecedent clause, certain conditions relating to physical apparatus, time, and the activity of an observer. Unless the experience reported by the confirmation statement is assumed to have occurred in accordance with the conditions thus stipulated, it cannot even be judged relevant to the prediction, much less to fulfill it with finality. On the other hand, if the assumption is made that these conditions have been satisfied in fact, this critical assumption itself shares in the uncertainty of the prediction, being itself clearly no more than a physical hypothesis. The question of whether a prediction has in fact come true is, then, just the question of whether a corrigible scientific statement, rather than a confirmation statement, is true. Such a question can always be reopened. The conclusion must be that the alleged certainty of confirmation statements no more enables them to provide absolutely certain completions for earlier scientific processes than it equips them to constitute absolute origins.

The alleged certainty of these statements must, finally, be called into question: What does such certainty amount to? According to Schlick, I cannot be deceived regarding the truth of my own confirmation statements, even though, as he writes, "the possibilities of error are innumerable" (p. 212). He admits, of course, that protocol statements are subject to error. Indeed, in one passage he concedes that a protocol statement saying "that N. N. used such and such an instrument to make such and such an observation" may be mistaken, because N. N. may "inadvertently . . . have described something that does not accurately represent the observed fact" (p. 212). Does this not imply that, in such a case, N. N. was himself deceived regarding the truth of his own confirmation statement? Such an implication is certainly unwelcome to Schlick, and contrary to his fundamental view. The question remains as to how it might reasonably be avoided. What is it, indeed, that precludes errors due to inadvertence and poor judgment in the case of confirmation statements alone, allowing them full scope in all other cases?

Schlick certainly does not suppose that one's own statements are generally immune to error. "Even in the case of statements which we ourselves have put forward," he writes, "we do not in principle exclude the possibility of error" (p. 213). However, he continues immediately to illustrate his point with specific and exclusive reference to protocol statements: "We grant that our mind at the moment the judgment was made may have been wholly confused, and that an experience which we now say we had two minutes ago may upon later examination be found to have been a hallucination, or even one that never took place at all" (p. 213). A statement by which we affirm the occurrence of our experience of two minutes earlier can, of course, in his scheme, not be a confirmation statement at all but only a protocol statement. The question persists, however: Is mental confusion possible only in the making of protocol statements? What protects us from confusion in the judgment of simultaneous experience? What necessity ensures us against error?

Concerning protocol statements occasioned by confirmation statements, Schlick writes that they are to be classed as hypotheses. "For, when we have such a statement before us, it is a mere assumption that it is true, that it agrees with the observation statements [confirmation statements] that give rise to it" (p. 220). The supposition is evident that if a protocol statement disagrees with the relevant confirmation statement, it must be the former and not the latter which is false. But why this asymmetry? What prevents the protocol statement from giving a truer account of a man's experience at a given moment than his own description at that moment? In one passage, Schlick suggests the curious doctrine that the protocol statement reports not a perception or an experience but rather the occurrence of a confirmation statement. The protocol statement, "M.S. perceived blue on the nth of April 1934 at such and such a time and such and such a place," he declares equivalent to "M.S. made . . . (here time and place are to be given) the confirmation 'here now blue'" (p. 226). Under such a doctrine, to be sure, if M.S.'s actual confirmation statement at the relevant time and place was "Here now yellow," the protocol statement must be false. It does not follow, however, that the confirmation statement is true. And the proposed equivalence must itself be rejected, for to perceive blue and to say "Here now blue," are surely different. If it is false that M.S. *said* "Here now blue," it is not therefore false that he *perceived* blue. Despite the fact that he actually said "Here now yellow," he may have perceived blue: his confirmation statement itself may have been false. What eliminates such a possibility?

The fundamental answer, in Schlick's theory, is given by his reference to the demonstrative terms included in confirmation statements. As he puts it, "'This here' has meaning only in connection with a gesture" (p. 225). To comprehend the meaning of a confirmation statement, "one must somehow point to reality" (p. 225). It follows, in his view, that I cannot understand a confirmation statement without thereby determining it to be true. Here is the fundamental source of the certainty of confirmation statements: their understanding presupposes their verification. Now it may perhaps be argued that the certainty thus yielded is weak because it is dependent upon the notion of "understanding." (I may, indeed, not be at all sure I understand a given confirmation statement when I make it, and may later decide that in fact I did not.) But the trouble, in any case, runs much deeper than this. Schlick's basic conception of the matter rests, I believe, upon a confusion.

For suppose it be granted that the meaning of demonstrative terms derives from their function as gestures, by which, as Schlick remarks, "the attention is directed upon something observed" (p. 225). Suppose it be admitted that "in order therefore to understand the meaning" of a confirmation statement, "one must simultaneously execute the gesture, one must somehow point to reality" (p. 225). What can be inferred from such admissions? They imply only that the comprehension of a confirmation statement requires attention to those observed elements indicated by its constituent demonstrative terms. In this and this sense only can comprehension of the statement be said to involve a "pointing to reality." By no means is it implied that we must point to reality in the wholly different sense of verifying the attribution represented by the statement as a whole. To attend to an indicated thing cannot be equated with determining the truth of any affirmation concerning it. It is therefore simply fallacious to infer, from the presumed necessity of attending to the things indicated by embedded demonstratives, the necessity of verifying the assertion made by a statement with the help of such demonstratives, in order to grasp its meaning.

The fallacy is concealed by the equivocal phrase "pointing to reality." For, in explaining the latter phrase, initially introduced to denote attention to the reference of a demonstrative term functioning as a gesture, Schlick writes: "In other words: I can understand the meaning of a 'confirmation' [confirmation statement] only by, and when, comparing it with the facts, thus carrying out that process which is necessary for the verification of all synthetic statements" (p. 225). Here is the easy, but illegitimate shift from the reference of a term to the reference of a statement, from things indicated to facts expressed, from attending to the object of a demonstrative to verifying the truth of a statement. Once this shift is exposed, Schlick's fundamental argument for the certainty of confirmation statements falls to the ground: the understanding of such statements does not, after all, presuppose their verification. I may understand a confirmation statement and be undecided as to its truth; what is more, I can understand, and even affirm, a confirmation statement that is false. Schlick's positive theory, no less than Neurath's, thus proves untenable.

The failure of both these theories may engender despair. For they seem, between them, to exhaust the possibilities for dealing with our basic dilemma between coherence and certainty. Either some of our beliefs must be transparently true of reality and beyond the scope of error and revision, or else we are free to choose any consistent set of beliefs whatever as our own, and to define "correctness" or "truth" accordingly. Either we suppose our beliefs to reflect the facts, in which case we beg the very question of truth and project our language gratuitously upon the world, or else we abandon altogether the intent to describe reality, in which case our scientific efforts reduce to nothing more than a word game. We can, in sum, neither relate our beliefs to a reality beyond them, nor fail so to relate them.

Despite this grim appraisal, I believe that despair is avoidable, and that the general approach of the previous lectures can be sustained. My view is that while rejecting certainty, it is yet possible to uphold the referential import of science; that to impose effective constraints upon coherence need beg no relevant questions nor people the world with ghostly duplicates of our language. In the remainder of the present lecture, I shall attempt to spell out the reasons for these views.

Let me turn first to the fundamental opposition between coherence and certainty. We have seen how central this opposition is in the thought of both Neurath and Schlick, who take contrary positions. Neurath insists that every scientific statement is subject to change, urging that "There is no way of taking conclusively established pure protocol sentences as the starting point of the sciences" (PS, 201). Rejecting certainty, he rejects, however, also the very idea of checking beliefs against experience or reality, taking coherence to be the only defensible alternative. Schlick, on the other hand, reacting against the absurdities of coherence, is driven to seek a class of "absolutely certain" (p. 223) statements capable of providing an "unshakeable point of contact between knowledge and reality" (p. 226). Affirming the need to relate science to fact, he assumes that only a doctrine of certainty can make such a relationship intelligible. Schlick and Neurath are thus agreed in binding extra-linguistic reference firmly to certainty and they join, therefore, in reducing the effective alternatives to two: (1) a rejection of certainty, as well as of appeals to extra-linguistic reference, yielding a coherence view, and (2) a rejection of the coherence view in favor of an appeal to extra-linguistic reference, yielding a commitment to certainty. Given such a reduction, we are driven to defend coherence if we find certainty repugnant, and impelled to defend certainty if appalled by the doctrine of coherence. The reduction makes it possible for these equally unpleasant alternatives thus to feed upon each other. But this reduction itself must be rejected. There is, in fact, no need to assume that the alternatives are exhausted by coherence and certainty; a third way lies open.

For what is required is simply a steady "referential" limitation upon unbridled coherence; certainty supplies much more than is required. In particular, it imports the notion of a fixity, a freedom from error and consequent revision, which cannot be defended for it is nowhere to be found. The supposition that certainty is required to restrain coherence is perhaps in part due to an ambiguity in the notion of "fixity": in one sense, a fixed point is simply one that is selectively designated, providing us with a frame of reference or a standard, for purposes of a given sort; in another sense, a fixed point is one that, in particular, does not undergo change over time. A point may be fixed in the first sense without being fixed in the second. There may be no temporally constant or *permanently* fixed points in a given context, and yet there may be fixed points that are relevant and effective in that context, at each moment. The scope of unrestrained coherence needs, indeed, to be supplemented by the introduction of relevantly "fixed" points at all times. However, the further supposition that there must be *some* points that are permanently fixed, that is, held forever immune to subsequent revision, is simply gratuitous.

We have earlier cited Schlick's remark that the coherence theory can be avoided only if we specify statements that "are to be maintained, to which the remainder have to be accommodated" (p. 216). That certain statements need to be *maintained* over time is an unwarrantedly strong demand. We need only recognize that statements have referential values for us, independent of their consistency relationships to other statements, and that these values, though subject to variation over time, provide us, at each moment, with sufficient "fixity" to constitute a frame of reference for choice of hypotheses.

How are these values of statements, compatible with lack of certainty, to be conceived? They may be thought of as representing our varied inclinations to affirm given statements as true or assert them as scientifically acceptable; equivalently, they may be construed as indicating the initial claims we recognize statements to make upon us, at any given time, for inclusion within our cognitive systems. A notion of this general sort has been put forward by Bertrand Russell in *Human Knowledge,* under the label "intrinsic credibility,"[8] and Nelson Goodman has spoken, analogously, of "initial credibility,"[9] the adjective serving in each case to differentiate the idea in question from the purely relative concept of "probability with respect to certain other statements." Goodman explains his conception as follows:

Internal coherence is obviously a necessary but not a sufficient condition for the truth of a system; for we need also some means of choosing between equally tight systems that are incompatible with each other. There must be a tie to fact through, it is contended, some immediately certain statements. Otherwise compatibility with a system is not even a probable indication of the truth of any statement.

Now clearly we cannot suppose that statements derive their credibility from other statements without ever bringing this string of statements to earth. Credibility may be transmitted from one statement to another through deductive or probability connections; but credibility does not spring from these connections by spontaneous generation. Somewhere along the line some statements, whether atomic sense reports or the entire system or something in between, must have initial credibility. So far the argument is sound. . . . Yet all that is indicated is credibility to some degree, not certainty. To say that some statements must be initially credible if any statement is ever to be credible at all is not to say that any statement is immune to withdrawal. For indeed, . . . no matter how strong its initial claim to preservation may be, a statement will be dropped if its retention— along with consequent adjustments in the interest of coherence—results in a system that does not satisfy as well as possible the totality of claims presented by all relevant statements. In the "search for truth" we deal with the clamoring demands of conflicting statements by trying, so to speak, to realize the greatest happiness of the greatest number of them. These demands constitute a different factor from coherence, the wanted means of choosing between different systems, the

missing link with fact; yet none is so strong that it may not be denied. That we
have probable knowledge, then, implies no certainty but only initial credibility.[10]

There is much in the above account that is metaphorical, but the fundamental point for present purposes seems to me quite simple and persuasive: while certainty is untenable, it is also excessive as a restraint upon
coherence. Such restraint does not require that any of the sentences we
affirm be guaranteed to be forever immune to revision; it is enough that
we find ourselves now impelled, in varying degrees, to affirm and retain
them, seeking to satisfy as best we can the current demands of all. That
these current demands vary for different, though equally consistent statements, and that we can distinguish, even roughly, the credibility-
preserving properties of alternative coherent systems, suffices to introduce
a significant limitation upon coherence. For it means that not all coherent
systems are equally acceptable; we are not free to make an arbitrary
choice among them. Nor, where what has hitherto been a satisfying system conflicts with a strong new candidate for inclusion, are we free to
decide the matter arbitrarily, discarding one or the other at will. There is
a price to be paid in either case in terms of overall credibility-preservation
and, though it may be difficult to determine in given circumstances, it
is a clearly relevant consideration.

In any event, it is the claims of sentences at a given time which set
the problem of systematic adjudication at that time, and so restrain the
arbitrariness of coherence. That these claims may vary in the future does
not alter the present task. That a sentence may be given up at a later time
does not mean that its present claim upon us may be blithely disregarded.
The idea that once a statement is acknowledged as theoretically revisable,
it can carry no cognitive weight at all, is no more plausible than the suggestion that a man loses his vote as soon as it is seen that the rules make
it possible for him to be outvoted.

There is, to be sure, a certain awkwardness in expressing a statement's
theoretical revisability in the same breath with asserting the statement
itself, and the difficulty this presents may be one source of the deep-rooted
feeling that certainty, rather than credibility, is required. If I say "There's
a horse but it may not be," I may appear to be at odds with myself in a
peculiar way; to remove the conflict I must presumably assert "There's a
horse" unqualifiedly and defend the immunity of this statement to pos-

sible withdrawal at any future time. Such a cure would, however, be worse than the disease, for by this argument all statements would be certain. The problem is more easily handled by finding a suitably circumspect form of interpretation, e.g., "There's a horse; and I recognize the possibility that the statement just made might be withdrawn under other circumstances than those now prevailing." The recognition of the latter possibility clearly does not conflict with the initial assertion; such possibility surely does not need to be eliminated in order to make the way clear for assertion generally.

It follows that the basic dilemma with which we started, between coherence and certainty, collapses. That none of the statements we assert can be freed of the possibility of withdrawal does not imply that no statement exercises any referential constraint at any time. That none can be *guaranteed* to be an absolutely reliable link to reality does not mean that we are free to assert any statements at will, provided only that they cohere. That the statement "There's a horse" cannot be rendered theoretically certain does not permit me to call anything a horse if only I do not thereby contradict any other statement of mine. On the contrary, if I have learned the term "horse," I have acquired distinctive habits of individuation and classification associated with it; I have learned what Quine refers to as its "built-in mode . . . of dividing [its] reference." [11] These habits do not guarantee that I will never be mistaken in applying the term, but it by no means therefore follows that they do not represent selective constraints upon my mode of employing the term. On the contrary, such constraints generate credibility claims which enter my reckoning critically as I survey my system of beliefs. I seek not consistency alone, but am bound to consider also the relative inclusiveness with which a system honors initial credibilities.

It follows, therefore, that the emphasis of earlier lectures on the *independence* of observation statements as the primary locus of their control does not, after all, have the consequence of committing us to the coherence theory. Such statements, as we urged, are not isolated certainties, but must be accommodated with other beliefs in a process during which they may themselves be overridden. It is, however, enough for the purposes of control that they may clash with these other beliefs in such a way as to force an unsettling systematic review of the situation. Such a review is not (contrary to the hypothetical fears earlier expressed) motivated simply by the wish to restore consistency. The need is, of course, to maintain consistency, but also to sacrifice as little as possible of overall credibility.

An observational expectation induced in us by our heretofore satisfying system may, for example, be challenged by an experimental observation which drastically increases the credibility of a statement incompatible with this expectation while radically reducing the credibility of the expectation itself. The problem in such a situation is to determine which consistent alternative strikes a more inclusive balance of relevant credibility claims. To drop the initial expectation in favor of the more credible incompatible statement demands internal systematic revision in the interests of consistency. To exclude the incompatible statement and maintain the system intact lowers the overall credibility value of the latter, for the credibility loss of its constituent expectation reverberates inward. Every clash-resolution, in short, has its price. In some such situations, the choice may be relatively easy; in others it may be exceedingly delicate; and it may even, in some circumstances, defy resolution.

Nevertheless, it is clear that we are in no case free simply to choose at will among all coherent systems whatever. And, further, it is clear that the control exercised by observation statements does not hinge on certainty. It requires only that the credibility they acquire at particular times be capable of challenging, in the manner above described, the expectations flowing from other sources. Such control is, surely, not absolute, since any observation statement may itself be outvoted in the end; in pressing their independent claims, however, such statements nevertheless contribute, along with other statements, to the restraint of arbitrariness in the choice of beliefs. Control is, moreover, released from distinctive ties to any special sort of statement, and diffused throughout the realm of statements as a whole.

What shall now be said concerning the difficult notions of truth and reality? Eschewing certainty, some philosophers, Neurath included, have rejected all talk of reality and truth. Having pointed out that appeal to an immediate comparison with the facts as a method of ascertaining truth is question-begging, and that facts, construed literally as entities, are mere ghostly doubles of true sentences, they have proceeded to cast doubt upon all thought of external reference, as embodied in philosophically innocent talk of reality and fact, and in innocent as well as serious talk of truth. Such skepticism leads, however, to insuperable difficulties, for without external reference, science has no point. If we stay within the circle of statements altogether, we are trapped in a game of words, with which even Neurath (as indicated by his reference to science as an instrument for life) cannot be wholly satisfied. Taken in its extreme form, Neurath's doctrine understandably evokes the sort of criticism which Russell offers:

> Neurath's doctrine, if taken seriously, deprives empirical propositions of all meaning. When I say 'the sun is shining', I do not mean that this is one of a number of sentences among which there is no contradiction; I mean something which is not verbal, and for the sake of which such words as 'sun' and 'shining' were invented. The purpose of words, though philosophers seem to forget this simple fact, is to deal with matters other than words. . . . The verbalist theories of some modern philosophers forget the homely practical purposes of every-day words, and lose themselves in a neo-neo-Platonic mysticism. I seem to hear them saying 'in the beginning was the Word,' not 'in the beginning was what the word means.' It is remarkable that this reversion to ancient metaphysics should have occurred in the attempt to be ultra-empirical.[12]

One source of the trouble is a persistent confusion between truth and estimation of the truth, between the import of our statements and the processes by which we choose among them. If, for example, appeal to reality or direct comparison with the facts is defective as a method of *ascertaining* truth, this does not show that the *purport* of a true statement cannot properly be described, in ordinary language, as "to describe reality" or "to state the facts." We may have no certain intuition of the truth, but this does not mean that our statements do not purport to be true. Now, if the sentence "Snow is white" is true, then snow is (really, or in fact) white, and vice versa, as Tarski insists.[13] As Quine has remarked, "Attribution of truth in particular to 'Snow is white', for example, is every bit as clear to us as attribution of whiteness to snow."[14] We may be unclear as to how to decide whether the sentence "Snow is white" is true, but the sentence in any case *refers* to snow and claims it to be white, and if we decide to hold the sentence to be true, we must be ready to hold snow to be (really, or in fact) white. The question of how we go about deciding what system of descriptive statements to accept in science is the question of how to estimate what statements are true. Whatever method we employ, our statements will refer to things quite generally and will purport to attribute to them what, *in reality, or in fact,* is attributable to them.

There is thus no way of staying wholly within the circle of statements, for in the very process of deciding which of these to affirm as true, we are deciding how to refer to, and describe things, quite generally. The *import* of our statements is inexorably referential. It is, however, quite another matter to suppose that, because this is so, the *methodology* by which we accept statements may be philosophically described in terms of an appeal to such supposed entities as facts, with which candidate statements are to be directly compared. For facts, postulated as special entities corresponding to truths, are generally suspect, and the determination of their existence is question-begging if proposed literally as a method of ascertaining the truth.

We thus separate the question of the *import* of scientific systems from the question of the *methods* by which we choose such systems. Can such methods be described without dependence upon the notion of direct comparison with the facts? Both Neurath and Schlick assume that any conception of science as referential must display such dependence. This supposition, however, is simply false. The conception of credibility above sketched represents a notion of choice among systems of statements, yet makes no use of any idea such as that of comparison with the facts. It is, nevertheless, perfectly compatible with the recognition that any system selected is referential in its *import.* Moreover, credibility considerations rest on the referential values which statements have for us at a given time, that is, on the inclinations we have, at that time, to affirm these statements as true.

Such inclinations as to statements are, surely, tempered by habits of individuation and classification acquired through the social process of learning our particular vocabulary of *terms.* In learning the term "horse," for example, I have incorporated selective habits of applying and withholding the term; these habits, operating upon what is before me, incline me to a greater or lesser degree to affirm the statement "There's a horse." If I have learned the term "white" as well as "horse," I may, further, be strongly inclined, on a given occasion, to affirm "That horse is white," and my inclination, on such an occasion, will be understandable in part, as a product of my applying both "horse" and "white" to what I see. I need, however, surely not recognize any such additional entity as *the fact that that horse is white,* nor need I have an applicable term for such a supposed entity in my vocabulary. Though it hinges in various ways on referential habits associated with a given vocabulary, the notion of initial credibility thus requires no reference to *facts,* in particular.

To be sure, whether I am to accept a statement depends not only on my initial inclination to accept it, but rather on its fitting coherently within a system of beliefs that is sufficiently preserving of relevant credibilities. Here again, however, there is no reference to any such entities as facts, with which statements are to be compared. In accepting a system I nevertheless take its *import* to be referential: I hold its statements to be true, and genuinely accept whatever attributions it makes to the entities mentioned in these statements. In a philosophically harmless sense, I may then say that I take the system as expressive of the facts. I have, at no time, any guarantees that my system will stand the test of the future, but the continual task of present evaluation is the only task it is possible for me to undertake. Science, generally, prospers not through seeking impossible guarantees, but through striving to systematize credibly a continuously expanding experience.

Notes

1. Otto Neurath, "Sociology and Physicalism," tr. Morton Magnus and Ralph Raico. Reprinted with permission of The Free Press from *Logical Positivism* by A. J. Ayer, ed., p. 285. Copyright © 1959 by The Free Press, A Corporation. Originally appeared as "Soziologie im Physikalismus," *Erkenntnis,* II (1931/2). Page references to this article in the text will be preceded by "SP."

2. Moritz Schlick, "The Foundation of Knowledge," tr. David Rynin. Reprinted with permission of The Free Press from *Logical Positivism* by A. J. Ayer, ed., p. 226. Copyright © 1959 by The Free Press, A Corporation. Originally appeared as "Über das Fundament der Erkenntnis," *Erkenntnis,* IV (1934). Page references to Schlick in the text refer to this article.

3. Otto Neurath, "Protocol Sentences," tr. Frederic Schick. Reprinted with permission of The Free Press from *Logical Positivism* by A. J. Ayer, ed., p. 201. Copyright © 1959 by The Free Press, A Corporation. Originally appeared as "Protokollsätze," *Erkenntnis,* III (1932/3). Page references to this article in the text will be preceded by "PS."

4. Otto Neurath, *Foundations of the Social Sciences* (Chicago: The University of Chicago Press, 1944), p. 5.

5. *Foundations of the Social Sciences*, p. 13.

6. On the parallelism of language and reality, see Ludwig Wittgenstein, *Tractatus Logico-Philosophicus* (London: Routledge & Kegan Paul, Ltd., 1922). For further discussion, see Edna Daitz, "The Picture Theory of Meaning," *Mind* (1953), reprinted in A. G. N. Flew, ed., *Essays in Conceptual Analysis* (London: Macmillan & Co., Ltd., 1960); John Passmore, *A Hundred Years of Philosophy* (London: Gerald Duckworth & Co. Ltd., 1957); and Nelson Goodman, "The Way the World Is," *Review of Metaphysics*, XIV (1960), 48–56.

7. There are problems in choosing a suitable translation; see David Rynin's note on these problems in Ayer, ed., *Logical Positivism*, p. 221. I choose "confirmation statements" to emphasize that statements are thus denoted, in preference to Rynin's "confirmations," though I believe the latter choice follows Schlick's own usage more closely.

8. Bertrand Russell, *Human Knowledge* (New York: Simon and Schuster, 1948), Part II, chap. 11, and Part V, chaps. 6 and 7.

9. Nelson Goodman, "Sense and Certainty," *Philosophical Review*, LXI (1952), 160–167.

10. *Ibid.*, pp. 162–163.

11. Willard Van Orman Quine, *Word and Object* (New York and London: The Technology Press of the Massachusetts Institute of Technology, and John Wiley & Sons, Inc., 1960), p. 91.

12. Bertrand Russell, *An Inquiry into Meaning and Truth* (London: Allen and Unwin, 1940), pp. 148–149; Penguin edn. (Harmondsworth: Penguin Books, Ltd., 1962), pp. 140–141.

13. Alfred Tarski, "The Semantic Conception of Truth," *Philosophy and Phenomenological Research* (1944); reprinted in Herbert Feigl and Wilfrid Sellars, eds., *Readings in Philosophical Analysis* (New York: Appleton-Century-Crofts, Inc., 1949), pp. 52–84.

14. Willard Van Orman Quine, *From A Logical Point of View* (Cambridge, Mass.: Harvard University Press, 1953), p. 138.

II

Worldmaking

4

Words, Works, Worlds

Nelson Goodman

4.1 Questions

Countless worlds made from nothing by use of symbols—so might a satirist summarize some major themes in the work of Ernst Cassirer. These themes—the multiplicity of worlds, the speciousness of 'the given', the creative power of the understanding, the variety and formative function of symbols—are also integral to my own thinking. Sometimes, though, I forget how eloquently they have been set forth by Cassirer,[1] partly perhaps because his emphasis on myth, his concern with the comparative study of cultures, and his talk of the human spirit have been mistakenly associated with current trends toward mystical obscurantism, anti-intellectual intuitionism, or anti-scientific humanism. Actually these attitudes are as alien to Cassirer as to my own skeptical, analytic, constructionalist orientation.

My aim in what follows is less to defend certain theses that Cassirer and I share than to take a hard look at some crucial questions they raise. In just what sense are there many worlds? What distinguishes genuine from spurious worlds? What are worlds made of? How are they made? What role do symbols play in the making? And how is worldmaking related to knowing? These questions must be faced even if full and final answers are far off.

4.2 Versions and Visions

As intimated by William James's equivocal title *A Pluralistic Universe*, the issue between monism and pluralism tends to evaporate under analysis. If there is but one world, it embraces a multiplicity of contrasting aspects; if there are many worlds, the collection of them all is one. The one world may be taken as many, or the many worlds taken as one; whether one or many depends on the way of taking.[2]

Why, then, does Cassirer stress the multiplicity of worlds? In what important and often neglected sense are there many worlds? Let it be clear that the question here is not of the possible worlds that many of my contemporaries, especially those near Disneyland, are busy making and manipulating. We are not speaking in terms of multiple possible alternatives to a single actual world but of multiple actual worlds. How to interpret such terms as "real," "unreal," "fictive," and "possible" is a subsequent question.

Consider, to begin with, the statements "The sun always moves" and "The sun never moves" which, though equally true, are at odds with each other. Shall we say, then, that they describe different worlds, and indeed that there are as many different worlds as there are such mutually exclusive truths? Rather, we are inclined to regard the two strings of words not as complete statements with truth-values of their own but as elliptical for some such statements as "Under frame of reference *A,* the sun always moves" and "Under frame of reference *B,* the sun never moves"—statements that may both be true of the same world.

Frames of reference, though, seem to belong less to what is described than to systems of description: and each of the two statements relates what is described to such a system. If I ask about the world, you can offer to tell me how it is under one or more frames of reference; but if I insist that you tell me how it is apart from all frames, what can you say? We are confined to ways of describing whatever is described. Our universe, so to speak, consists of these ways rather than of a world or of worlds.

The alternative descriptions of motion, all of them in much the same terms and routinely transformable into one another, provide only a minor and rather pallid example of diversity in accounts of the world. Much more striking is the vast variety of versions and visions in the several sciences, in the works of different painters and writers, and in our perceptions as informed by these, by circumstances, and by our own insights, interests, and past experiences. Even with all illusory or wrong or dubious versions dropped, the rest exhibit new dimensions of disparity. Here we have no neat set of frames of reference, no ready rules for transforming physics, biology, and psychology into one another, and no way at all of transforming any of these into Van Gogh's vision, or Van Gogh's into Canaletto's. Such of these versions as are depictions rather than descriptions have no truth-value in the literal sense, and cannot be combined by conjunction. The difference between juxtaposing and conjoining two statements has no evident analogue for two pictures or for a picture and a statement. The dramatically contrasting versions of the world can of course be relativized: each is right under a given system—for a given science, a given artist, or a given perceiver and situation. Here again we turn from describing or depicting 'the world' to talking of descriptions and depictions, but now without even the consolation of intertranslatability among or any evident organization of the several systems in question.

Yet doesn't a right version differ from a wrong one just in applying to the world, so that rightness itself depends upon and implies a world? We might better say that 'the world' depends upon rightness. We cannot test a version by comparing it with a world undescribed, undepicted, unperceived, but only by other means that I shall discuss later. While we may speak of determining what versions are right as 'learning about the world', 'the world' supposedly being that which all right versions describe, all we learn about the world is contained in right versions of it; and while the underlying world, bereft of these, need not be denied to those who love it, it is perhaps on the whole a world well lost. For some purposes, we may want to define a relation that will so sort versions into clusters that each cluster constitutes a world, and the members of the cluster are versions of that world; but for many purposes, right world-descriptions and world-depictions and world-perceptions, the ways-the-world-is, or just versions, can be treated as our worlds.[3]

Since the fact that there are many different world-versions is hardly debatable, and the question how many if any worlds-in-themselves there are is virtually empty, in what non-trivial sense are there, as Cassirer and like-minded pluralists insist, many worlds? Just this, I think: that many different world-versions are of independent interest and importance, without any requirement or presumption of reducibility to a single base. The pluralist, far from being anti-scientific, accepts the sciences at full value. His typical adversary is the monopolistic materialist or physicalist who maintains that one system, physics, is preeminent and all-inclusive, such that every other version must eventually be reduced to it or rejected as false or meaningless. If all right versions could somehow be reduced to one and only one, that one might with some semblance of plausibility[4] be regarded as the only truth about the only world. But the evidence for such reducibility is negligible, and even the claim is nebulous since physics itself is fragmentary and unstable and the kind and consequences of reduction envisaged are vague. (How do you go about reducing Constable's or James Joyce's world-view to physics?) I am the last person likely to underrate construction and reduction.[5] A reduction from one system to another can make a genuine contribution to understanding the interrelationships among world-versions; but reduction in any reasonably strict sense is rare, almost always partial, and seldom if ever unique. To demand full and sole reducibility to physics or any other one version is to forego nearly all other versions. The pluralists' acceptance of versions other than physics implies no relaxation of rigor but a recognition that standards different from yet no less exacting than those applied in science are appropriate for appraising what is conveyed in perceptual or pictorial or literary versions.

So long as contrasting right versions not all reducible to one are countenanced, unity is to be sought not in an ambivalent or neutral *something* beneath these versions but in an overall organization embracing them. Cassirer undertakes the search through a cross-cultural study of the development of myth, religion, language, art, and science. My approach is rather through an analytic study of types and functions of symbols and symbol systems. In neither case should a unique result be anticipated; universes of worlds as well as worlds themselves may be built in many ways.

4.3   How Firm a Foundation?

The non-Kantian theme of multiplicity of worlds is closely akin to the Kantian theme of the vacuity of the notion of pure content. The one denies us a unique world, the other the common stuff of which worlds are made. Together these theses defy our intuitive demand for something solid underneath, and threaten to leave us uncontrolled, spinning out our own inconsequent fantasies.

The overwhelming case against perception without conception, the pure given, absolute immediacy, the innocent eye, substance as substratum, has been so fully and frequently set forth—by Berkeley, Kant, Cassirer, Gombrich,[6] Bruner,[7] and many others—as to need no restatement here. Talk of unstructured content or an unconceptualized given or a substratum without properties is self-defeating; for the talk imposes structure, conceptualizes, ascribes properties. Although conception without perception is merely *empty*, perception without conception is *blind* (totally inoperative). Predicates, pictures, other labels, schemata, survive want of application, but content vanishes without form. We can have words without a world but no world without words or other symbols.

The many stuffs—matter, energy, waves, phenomena—that worlds are made of are made along with the worlds. But made from what? Not from nothing, after all, but *from other worlds*. Worldmaking as we know it always starts from worlds already on hand; the making is a remaking. Anthropology and developmental psychology may study social and individual histories of such world-building, but the search for a universal or necessary beginning is best left to theology.[8] My interest here is rather with the processes involved in building a world out of others.

With false hope of a firm foundation gone, with the world displaced by worlds that are but versions, with substance dissolved into function, and with the given acknowledged as taken, we face the questions how worlds are made, tested, and known.

4.4 Ways of Worldmaking

Without presuming to instruct the gods or other worldmakers, or attempting any comprehensive or systematic survey, I want to illustrate and comment on some of the processes that go into worldmaking. Actually, I am concerned more with certain relationships among worlds than with how or whether particular worlds are made from others.

Composition and Decomposition

Much but by no means all worldmaking consists of taking apart and putting together, often conjointly: on the one hand, of dividing wholes into parts and partitioning kinds into subspecies, analyzing complexes into component features, drawing distinctions; on the other hand, of composing wholes and kinds out of parts and members and subclasses, combining features into complexes, and making connections. Such composition or decomposition is normally effected or assisted or consolidated by the application of labels: names, predicates, gestures, pictures, etc. Thus, for example, temporally diverse events are brought together under a proper name or identified as making up 'an object' or 'a person'; or snow is sundered into several materials under terms of the Eskimo vocabulary. Metaphorical transfer—for example, where taste predicates are applied to sounds—may effect a double reorganization, both re-sorting the new realm of application and relating it to the old one (*Languages of Art* [*LA*], 2d ed. [Indianapolis Hackett, 1976]: II).

Identification rests upon organization into entities and kinds. The response to the question "Same or not the same?" must always be "Same what?"[9] Different so-and-so's may be the same such-and-such: what we point to or indicate, verbally or otherwise, may be different events but the same object, different towns but the same state, different members but the same club or different clubs but the same members, different innings but the same ball game. 'The ball-in-play' of a single game may be comprised of temporal segments of a dozen or more baseballs. The psychologist asking the child to judge constancy when one vessel is emptied into another must be careful to consider *what* constancy is in question—constancy of volume or depth or shape or kind of material, etc.[10] Identity or constancy in a world is identity with respect to what is within that world as organized.

Motley entities cutting across each other in complicated patterns may belong to the same world. We do not make a new world every time we take things apart or put them together in another way; but worlds may *differ* in that not everything belonging to one belongs to the other. The world of the Eskimo who has not grasped the comprehensive concept of snow differs not only from the world of the Samoan but also from the world of the New Englander who has not grasped the Eskimo's distinctions. In other cases, worlds differ in response to theoretical rather than practical needs. A world with points as elements cannot be the Whiteheadian world having points as certain classes of nesting volumes or having points as certain pairs of intersecting lines or as certain triples of intersecting planes. That the points of our everyday world can be equally well defined in any of these ways does not mean that a point can be identified in any one world with a nest of volumes and a pair of lines and a triple of planes; for all these are different from each other. Again the world of a system taking minimal concrete phenomena as atomic cannot admit qualities as atomic parts of these concreta.[11]

Repetition as well as identification is relative to organization. A world may be unmanageably heterogeneous or unbearably monotonous according to how events are sorted into kinds. Whether or not today's experiment repeats yesterday's, however much the two events may differ, depends upon whether they test a common hypothesis; as Sir George Thomson puts it:

> There will always be something different. . . . What it comes to when you say you repeat an experiment is that you repeat all the features of an experiment which a theory determines are relevant. In other words you repeat the experiment as an example of the theory.[12]

Likewise, two musical performances that differ drastically are nevertheless performances of the same work if they conform to the same score. The notational system distinguishes constitutive from contingent features, thus picking out the performance-kinds that count as works (*LA*, pp. 115–130). And things 'go on in the same way' or not according to what is regarded as the same way; 'now I can go on',[13] in Wittgenstein's sense, when I have found a familiar pattern, or a tolerable variation of one, that fits and goes beyond the cases given. Induction requires taking some classes to the exclusion of others as relevant kinds. Only so, for example, do our observations of emeralds exhibit any regularity and confirm that all emeralds are green rather than that all are grue (i.e., examined before a given date and green, or not so examined and blue—*FFF*, pp. 72–80). The uniformity of nature we marvel at or the unreliability we protest belongs to a world of our own making.

In these latter cases, worlds differ in the relevant kinds they comprise. I say "relevant" rather than "natural" for two reasons: first, "natural" is an inapt term to cover not only biological species but such artificial kinds as musical works, psychological experiments, and types of machinery; and second, "natural" suggests some absolute categorical or psychological priority, while the kinds in question are rather habitual or traditional or devised for a new purpose.

Weighting

While we may say that in the cases discussed some relevant kinds[14] of one world are missing from another, we might perhaps better say that the two worlds contain just the same classes sorted differently into relevant and irrelevant kinds. Some relevant kinds of the one world, rather than being absent from the other, are present as irrelevant kinds; some differences among worlds are not so much in entities comprised as in emphasis or accent, and these differences are no less consequential. Just as to stress all syllables is to stress none, so to take all classes as relevant kinds is to take none as such. In one world there may be many kinds serving different purposes; but conflicting purposes may make for irreconcilable accents and contrasting worlds, as may conflicting conceptions of what kinds serve a given purpose. Grue cannot be a relevant kind for induction in the same world as green, for that would preclude some of the decisions, right or wrong, that constitute inductive inference.

Some of the most striking contrasts of emphasis appear in the arts. Many of the differences among portrayals by Daumier, Ingres, Michelangelo, and Rouault are differences in aspects accentuated. What counts as emphasis, of course, is departure from the relative prominence accorded the several features in the current world of our everyday seeing. With changing interests and new insights, the visual weighting of features of bulk or line or stance or light alters, and yesterday's level world seems strangely perverted—yesterday's realistic calendar landscape becomes a repulsive caricature.

These differences in emphasis, too, amount to a difference in relevant kinds recognized. Several portrayals of the same subject may thus place it according to different categorial schemata. Like a green emerald and a grue one, even if the same emerald, a Piero della Francesca *Christ* and a Rembrandt one belong to worlds organized into different kinds.

Works of art, though, characteristically illustrate rather than name or describe relevant kinds. Even where the ranges of application—the things described or depicted—coincide, the features or kinds exemplified or expressed may be very different. A line drawing of softly draped cloth may exemplify rhythmic linear patterns; and a poem with no words for sadness and no mention of a sad person may in the quality of its language be sad and poignantly express sadness. The distinction between saying or representing on the one hand and showing or exemplifying on the other becomes even more evident in the case of abstract painting and music and dance that have no subject-matter but nevertheless manifest—exemplify or express—forms and feelings. Exemplification and expression though running in the opposite direction from denotation—that is, from the symbol to a literal or metaphorical feature of it instead of to something the symbol applies to—are no less symbolic referential functions and instruments of worldmaking.[15]

Emphasis or weighting is not always binary as is a sorting into relevant and irrelevant kinds or into important and unimportant features. Ratings of relevance, importance, utility, value often yield hierarchies rather than dichotomies. Such weightings are also instances of a particular type of ordering.

Ordering

Worlds not differing in entities or emphasis may differ in ordering; for example, the worlds of different constructional systems differ in order of derivation. As nothing is at rest or is in motion apart from a frame of reference, so nothing is primitive or is derivationally prior to anything apart from a constructional system. However, derivation unlike motion is of little immediate practical interest; and thus in our everyday world, although we almost always adopt a frame of reference at least temporarily, we seldom adopt a derivational basis. Earlier I said that the difference between a world having points as pairs of lines and a world having lines as composed of points is that the latter but not the former admits as entities nonlinear elements comprised within lines. But alternatively we may say that these worlds differ in their derivational ordering of lines and points of the not-derivationally-ordered world of daily discourse.

Orderings of a different sort pervade perception and practical cognition. The standard ordering of brightness in color follows the linear increase in physical intensity of light, but the standard ordering of hues curls the straight line of increasing wavelength into a circle. Order includes periodicity as well as proximity; and the standard ordering of tones is by pitch and octave. Orderings alter with circumstances and objectives. Much as the nature of shapes changes under different geometries, so do perceived patterns change under different orderings; the patterns perceived under a twelve-tone scale are quite different from those perceived under the traditional eight-tone scale, and rhythms depend upon the marking off into measures.

Radical reordering of another sort occurs in constructing a static image from the input on scanning a picture, or in building a unified and comprehensive image of an object or a city from temporally and spatially and qualitatively heterogeneous observations and other items of information.[16] Some very fast readers recreate normal word-ordering from a series of fixations that proceed down the left-hand page and then up the right-hand page of a book.[17] And spatial order in a map or a score is translated into the temporal sequence of a trip or a performance.

All measurement, furthermore, is based upon order. Indeed, only through suitable arrangements and groupings can we handle vast quantities of material perceptually or cognitively. Gombrich discusses the decimal periodization of historical time into decades, centuries, and millennia.[18] Daily time is marked off into twenty-four hours, and each of these into sixty minutes of sixty seconds each. Whatever else may be said of these modes of organization, they are not 'found in the world' but *built into a world*. Ordering, as well as composition and decomposition and weighting of wholes and kinds, participates in worldmaking.

Deletion and Supplementation

Also, the making of one world out of another usually involves some extensive weeding out and filling—actual excision of some old and supply of some new material. Our capacity for overlooking is virtually unlimited, and what we do take in usually consists of significant fragments and clues that need massive supplementation. Artists often make skillful use of this: a lithograph by Giacometti fully presents a walking man by sketches of nothing but the head, hands, and feet in just the right postures and positions against an expanse of blank paper; and a drawing by Katharine Sturgis conveys a hockey player in action by a single charged line.

That we find what we are prepared to find (what we look for or what forcefully affronts our expectations), and that we are likely to be blind to what neither helps nor hinders our pursuits, are commonplaces of everyday life and amply attested in the psychological laboratory.[19] In the painful experience of proofreading and the more pleasurable one of watching a skilled magician, we incurably miss something that is there and see something that is not there. Memory edits more ruthlessly: a person with equal command of two languages may remember a learned list of items while forgetting in which language they were listed.[20] And even within what we do perceive and remember, we dismiss as illusory or negligible what cannot be fitted into the architecture of the world we are building.

The scientist is no less drastic, rejecting or purifying most of the entities and events of the world of ordinary things while generating quantities of filling for curves suggested by sparse data, and erecting elaborate structures on the basis of meagre observations. Thus does he strive to build a world conforming to his chosen concepts and obeying his universal laws.

Replacement of a so-called analog by a so-called digital system through the articulation of separate steps involves deletion; for example, to use a digital thermometer with readings in tenths of a degree is to recognize no temperature as lying between 90 and 90.1 degrees. Similar deletion occurs under standard musical notation, which recognizes no pitch between c and $c\#$ and no duration between a sixty fourth and a one hundred-and-twenty-eighth note. On the other hand, supplementation occurs when, say, an analog replaces a digital instrument for registering attendance, or reporting money raised, or when a violinist performs from a score.

Perhaps the most spectacular cases of supplementation, though, are found in the perception of motion. Sometimes motion in the perceptual world results from intricate and abundant fleshing out of the physical stimuli. Psychologists have long known of what is called the "phi phenomenon": under carefully controlled conditions, if two spots of light are flashed a short distance apart and in quick succession, the viewer normally sees a spot of light moving continuously along a path from the first position to the second. That is remarkable enough in itself since of course the direction of motion cannot have been determined prior to the second flash; but perception has even greater creative power. Paul Kolers has recently shown[21] that if the first stimulus spot is circular and the second square, the seen moving spot transforms smoothly from circle to square; and transformations between two-dimensional and three-dimensional shapes are often effected without trouble. Moreover, if a barrier of light is interposed between the two stimulus spots, the moving spot detours around the barrier. Just why these supplementations occur as they do is a fascinating subject for speculation.

Deformation

Finally, some changes are reshapings or deformations that may according to point of view be considered either corrections or distortions. The physicist smooths out the simplest rough curve that fits all his data. Vision stretches a line ending with arrowheads pointing *in* while shrinking a physically equal line ending with arrowheads pointing *out,* and tends to expand the size of a smaller more valuable coin in relation to that of a larger less valuable one.[22] Caricaturists often go beyond overemphasis to actual distortion. Picasso starting from Velasquez's *Las Meninas,* and Brahms starting from a theme of Haydn's, work magical variations that amount to revelations.

These then are ways that worlds are made. I do not say *the* ways. My classification is not offered as comprehensive or clearcut or mandatory. Not only do the processes illustrated often occur in combination but the examples chosen sometimes fit equally well under more than one heading; for example, some changes may be considered alternatively as re-weightings or reorderings or reshapings or as all of these, and some deletions are also matters of differences in composition. All I have tried to do is to suggest something of the variety of processes in constant use. While a tighter systematization could surely be developed, none can be ultimate; for as remarked earlier, there is no more a unique world of worlds than there is a unique world.

4.5   Trouble with Truth

With all this freedom to divide and combine, emphasize, order, delete, fill in and fill out, and even distort, what are the objectives and the constraints? What are the criteria for success in making a world?

Insofar as a version is verbal and consists of statements, truth may be relevant. But truth cannot be defined or tested by agreement with 'the world'; for not only do truths differ for different worlds but the nature of agreement between a version and a world apart from it is notoriously nebulous. Rather—speaking loosely and without trying to answer either Pilate's question or Tarski's—a version is taken to be true when it offends no unyielding beliefs and none of its own precepts. Among beliefs unyielding at a given time may be long-lived reflections of laws of logic, short-lived reflections of recent observations, and other convictions and prejudices ingrained with varying degrees of firmness. Among precepts, for example, may be choices among alternative frames of reference, weightings, and derivational bases. But the line between beliefs and precepts is neither sharp nor stable. Beliefs are framed in concepts informed by precepts; and if a Boyle ditches his data for a smooth curve just missing them all, we may say either that observational volume and pressure are different properties from theoretical volume and pressure or that the truths about volume and pressure differ in the two worlds of observation and theory. Even the staunchest belief may in time admit alternatives; "The earth is at rest" passed from dogma to dependence upon precept.

Truth, far from being a solemn and severe master, is a docile and obedient servant. The scientist who supposes that he is single-mindedly dedicated to the search for truth deceives himself. He is unconcerned with the trivial truths he could grind out endlessly; and he looks to the multifaceted and irregular results of observations for little more than suggestions of overall structures and significant generalizations. He seeks system, simplicity, scope; and when satisfied on these scores he tailors truth to fit (*PP*:VII, 6–8). He as much decrees as discovers the laws he sets forth, as much designs as discerns the patterns he delineates.

Truth, moreover, pertains solely to what is said, and literal truth solely to what is said literally. We have seen, though, that worlds are made not only by what is said literally but also by what is said metaphorically, and not only by what is said either literally or metaphorically but also by what is exemplified and expressed—by what is shown as well as by what is said. In a scientific treatise, literal truth counts most; but in a poem or novel, metaphorical or allegorical truth may matter more, for even a literally false statement may be metaphorically true (*LA*, pp. 51, 68–70) and may mark or make new associations and discriminations, change emphases, effect exclusions and additions. And statements whether literally or metaphorically true or false may show what they do not say, may work as trenchant literal or metaphorical examples of unmentioned features and feelings. In Vachel Lindsay's *The Congo*, for example, the pulsating pattern of drumbeats is insistently exhibited rather than described.

Finally, for nonverbal versions and even for verbal versions without statements, truth is irrelevant. We risk confusion when we speak of pictures or predicates as "true of" what they depict or apply to; they have no truth-value and may represent or denote some things and not others, while a statement does have truth-value and is true of everything if of anything.[23] A nonrepresentational picture such as a Mondrian says nothing, denotes nothing, pictures nothing, and is neither true nor false, but shows much. Nevertheless, showing or exemplifying, like denoting, is a referential function; and much the same considerations count for pictures as for the concepts or predicates of a theory: their relevance and their revelations, their force and their fit—in sum their *rightness*. Rather than speak of pictures as true or false we might better speak of theories as right or wrong; for the truth of the laws of a theory is but one special feature and is often, as we have seen, overridden in importance by the cogency and compactness and comprehensiveness, the informativeness and organizing power of the whole system.

"The truth, the whole truth, and nothing but the truth" would thus be a perverse and paralyzing policy for any worldmaker. The whole truth would be too much; it is too vast, variable, and clogged with trivia. The truth alone would be too little, for some right versions are not true—being either false or neither true nor false—and even for true versions rightness may matter more.

4.6   Relative Reality

Shouldn't we now return to sanity from all this mad proliferation of worlds? Shouldn't we stop speaking of right versions as if each were, or had, its own world, and recognize all as versions of one and the same neutral and underlying world? The world thus regained, as remarked earlier, is a world without kinds or order or motion or rest or pattern—a world not worth fighting for or against.

We might, though, take the real world to be that of some one of the alternative right versions (or groups of them bound together by some principle of reducibility or translatability) and regard all others as versions of that same world differing from the standard version in accountable ways. The physicist takes his world as the real one, attributing the deletions, additions, irregularities, emphases of other versions to the imperfections of perception, to the urgencies of practice, or to poetic license. The phenomenalist regards the perceptual world as fundamental, and the excisions, abstractions, simplifications, and distortions of other versions as resulting from scientific or practical or artistic concerns. For the man-in-the-street, most versions from science, art, and perception depart in some ways from the familiar serviceable world he has jerry-built from fragments of scientific and artistic tradition and from his own struggle for survival. This world, indeed, is the one most often taken as real; for reality in a world, like realism in a picture, is largely a matter of habit.

Ironically, then, our passion for *one* world is satisfied, at different times and for different purposes, in *many* different ways. Not only motion, derivation, weighting, order, but even reality is relative. That right versions and actual worlds are many does not obliterate the distinction between right and wrong versions, does not recognize merely possible worlds answering to wrong versions, and does not imply that all right alternatives are equally good for every or indeed for any purpose. Not even a fly is likely to take one of its wing-tips as a fixed point; we do not welcome molecules or concreta as elements of our everyday world, or combine tomatoes and triangles and typewriters and tyrants and tornadoes into a single kind; the physicist will count none of these among his fundamental particles; the painter who sees the way the man-in-the-street does will have more popular than artistic success. And the same philosopher who here metaphilosophically contemplates a vast variety of worlds finds that only versions meeting the demands of a dogged and deflationary nominalism suit his purposes in constructing philosophical systems.

Moreover, while readiness to recognize alternative worlds may be liberating, and suggestive of new avenues of exploration, a willingness to welcome all worlds builds none. Mere acknowledgement of the many available frames of reference provides us with no map of the motions of heavenly bodies; acceptance of the eligibility of alternative bases produces no scientific theory or philosophical system; awareness of varied ways of seeing paints no pictures. A broad mind is no substitute for hard work.

4.7   Notes on Knowing

What I have been saying bears on the nature of knowledge. On these terms, knowing cannot be exclusively or even primarily a matter of determining what is true. Discovery often amounts, as when I place a piece in a jigsaw puzzle, not to arrival at a proposition for declaration or defense, but to finding a fit. Much of knowing aims at something other than true, or any, belief. An increase in acuity of insight or in range of comprehension, rather than a change in belief, occurs when we find in a pictured forest a face we already knew was there, or learn to distinguish stylistic differences among works already classified by artist or composer or writer, or study a picture or a concerto or a treatise until we see or hear or grasp features and structures we could not discern before. Such growth in knowledge is not by formation or fixation or belief[24] but by the advancement of understanding.[25]

Furthermore, if worlds are as much made as found, so also knowing is as much remaking as reporting. All the processes of worldmaking I have discussed enter into knowing. Perceiving motion, we have seen, often consists in producing it. Discovering laws involves drafting them. Recognizing patterns is very much a matter of inventing and imposing them. Comprehension and creation go on together.

Notes

1. E.g., in *Language and Myth,* translated by Susanne Langer (Harper, 1946).

2. But see further VII:1 in *Ways of Worldmaking.*

3. Cf. "The Way the World Is" (1960), *Problems and Projects* [hereinafter *PP*], pp. 24–32, and Richard Rorty, "The World Well Lost," *Journal of Philosophy,* Vol. 69 (1972), pp. 649–665.

4. But not much, for no one type of reducibility serves all purposes.

5. Cf. "The Revision of Philosophy" (1956), *PP,* pp. 5–23; and also *The Structure of Appearance* [hereinafter SA], 3d ed.

6. In *Art and Illusion* (Pantheon Books, 1960), E. H. Gombrich argues in many passages against the notion of 'the innocent eye'.

7. See the essays in Jerome S. Bruner's *Beyond the Information Given* [hereinafter *BI*], Jeremy M. Anglin, ed. (W. W. Norton, 1973), Chap. 1.

8. Cf. *SA,* pp. 127–145; and "Sense and Certainty" (1952) and "The Epistemological Argument" (1967), *PP,* pp. 60–75. We might take construction of a history of successive development of worlds to involve application of something like a Kantian regulative principle, and the search for a first world thus to be as misguided as the search for a first moment of time.

9. This does not, as sometimes is supposed, require any modification of the Leibniz formula for identity, but merely reminds us that the answer to a question "Is this the same as that?" may depend upon whether the "this" and the "that" in the question refer to thing or event or color or species, etc.

10. See *BI*, pp. 331–340.

11. See further *SA*, pp. 3–22, 132–135, 142–145.

12. In "Some Thoughts on Scientific Method" (1963), in *Boston Studies in the Philosophy of Science*, Vol. 2 (Humanities Press, 1965), p. 85.

13. Discussion of what this means occupies many sections, from about Sec. 142 on, of Ludwig Wittgenstein's *Philosophical Investigations*, translated by G. E. M. Anscombe, (Blackwell, 1953). I am not suggesting that the answer I give here is Wittgenstein's.

14. I speak freely of kinds here. Concerning ways of nominalizing such talk, see *SA*:II and *PP*:IV.

15. On exemplification and expression as referential relations see *Languages of Art*, 2d ed., pp. 50–57, 87–95.

16. See *The Image of the City* by Kevin Lynch (Cambridge, Technology Press, 1960).

17. See E. Llewellyn Thomas, "Eye Movements in Speed Reading," in *Speed Reading: Practices and Procedures* (University of Delaware Press, 1962), pp. 104–114.

18. In "Zeit, Zahl, und Zeichen," delivered at the Cassirer celebration in Hamburg, 1974.

19. See "On Perceptual Readiness" (1957) in *BI*, pp. 7–42.

20. See Paul Kolers, "Bilinguals and Information Processing," *Scientific American* 218 (1968), 78–86.

21. *Aspects of Motion Perception* (Pergamon Press, 1972), pp. 4/ff.

22. See "Value and Need as Organizing Factors in Perception" (1947), in *BI*, pp. 43–56.

23. E.g., "2 + 2 = 4" is true of everything in that for every x, x is such that $2 + 2 = 4$. A statement S will normally not be *true about x* unless S is about x in one of the senses of "about" defined in "About" (*PP*, pp. 246–272); but definition of "about" depends essentially on features of statements that have no reasonable analogues for pictures. See further: Joseph Ullian and Nelson Goodman, "Truth about Jones," *Journal of Philosophy*, Vol. 74 (1977), pp. 317–338.

24. I allude here to Charles S. Peirce's paper, "The Fixation of Belief" (1877), in *Collected Papers of Charles Sanders Peirce*, Vol. 5 (Harvard University Press, 1934), pp. 223–247.

25. On the nature and importance of understanding in the broader sense, see M. Polanyi, *Personal Knowledge* (University of Chicago Press, 1960).

5

On Rightness of Rendering

Nelson Goodman

5.1 Worlds in Conflict

With multiple and sometimes unreconciled and even unreconcilable theories and descriptions recognized as admissible alternatives, our notions about truth call for some reexamination. And with our view of worldmaking expanded far beyond theories and descriptions, beyond statements, beyond language, beyond denotation even, to include versions and visions metaphorical as well as literal, pictorial and musical as well as verbal, exemplifying and expressing as well as describing and depicting, the distinction between true and false falls far short of marking the general distinction between right and wrong versions. What standard of rightness then, for example, is the counterpart of truth for works without subjects that present worlds by exemplification or expression? I shall have to approach such forbidding questions circumspectly.

In the title of this chapter, both "rendering" and "rightness" are to be taken rather generally. Under "rendering," I include not just what a draftsman does but all the ways of making and presenting worlds—in scientific theories, works of art, and versions of all sorts. I choose the term to counteract any impression that I shall be discussing moral or ethical rightness.[1] Under "rightness" I include, along with truth, standards of acceptability that sometimes supplement or even compete with truth where it applies, or replace truth for nondeclarative renderings.

Although my main concern here is with these other standards, I must begin with another and closer look at truth. Most of us learned long ago such fundamental principles as that truths never really conflict, that all true versions are true in[2] the only actual world, and that apparent disagreements among truths amount merely to differences in the frameworks or conventions adopted. While most of us also learned a little later to mistrust fundamental principles learned earlier, I am afraid that my remark above about conflicting truths and multiple actual worlds may be passed over as purely rhetorical. They are not; and even at the cost of some repetition, I must make that clearer by a more consecutive account of certain points already often urged throughout these pages. We shall need a sound basis for comparison when we come to the main business of this chapter.

To anyone but an arrant absolutist, alternative ostensibly conflicting versions often present good and equal claims to truth. We can hardly take conflicting statements as true in the same world without admitting all statements whatsoever (since all follow from any contradiction) as true in the same world, and that world itself as impossible. Thus we must either reject one of two ostensibly conflicting versions as false, or take them as true in different worlds, or find if we can another way of reconciling them.

In some cases, apparently conflicting truths can be reconciled by clearing away an ambiguity of one sort or another.[3] Sometimes, for example, sentences seem incompatible only because they are elliptical, and when expanded by explicit inclusion of erstwhile implicit restrictions, they plainly speak of different things or different parts of things. Statements affirming that all soldiers are equipped with bows and arrows and that none are so equipped are both true—for soldiers of different eras; the statements that the Parthenon is intact and that it is ruined are both true—for different temporal parts of the building; and the statement that the apple is white and that it is red are both true—for different spatial parts of the apple. Sentences at odds with one another get along better when kept apart. In each of these cases, the two ranges of application combine readily into a recognized kind or object; and the two statements are true in different parts or subclasses of the same world.

But peace cannot always be made so easily. Consider again descriptions of the motion (or nonmotion) of the earth. On the face of it, the two statements

(1)   The earth always stands still

(2)   The earth dances the role of Petrouchka

conflict since the negate of each follows from the other. And they seem to be about the same earth. Yet each is true—within an appropriate system.[4]

Now we shall surely be told that those last four words point the way out: that here again the statements are elliptical, and when expanded by explicit relativization so that they read, for example,

(3)   In the Ptolemaic system, the earth stands always still

(4)   In a certain Stravinsky-Fokine-like system, the earth dances the role of Petrouchka,

they are seen to be entirely compatible. But this argument works too well. To see why (3) and (4) cannot by any means be accepted as—or even among—fuller formulations of (1) and (2), notice that while at least one of the conflicting statements

(5)   The kings of Sparta had two votes

(6)   The kings of Sparta had only one vote

is false, both of the following are true:

(7)   According to Herodotus, the kings of Sparta had two votes

(8)   According to Thucydides, the kings of Sparta had only one vote.

Clearly (7) and (8), unlike (5) and (6), are entirely noncommittal as to how many votes the kings had. Whether someone makes a statement and whether that statement is true are altogether different questions. Similarly (3) and (4), unlike (1) and (2), are entirely noncommittal as to the earth's motion; they do not tell us how or whether the earth moves unless a clause is added to each affirming that what the system in question says is true. But if that is done, then of course (1) and (2) are themselves affirmed and no resolution of the conflict is achieved. The apparently powerful and universal device of relativization to system or version thus misses the mark.

Perhaps, though, we can reconcile sentences like (1) and (2) by relativization to points or frames of reference rather than to systems or versions. A simpler example will be easier to handle here. The equally true conflicting sentences concerning the daily motion[5] of the earth and sun

(9)   The earth rotates, while the sun is motionless

(10)   The earth is motionless, while the sun revolves around it

might be interpreted as amounting to

(11)   The earth rotates relative to the sun

(12)   The sun revolves relative to the earth,

which are nonconflicting truths.

What must be noticed, however, is that (11) does not quite say, as (9) does, that the earth rotates; and (12) does not quite say, as (10) does, that the earth is motionless. That an object moves relative to another does not imply either that the first one moves or that the second does not.[6] Indeed, where f is an appropriate formula, (11) and (12) alike amount to the single statement

(13)   The spatial relationships between the earth and the sun vary with time according to formula f,[7]

and this does not attribute motion or rest to the earth or the sun but is entirely compatible not only with (9) and (10) but also with the statement that the earth rotates for a time and then stops while the sun moves around it. The reconciliation of (9) and (10) is here effected by cancelling out those features responsible for their disagreement; (11), (12), (13) dispense with motion in any sense such that we can ask whether or not or how much a given object moves.

At this juncture we may be inclined to say "Good riddance; such questions are obviously empty anyway." On the other hand, we are severely handicapped if rather than saying whether or how a given object moves, we are restricted to describing changes in relative position. A frame of reference is practically indispensable in most contexts. An astronomer can no more work with a neutral statement like (13) in conducting his observations than we can use a map without locating ourselves on it in finding our way around a city. If there is no difference in what (9) and (10) describe still there seems to be a significant difference in how they describe it. And so on second thought we are tempted to say that the 'empty' questions are rather 'external' as contrasted with 'internal' questions,[8] that they pertain to discourse as contrasted with fact, to convention as contrasted with content. But then we may well have qualms about resting anything on such notoriously dubious dichotomies. For the moment, though, let's leave it at that and consider a different case.

Suppose for now that our universe of discourse is limited to a square segment of a plane, with the two pairs of boundary lines labelled "vertical" and "horizontal." If we assume that there are points, whatever they may be, then the two sentences

(14)   Every point is made up of a vertical and a horizontal line

(15)   No point is made up of lines or anything else[9]

conflict, but are equally true under appropriate systems. We know that simple relativization to system, as in (3) and (4), is a specious way of resolving the conflict. The truth of the statement in question made by each system must also be affirmed; and if the systems, respectively, say (14) and (15) as they stand, the conflict remains.

Can we, then, perhaps reconcile (14) and (15) by restricting their ranges of application? If in our space there are only lines and combinations of lines then (14) but not (15) may be true, while if there are only points then (15) but not (14) may be true. The trouble is, though, that if there are both lines and points, (14) and (15) still cannot both be true, though neither is singled out as the false one. If (14) and (15) are alternative truths they are so within different realms, and these realms cannot be combined into one where both statements are true.[10] This case is thus radically different from those where ostensibly conflicting statements about the color of an object or the equipment of soldiers can be reconciled by confinement of scope to different parts of the object or to different soldiers; for (14) and (15) cannot easily be construed as applying to different points or different parts of a point. Together they say that every point is, but that no point is, made up of lines. Although (14) may be true in our sample space taken as consisting solely of lines, and (15) true in that space taken as consisting solely of points, still both cannot be true in that space or any subregion of it taken as consisting of both points and lines. Where we have more comprehensive systems or versions that conflict as do (14) and (15), their realms are thus less aptly regarded as within one world than as two different worlds, and even—since the two refuse to unite peaceably—as worlds in conflict.

5.2   Convention and Content

Since that conclusion may not be widely and warmly welcomed, let us look for some way of dealing with the conflict between (14) and (15) without confining them to antagonistic worlds. Our earlier efforts at reconciliation by relativization to system were perhaps not so much in the wrong direction as too simple-minded. Not only must we suppose that the correctness of the systems in question is tacitly affirmed, but we must examine more closely what (14) and (15) say as statements within those systems.

If, as I have argued before, the criterion for correctness of such systems is that they set up an overall correlation meeting certain conditions of extensional isomorphism, then our two statements may be replaced by

(16)   Under the correct system in question, every point has correlated with it a combination of a vertical and a horizontal line.

(17)   Under the (another) correct system in question, no point has correlated with it a combination of any other elements;

and these are entirely compatible with each other. They say nothing about what makes up a point; each speaks only about what makes up whatever is correlated with a point in the correct system in question. Furthermore, since isomorphism neither guarantees nor precludes identity (though guaranteed by it), (16) makes no commitment, positive or negative, concerning anything but lines and combinations of lines, while (17) makes none concerning anything but points. Thus these statements, which unlike (14) and (15) do not together claim that points are and are not made up of lines, may both be true in a world containing both lines and points—and indeed only in such a world.

Obviously, just as in passing from (9) and (10) to (11) and (12), we have lost something in passing from (14) and (15) to (16) and (17). In both cases we have effected a reconciliation by dispensing with the features responsible for the disagreement. There we abstracted from motion and contented ourselves with variations of distance with time; here we have abstracted from composition and contented ourselves with correlation. We have cancelled out the counterclaims of (14) and (15) and retreated to neutral statements.

And we may feel small loss. Whether a point is atomic or compound, and if compound what it comprises, depend heavily upon the basis and means of composition adopted for a system. Isn't this plainly, like frame of reference for motion, a matter of choice, while isomorphism of a correlation, like variation in distance with time, is a matter of fact? Most of us talk that way now and then, sometimes just before or just after decrying or denying the very distinction between convention and content. Which way shall we have it?

In any case, if the composition of points out of lines or of lines out of points is conventional rather than factual, points and lines themselves are no less so. Statements like (16) and (17) are not only neutral as to what makes up points or lines or regions but also neutral as to what these are. If we say that our sample space is a combination of points, or of lines, or of regions, or a combination of combinations of points, or lines, or regions, or a combination of all these together, or is a single lump, then since none of these is identical with any of the rest, we are giving one among countless alternative conflicting descriptions of what the space is. And so we may regard the disagreements as not about the facts but as due to differences in the conventions—of lines, points, regions, and modes of combination—adopted in organizing or describing the space. What, then, is the neutral fact or thing described in these different terms? Neither the space as (*a*) an undivided whole nor (*b*) as a combination of everything involved in the several accounts; for (*a*) and (*b*) are but two among the various ways of organizing it. But what is *it* that is so organized? When we strip off as layers of convention all differences among ways of describing *it,* what is left? The onion is peeled down to its empty core.

When we widen our purview to take in not just our sample space but all of space and everything else, the variety of contrasting versions multiplies enormously, and further reconciliations are sought by like means. Look back at our familiar example of apparent motion:

(18)   A spot moves across the screen

(19)   No spot so moves.

If we suppose that the realms of stimuli and of vision are entirely separate, the statements can be reconciled by segregation, mush as in the case of opposing color descriptions applied to different parts of an object. But if, as is more usual, we regard the stimulus version and the visual version that these statements respectively belong to as covering the same territory in different ways, as different reports on a common world, then both the seen spot and the unseen stimuli will be missing from that common world. Again, statement (13) concerning variation in distance with time, although neutral relative to the opposing descriptions of the earth's motion in (9) and (10), is at odds with perceptual versions that admit no such physical objects as the earth. Physical objects and events and perceptual phenomena go the way of points and lines and regions and space.

In short, if we abstract from all features responsible for disagreements between truths we have nothing left but versions without things or facts or worlds. As Heraclitus or Hegel might have said, worlds seem to depend upon conflict for their existence. On the other hand, if we accept any two truths as disagreeing on the facts, and thus as true in different worlds, the grounds are not clear for discounting other conflicts between truths as mere differences in manner of speaking. To say for example that conflicting statements apply to the same world just insofar as they are about the same things would, reasonably, make (9) and (10) statements about the same world but would help very little in most cases. Do (14) and (15), for instance, speak of the same points? Is the screen that a dot moves across the same as the one no dot moves across? Is the seen table the same as the mess of molecules? To such questions, discussed at length in the philosophical literature, I suspect that the answer is a firm *yes* and a firm *no*. The realist will resist the conclusion that there is no world; the idealist will resist the conclusion that all conflicting versions describe different worlds. As for me, I find these views equally delightful and equally deplorable—for after all, the difference between them is purely conventional!

In practice, of course, we draw the line wherever we like, and change it as often as suits our purposes. On the level of theory, we flit back and forth between extremes as blithely as a physicist between particle and field theories. When the verbiage view threatens to dissolve everything into nothing, we insist that all true versions describe worlds. When the right-to-life sentiment threatens an overpopulation of worlds, we call it all talk.

Or to put it another way, the philosopher like the philanderer is always finding himself stuck with none or too many.

Incidentally, recognition of multiple worlds or true versions suggests innocuous interpretations of necessity and possibility. A statement is necessary in a universe of worlds or true versions if true in all, necessarily false if true in none, and contingent or possible if true in some. Iteration would be construed in terms of universes of universes: a statement is necessarily necessary in such a superuniverse if necessarily true in all the member universes, etc. Analogues of theorems of a modal calculus follow readily. But such an account will hardly satisfy an avid advocate of possible worlds any more than spring water will satisfy an alcoholic.

5.3   Tests and Truth

Our foregoing conclusions or observations or suspicions bear upon the treatment of truth in at least three ways: A standard though uninformative formula concerning truth requires modification to a no more informative one; considerations other than truth take on added importance in the choice among statements or versions; and a hard problem concerning the relation between truth and tests for it may be slightly softened.

First, and of least importance, the familiar dictum " 'Snow is white' is true if and only if snow is white" must be revised to something like " 'Snow is white' is true in a given world if and only if snow is white in that world," which in turn, if differences between true versions cannot be firmly distinguished from differences between worlds, amounts merely to " 'Snow is white' is true according to a true version if and only if snow is white according to that version."

Second, that truths conflict reminds us effectively that truth cannot be the only consideration in choosing among statements or versions. As we have observed earlier, even where there is no conflict, truth is far from sufficient. Some truths are trivial, irrelevant, unintelligible, or redundant; too broad, too narrow, too boring, too bizarre, too complicated; or taken from some other version than the one in question, as when a guard, ordered to shoot any of his captives who moved, immediately shot them all and explained that they were moving rapidly around the earth's axis and around the sun.

Furthermore, we no more characteristically proceed by selecting certain statements as true and then applying other criteria to choose among them than by selecting certain statements as relevant and serviceable and then considering which among them are true. Rather we begin by excluding statements initially regarded as either false though perhaps otherwise right, or wrong though perhaps true, and go on from there. This account does not deny that truth is a necessary condition but deprives it of a certain preeminence.

But, of course, truth is no more a necessary than a sufficient consideration for a choice of a statement. Not only may the choice often be of a statement that is the more nearly right in other respects over one that is the more nearly true, but where truth is too finicky, too uneven, or does not fit comfortably with other principles, we may choose the nearest amenable and illuminating lie. Most scientific laws are of this sort: not assiduous reports of detailed data but sweeping Procrustean simplifications.

So irreverent a view of scientific laws is often resisted on the ground that they are implicitly only statements of approximation—that the "$=$" in "$v = p \cdot t$," for example, is to be read not as "equals" but as "approximately equals." Thus the sanctity and preeminence of truth is preserved. But whether we say that such a law is an approximation to truth or a true approximation matters very little. What does matter is that the approximations are preferred to what may be regarded either as truths or as more exact truths.

So far, I have been taking other criteria of rightness as supplementary to truth, and even at times contending with it. But do some of these other considerations serve also, or even rather, as tests for truth? After all, we must use some tests in judging truths; and such features as utility and coherence are prominent candidates. That we can readily produce ostensible examples of useless tangled truths and of useful neat falsehoods shows at most only that the tests are corroborative rather than conclusive. And good tests need not be conclusive; attraction by a magnet is a good but not conclusive test for iron. Nor need we be able to explain why utility or coherence or some other feature is any indication of truth. We may use the attraction as a test for iron without understanding at all the connection between the attraction and the composition of iron; all we need is to be satisfied that there is a reasonably reliable correlation between the two.

And if the attraction is adopted as a test before we know the composition of iron, the correlation in question is between the attraction and either the results of other tests or a prior classification of objects as iron and not iron. Much the same may be said for truth; in the absence of any definitive and informative characterization, we apply various tests that we check against each other and against a rough and partial antecedent classification of statements as true and false. Truth, like intelligence, is perhaps just what the tests test; and the best account of what truth is may be an 'operational' one in terms of tests and procedures used in judging it.

Philosophers would like, though, to arrive at a characterization of truth as definitive as the scientific definition of iron; and some have argued with considerable ingenuity for the identification of truth with one or another accessible feature.

Notable among such efforts is the pragmatists' proposed interpretation of truth in terms of utility.[11] The thesis that true statements are those that enable us to predict or manage or defeat nature has no little appeal; but some conspicuous discrepancies between utility and truth have to be explained away. That utility unlike truth is a matter of degree can perhaps be dealt with by taking utility as measuring nearness to truth rather than as a criterion of truth itself. That utility unlike truth is relative to purpose might seem less serious when truth is recognized, as in the preceding pages, to be relative rather than absolute. But relativity to purpose does not align in any obvious way with relativity to world or version; for among alternative true versions or statements, some may be highly useful for many purposes, others for almost none and indeed much less useful than some falsehoods. Here a master argument will perhaps be put forth: that utility for one primary purpose—the acquisition of knowledge—can be identified with truth. But then the pragmatic thesis would seem to expire as it triumphs; that truths best satisfy the purpose of acquiring truths is as empty as evident.

Attempts to construe truth in terms of confident belief, or of credibility as some codification of belief—in terms of initial credibility together with inference, confirmation, probability, etc.[12]—face the obvious objection that the most credible statements often turn out to be false and the least credible ones true. Credibility thus seems no measure even of nearness to truth. But this obstacle may not be insurmountable. Consider for a moment the notion of permanence—taken here to mean lasting forever after some given time. Although we can never establish permanence of an object or material, we can establish durability in varying degrees short of permanence. Likewise, although we can never establish total and permanent credibility, we can establish strength and durability of credibility in varying degrees short of that. Shall we then identify unattainable total and permanent credibility with unattainable truth? To the ready protest that we might have total and permanent belief in a falsehood—that what is totally and permanently credible might not be true—perhaps the answer is that so long as the belief or credibility is indeed total and permanent, any divergence from the truth could never matter to us at all. Then if there is any such divergence, so much the worse for truth: scrap it in favor of total and permanent credibility. But, as Hartry Field has pointed out to me, total and permanent credibility can hardly be taken as a necessary condition for truth since a disjunction may be permanently and totally credible even though none of its components is.[13]

More venerable than either utility or credibility as definitive of truth is coherence, interpreted in various ways but always requiring consistency. The problems here, too, have been enormous. But the classic and chilling objection that for any coherent world version there are equally coherent conflicting versions weakens when we are prepared to accept some two conflicting versions as both true. And the difficulty of establishing any correlation between internal coherence and external correspondence diminishes when the very distinction between the 'internal' and the 'external' is in question. As the distinction between convention and content—between what is said and how it is said—wilts, correspondence between version and world loses its independence from such features of versions as coherence. Of course coherence, however defined, rather than being sufficient for truth seems to operate conjointly with judgments of initial credibility in our efforts to determine truth.[14] But at least—and this is the third of the points mentioned at the beginning of the section—coherence and other so-called internal features of versions are no longer disqualified as tests for truth.

So much for this rather roller-coaster view of truth in relation to its companions and competitors. Now let us look at some clear cases where we judge with considerable confidence and constancy the rightness of what is neither true nor false.

5.4   Veracity and Validity

Among the most explicit and clearcut standards of rightness we have anywhere are those for validity of a deductive argument; and validity is of course distinct from truth in that the premises and conclusions of a valid argument may be false. Validity consists of conformity with rules of inference—rules that codify deductive practice in accepting or rejecting particular inferences.[15] Yet deductive validity, though different from is not altogether independent of truth, but so relates statements that valid inference from true premises gives true conclusions. Indeed, the primary function of valid inference is to relate truths to truths. Furthermore, validity is not the only requirement upon a right deductive argument. A deductive argument is right in a fuller sense only if the premises are true and the inferences valid. Thus rightness of deductive argument, while involving validity, is still closely allied with truth.

Now consider inductive validity. Here again, neither truth of premises nor truth of conclusion is required; and inductive like deductive validity consists of conformity with principles that codify practice. But inductive validity is one step further removed from truth than is deductive validity; for valid inductive inference from true premises need not yield a true conclusion.

On the other hand, while inductive *rightness* like deductive rightness does require truth of the premises as well as validity, it also requires something more.[16] To begin with, a right inductive argument must be based not only on true premises but upon all the available genuine evidence. An inductive argument from positive instances of a hypothesis is not right if negative instances are omitted; all the examined instances must be taken into account. No parallel requirement is imposed upon a deductive argument, which is right if it proceeds validly from any true premises, however incomplete.

Still, inductive rightness is not fully characterized as inductive validity plus use of all examined instances. If all examined instances have been examined before 1977, the argument that all instances whatever will be examined before 1977 is still inductively wrong; and even if all examined emeralds have been grue, still inductive argument to the hypothesis that all emeralds are grue is wrong. Inductive rightness requires evidence statements and the hypothesis to be in terms of 'genuine' or 'natural' kinds—or in my terminology, to be in terms of projectible predicates like "green" and "blue" rather than in terms of nonprojectible predicates like "grue" and "bleen." Without such a restriction, right inductive arguments could always be found to yield countless conflicting conclusions: that all emeralds are green, are grue, are gred, etc.

In sum, then, inductive rightness requires that the argument proceed from premises consisting of all such true reports on examined instances as are in terms of projectible predicates. Thus inductive rightness, while still demanding truth of premises, makes severe additional demands. And although we hope by means of inductive argument to arrive at truth, inductive rightness unlike deductive rightness does not guarantee truth. A deductive argument is wrong and its inferences invalid if it reaches a false conclusion from true premises, but an inductive argument that is valid and right in all respects may yet reach a false conclusion from true premises. This vital difference has inspired some frantic and futile attempts to justify induction in the sense of showing that right induction will always, or more often than not, yield true conclusions. Any feasible justification of induction must consist rather of showing that the rules of inference codify inductive practice—that is, of effecting a mutual adjustment between rules and practice—and of distinguishing projectible predicates or inductively right categories from others.

This brings us, then, to the question what are inductively right categories, and so to a third kind of rightness in general: rightness of categorization. Such rightness is one step further removed from truth; for while deductive and inductive rightness still have to do with statements, which have truth-value, rightness of categorization attaches to categories or predicates—or systems thereof—which have no truth-value.

On the question what distinguishes right inductive categories from others, I can only indicate the nature of a tentative reply I have outlined elsewhere (*FFF:* IV). A primary factor in projectibility is habit; where otherwise equally well-qualified hypotheses conflict, the decision normally goes to the one with the better entrenched predicates. Obviously there must be leeway for progress, for the introduction of novel organizations that make, or take account of, newly important connections and distinctions. Inertia is modified by inquiry and invention, somewhat restrained in turn by entrenched general 'background' principles or metaprinciples, and so on.[17] The formulation of rules, based on these factors, that in effect define projectibility or right inductive categorization is a difficult and intricate task. Categories that are inductively right tend to coincide with categories that are right for science in general; but variations in purpose may result in variations in relevant kinds.

Sometimes the choice among versions adopting different categorizations, like the choice among descriptions of motion adopting different frames of reference, may be mainly for convenience. After all, we can somewhat awkwardly restate our ordinary inductive arguments in terms like "grue" and "bleen" much as we can translate a heliocentric into a geocentric system. We need only replace "green" by "grue if examined before *t* and otherwise bleen" and replace "blue" by "bleen if examined before *t* and otherwise grue." Nevertheless, according to present practice, the blue-green categorization is right and the grue-bleen categorization wrong as marking the lines along which we make our inductive inferences. The penalty for using wrong categories is not merely an inconvenience any more than the result of the guard's choice of a wrong frame of reference was merely an inconvenience to the slaughtered captives. "Shoot if they change in color" could have been equally fatal if the guard were projecting abnormal color predicates. Induction according to nonprojectible categories is not merely awkward but wrong, whatever may be the outcome of the inductive conclusion drawn. Rightness of induction requires rightness of predicates projected, and that in turn may vary with practice.

Every so often a critic of one of my writings complains that on some topic I 'state without argument that . . .'. A particular example I vaguely remember from somewhere reads something like: "Goodman states without argument that the core of representation is denotation." This led me to reflect on why I made so crucial a declaration without argument. And the reason is that argument in any sense that involves inference from premises would be utterly inappropriate here. In such a context, I am not so much stating a belief or advancing a thesis or a doctrine as proposing a categorization or scheme of organization, calling attention to a way of setting our nets to capture what may be significant likenesses and differences. Argument for the categorization, the scheme, suggested could not be for its truth, since it has no truth-value, but for its efficacy in worldmaking and understanding. An argument would consist rather of calling attention to important parallels between pictorial representation and verbal denotation, of pointing out obscurities and confusions that are clarified by this association, of showing how this organization works with other aspects of the theory of symbols. For a categorial system, what needs to be shown is not that it is true but what it can do. Put crassly, what is called for in such cases is less like arguing than selling.

5.5   Right Representation

Validity of deductive and inductive inference and projectibility of predicates are in varying degrees independent of truth, but not of language. All are standards applicable to versions in words. What about rightness of nonverbal versions? When, for example, is a pictorial representation correct?

Two familiar answers are that a representation is right to the extent that it resembles what it depicts, and that a representation is right if in effect it makes a true statement. Neither answer is satisfactory.

The shortcomings of the first answer, in terms of resemblance, have been so fully set forth in the literature[18] as to make any detailed discussion here superfluous. Correctness of representation like correctness of description varies with system or framework; the question "Is the picture correct?" is in this way like the question "Does the earth move?" A picture drawn in reversed or otherwise distorted perspective,[19] or replacing colors by their complementaries, can be as correct under the given system as a picture we call realistic under the current standard Western system of representation. But here we must remember that there are two different uses of "realistic." According to the more frequent usage, a picture is realistic to the extent that it is correct under the accustomed system of representation; for example, in the present Western culture, a picture by Dürer is more realistic than a picture by Cézanne. Realistic or right representation in this sense, like right categorization, requires observance of custom and tends to correlate loosely with ordinary judgments of resemblance, which likewise rest upon habit. On the other hand, a representation unrealistic by this standard may picture quite correctly under a different system, much as the earth may dance the role of Petrouchka under a certain unusual frame of reference. And an 'unnatural' frame or system may be right in some circumstances through prevailing in another culture or winning adoption for special purposes. When a painter or photographer makes, or discloses to us, erstwhile unseen aspects of a world, he is sometimes said to have achieved a new degree of realism by discovering and presenting new aspects of reality. What we have here, in representation under a right system strange to us, is realism in the sense not of habituation but of revelation. The two senses of "realistic" reflect the factors of inertia and initiative we saw contending in the case of rightness of induction and categorization.

The trouble with the other answer to the question of rightness of representation—the answer in terms of the truth of a statement supposedly made by a picture—is that a picture makes no statement. The picture of a huge yellow wrecked antique car, like the description "the huge yellow wrecked antique car," does not commit itself to any of the following statements:

The huge yellow wrecked car is antique

The huge yellow antique car is wrecked

The huge wrecked antique car is yellow

The yellow wrecked antique car is huge,

or to any other. Although representations and descriptions differ in important ways, in neither case can correctness be a matter of truth.

For descriptive as well as for declarative versions, conflict can be construed in terms of negation: "always red everywhere" and "never red anywhere" conflict, while "green" and "round" do not. And where two right versions conflict and cannot be reconciled in some such way as illustrated earlier, they are of different worlds if any. But for representational versions, where there is no explicit negation, what distinguishes between a pair of right pictures of different things and a pair of different right pictures of the same thing? Do a Soutine painting and a Utrillo drawing, the one in thick impasto and curved lines showing a facade with two twisted windows, the other in straight black lines showing a facade with a door and five windows, represent different buildings or the same building in different ways? We must bear in mind here that even for declarative versions we could draw no clear and firm general distinction between the matter and the manner of discourse. Sometimes a sentence and its negate are reconcilable in one way or another—for example, as applying to different parts or periods of a world. Likewise two moving pictures, one of a sphere rotating clockwise and the other of a sphere rotating counterclockwise, may picture the earth equally correctly from different points of view. Showing that two versions are of the same world involves showing how they fit together. And the question about the Soutine and the Utrillo is much like the question whether a certain mess of molecules and my table are the same.

Such matters aside, a statement is true, and a description or representation right, for a world it fits. And a fictional version, verbal or pictorial, may if metaphorically construed fit and be right for a world. Rather than attempting to subsume descriptive and representational rightness under truth, we shall do better, I think, to subsume truth along with these under the general notion of rightness of fit.[20] That brings us, before we examine further the nature and criteria of right fit, to versions that are neither factual nor fictional statements, descriptions, or representations.

5.6   The Fair Sample

Rightness of abstract visual or musical works will have such aspects as rightness of design, and here we risk an accusation of invading the sacrosanct realm of beauty rather than keeping to kinds of rightness at all comparable to truth. Any such protest would betray an attitude antithetical to my insistence on the very continuity and unity, the very affinity, of art and science and perception as branches of worldmaking. Rightness of abstract works, or of nondenotational aspects of nonabstract works, is neither identical with nor utterly alien to truth; both are species of a more general notion of rightness. To say that beauty or aesthetic rightness is truth or that it is incomparable with truth seem to me equally misleading slogans, and I mention beauty here only to exclude it from further consideration.

We saw earlier that works or other symbols that do not declare or describe or represent anything, literally or metaphorically, or even purport to denote anything, may present worlds by exemplification. What constitutes rightness or wrongness of such exemplification? When is a sample right?

Most obviously, just as a predicate or other label may be wrongly applied to a given object—as say, "red" to a green object—so an object may be a wrong sample in that it is not even an instance of the label, does not possess the property in question. But also, something may be an instance of a predicate or property without being a sample of it, as in the case of the tailor's swatch that is an instance of a certain size and shape but not, since it does not refer to these features, a sample of them.

A further question, therefore, is whether what actually is a sample of a feature[21] may still not be a right sample of it. We have noticed that even though all examined emeralds are grue, inductive argument to "All emeralds are grue" is wrong, and that even though the captives did move, the guard should not have shot them. But this, while it may offer some hints toward an approach to our present question, suggests no immediate answer.

In common parlance, we do distinguish between not being a sample of a feature and being a sample but not a fair sample. A swatch cut from a bolt and used as a sample is not always a fair sample. It may be too small to show the pattern at all or else so cut as to show a component motif only partially or in a misleading orientation. The five samples sketched in figure 5.1 may all have come from the same bolt. Each contains the same amount of material as the rest, and of course none contains the whole pattern, which may consist of many long bands.[22] Yet among the five, the one at the lower right may be the only fair sample. Why is this so? What does it mean?

Before we try to answer, let us look at the somewhat different case of samples of the grass seed mixture in a given barrel. On occasion, we may apply either of two criteria for being a fair sample of the mixture: first, that the mixture in the sample is in the same proportion as in the barrel; or second, that the sample has been fairly drawn in that the contents of the barrel have been thoroughly stirred, parts of the sample taken without prejudice from various levels, etc. Although the rationale for the first

Figure 5.1

criterion is clear, such criteria are inapplicable in many cases and we re-sort to much less easily defended criteria like the second. When we know the proportion of the various kinds of seed in the barrel, we can make a sample fair in the first sense by keeping the proportions in the sample the same. But when we take samples of sea water or drinking water, we can-not know—though we hope—that the samples are fair in the first sense; we rely upon what we consider to be fairness in taking the samples as a basis for supposing that the samples accurately reflect the mixture in the harbor or reservoir. But what determines such fairness in sampling?

The question—and the answer—should have a familiar ring. A sample fair in this sense is one that may be rightly projected to the pattern or mixture or other relevant feature of the whole or of further samples. Such fairness or projectibility, rather than requiring or guaranteeing agreement between the projection made and an actual feature of the whole or of further samples, depends upon conformity to good practice in interpre-ting samples—that is, both in proceeding from sample to feature in ques-tion[23] and in determining whether that feature is projectible. Good practice, in turn, depends upon habit in continual revision under frustra-tion and invention. When the outcomes of rightly made predictions are wrong, the failures may be blamed on bad luck or, if they are prominent or plentiful, may call for amendment of what constitutes good practice. Some accord among samples is a test of good practice and of fairness of sample; but also such accord depends heavily upon what labels or kinds are relevant and right. Thus here as well as in ordinary induction en-trenchment-novelty is a major factor, entering into the determination of what is exemplified, of whether the sample is fairly taken, of whether the exemplified feature is projectible, and of what constitutes accord among samples. Indeed, projectibility from evidence differs from fairness of sample primarily in that while evidence and hypotheses are statements, samples and what they exemplify may be nonlinguistic. Thus some samples and the nonverbal labels or features exemplified by or projectible from them may, unlike evidence statements and hypotheses, belong to symbol systems that are neither denotational nor articulate.[24]

Although in the case of the cloth and the seed, I have usually been speaking as if the projection of pattern or mixture were to the whole bolt or barrel or reservoir, we more typically project rather to other fairly taken portions: to packages of seed, or suit-lengths of cloth, or drinks of water. And this is worth noting for several reasons. First, such portions, which are often of primary interest to us, may all be quite different from the whole in the required respect; for instance, even if the barrel mix is 50–50, each package might contain seed all of one kind or the other. Second, accord among samples, not satisfied in such an event, is thus a more direct test of fairness of sample for normal projection. And third, our attention is called to the sort of accord called for among samples: the swatches need not all be the same so long as the same pattern results from them by appropriate construction; and the packages of seed need not all have exactly the same mixture, say 50–50, but only need center around this ratio in a preferred statistical way (as median, mean, or mode) or just in that the logical sum of all the samples taken has approximately the 50–50 mix.

Works of art are not specimens from bolts or barrels but samples from the sea. They literally or metaphorically exemplify forms, feelings, affinities, contrasts, to be sought in or built into a world. The features of the whole are undetermined; and fairness of sample is no matter of shaking a barrel thoroughly or taking water from scattered places but rather of coordination of samples. In other words, rightness of design, color, harmonics—fairness of a work as a sample of such features—is tested by our success in discovering and applying what is exemplified. What counts as success in achieving accord depends upon what our habits, progressively modified in the face of new encounters and new proposals, adopt as projectible kinds. A Mondrian design is right if projectible to a pattern effective in seeing a world. When Degas painted a woman seated near the edge of the picture and looking out of it, he defied traditional standards of composition but offered by example a new way of seeing, of organizing experience. Rightness of design differs from rightness of representation or description not so much in nature or standards as in the type of symbolization and mode of reference involved.

5.7   Rightness Reviewed

Briefly, then, truth of statements and rightness of descriptions, representations, exemplifications, expressions—of design, drawing, diction, rhythm—is primarily a matter of fit: fit to what is referred to in one way or another, or to other renderings, or to modes and manners of organization. The differences between fitting a version to a world, a world to a version, and a version together or to other versions fade when the role of versions in making the worlds they fit is recognized. And knowing or understanding is seen as ranging beyond the acquiring of true beliefs to the discovering and devising of fit of all sorts.

Procedures and tests used in the search for right versions range from deductive and inductive inference through fair sampling and accord among samples. Despite our faith in such tests, their claims as means for determining rightness may often seem obscure. Indeed, rather than being able to justify our confidence in inductive inference or in the procedures for taking fair samples, we look to the confidence itself for whatever justification there may be for these procedures. Choosing "green" rather than "grue" as projectible, or stirring and shaking a barrel of seed, may seem like rain-dancing—ritual with some celebrated successes and some dismissed failures that is cherished until too disastrous or disreputable. But so sour a view betrays a discredited demand for justification as convincing argument that a test or procedure will ensure, or at least improve our chances of, reaching right conclusions. We have seen, on the contrary, that rightness of categorization, which enters into most other varieties of rightness, is rather a matter of fit with practice; that without the organization, the selection of relevant kinds, effected by evolving tradition, there is no rightness or wrongness of categorization, no validity or invalidity of inductive inference, no fair or unfair sampling, and no uniformity or disparity among samples. Thus justifying such tests for rightness may consist primarily in showing not that they are reliable but that they are authoritative.

All the same, tests results are transient while we think of truth and rightness as eternal. The passing of many and varied tests increases acceptability; but what is once maximally acceptable may later be unacceptable. Total and permanent acceptability, though, may be taken as a sufficient condition of rightness. Such ultimate acceptability, while as inaccessible as absolute rightness, is nevertheless explicable in terms of the tests and their results.

Whether a picture is rightly designed or a statement correctly describes is tested by examination and reexamination of the picture or statement and what it refers to in one way or another, by trying its fit in varied applications and with other patterns and statements. One thinks again of Constable's intriguing remark, stressed by Gombrich,[25] that painting is a science of which pictures are the experiments. Agreement on or among initial untested judgments,[26] and their survival upon testing, is rather rare for either designs or statements. Furthermore, rightness of design and truth of statement are alike relative to system: a design that is wrong in Raphael's world may be right in Seurat's, much as a description of the stewardess's motion that is wrong from the control tower may be right from the passenger's seat; and such relativity should not be mistaken for subjectivity in either case. The vaunted claim of community of opinion among scientists is mocked by fundamental controversies raging in almost every science from psychology to astrophysics. And judgments of the Parthenon and the Book of Kells have hardly been more variable than judgments of the laws of gravitation.[27] I am not claiming that rightness in the arts is less subjective, or even no more subjective, than truth in the sciences, but only suggesting that the line between artistic and scientific judgment does not coincide with the line between subjective and objective, and that any approach to universal accord on anything significant is exceptional.

My readers could weaken that latter conviction by agreeing unanimously with the foregoing somewhat tortuous and in a double sense trying course of thought.

Notes

1. Any treatment of rightness may, of course, give rise to speculation concerning an application to moral rightness; but I willingly leave that to others. One point might be pondered, though: in the present context at least, relativity of rightness and the admissibility of conflicting right renderings in no way precludes rigorous standards for distinguishing right from wrong.

2. I say that a statement is true *in* (or *for*) a given actual world if that statement is true insofar as that world alone is taken into consideration. On the different locutions "true of" and "true about" see my paper with Joseph Ullian, "Truth About Jones," *Journal of Philosophy*, Vol. 74 (1977) pp. 317–338.

3. On various types of ambiguity, see Israel Scheffler, "Ambiguity: An Inscriptional Approach" in *Logic and Art*, Rudner and Scheffler, eds. (Bobbs-Merrill, 1972), pp. 251–272; and also a forthcoming book by Scheffler.

4. I am not concerned here with controversies over whether in some absolute sense the earth is still or moves in a particular way. The reader who holds that neither or only one of (1) and (2) is true may substitute his own example; for instance he will perhaps agree that "The earth rotates clockwise" and "The earth rotates counterclockwise" are both true, from different points of view.

5. I am purposely and harmlessly oversimplifying here by ignoring all other motion such as annual revolution.

6. The temptation is to replace such a phrase as "relative to the sun" by something like "taking the sun as fixed." But what does that mean? Perhaps something like "representing the sun by a fixed dot on a sheet of paper"; but that is only to say "representing the sun by a dot fixed relative to the sheet of paper," and the original problem recurs.

7. For the moment I purposely pass over the relativity to observer or framework of distance between objects; but see Section 5.2 below.

8. See the controversy between Carnap and Quine in *The Philosophy of Rudolph Carnap*, Schilpp, ed. (La Salle, 1963), pp. 385–406; 915–922.

9. Cf. *The Structure of Appearance*: 1. In the present context, I use such informal terms as "made up of," "combination of," "contains," as indeterminate between the terminology of individuals and that of classes.

   Of course there are countless alternatives other than (14) and (15) that conflict with both; points may be construed as made up of opposing diagonals, or of any other two or more lines having a common intersection, or construed in various ways in terms of regions.

10. Nor, again, can (14) and the conflicting statement (call it "14*a*") that points are made up of opposing diagonals both be true in the realm of all lines and all combinations thereof. The realms for (14) and (14*a*) must be differently restricted; for example, that for (14) to lines parallel to the boundaries and that for (14*a*) to diagonals. Or all these lines may be admitted for both, but combinations of cross-

ing lines restricted for (14) to vertical-horizontal cases and for (14*a*) to opposing diagonals. Incidentally, notice that "realm" is not used here in the special technical sense given it in *Languages of Art* [hereinafter *LA*], p. 72.

11. Nothing in this or the immediately following paragraphs is meant as a summary or caricature or defense or cavalier dismissal of any of the views discussed but only as a reminder of some of the problems and possibilities involved.

12. Credibility, though not identical with confidence, is here taken to be explicated in terms of it. We may be rather unsure of some statements that are highly confirmed, and stubbornly sure of others that are ill-confirmed; but confirmation and probability are the results of efforts to codify—and establish standards for—belief. See further "Sense and Certainty," *Problems and Projects* [hereinafter *PP*], pp. 60–68; also *Fact, Fiction, and Forecast* [hereinafter *FFF*], pp. 62–65.

13. Compare C. S. Peirce's "Fixation of Belief" in *Collected Papers of Charles Sanders Peirce* (Cambridge, Mass., 1931–1958), Vol. V, pp. 223–247; but see Israel Scheffler's discussion of that paper in his *Four Pragmatists* (London, 1974), pp. 60–75.

Note added in fifth printing: In the present text, the end of the first paragraph has been revised, as have the last two sentences of the first full paragraph on page 139. The discussion of truth and acceptability here has been replaced by a drastically different treatment in *Reconceptions* by Nelson Goodman and Catherine Z. Elgin (Hackett, 1988), Chapter X.

14. See *PP*, pp. 60–68.

15. On this and other matters to be discussed in this section, see further *FFF*: III and IV. Incidentally, although validity is above identified with conformity to rules of inference, it is sometimes even in my own writings identified rather with overall rightness, which includes satisfaction of other requirements as well.

16. A singular statement derived by instantiation from a hypothesis is a positive instance when determined by examination to be true, a negative instance when so determined to be false.

17. See *FFF*, p. 97; also "On Kahane's Confusions," *Journal of Philosophy*. Vol. 69 (1972), pp. 83–84, and my comments on Kutschera's paper, *Erkenntnis*, Vol. 12 (1978), pp. 282–284.

18. E.g., in E. H. Gombrich, *Art and Illusion* (New York, 1960), various passages, and in *LA*: I.

19. See my note "On J. J. Gibson's New Perspective," *Leonardo*, Vol. 4 (1971), pp. 359–360.

20. Readers of foregoing pages will be well aware that none of this implies either that any ready-made world lies waiting to be described or represented, or that wrong as well as right versions make worlds they fit. See further Section 5.7 below.

21. Since "property" is customarily so closely associated with "predicate," I often use the term "feature" in the hope that it may come to serve as a reminder that not all labels are verbal.

22. Patterns exemplified may vary greatly in specificity, as, e.g., striped, pin-striped, blue and white quarter-inch pin-striped, etc. Exemplification like denotation may thus be more or less general; but whereas generality of a predicate is a matter of scope of application, generality of a sample is a matter of scope of exemplified feature.

23. Requirements upon procedure will vary with need in different cases: for the seed samples, the proportion of types of seed must be selected rather than such other features as the actual count; for the tailor's swatch, the pattern in question might be constructed by a standard juxtaposition of iterations of the patch.

24. On articulate or finitely differentiated as contrasted with dense symbol systems, see *LA:* IV.

25. *Art and Illusion,* p. 33 and elsewhere.

26. "Judgment" as used here must be freed of exclusive association with statements; it includes, for example, apprehension of the fit of a design, and the decisions a pool-player takes in aiming his shots.

27. Curiously, such observations are sometimes adduced to show that since science progresses while art does not, judgments of scientific truth are more objective than judgments of artistic rightness. The reason that earlier theories but not older works may be rendered obsolete by later ones is often, I think, that the earlier theories, insofar as sound, are absorbed into and are rederivable from the later while works of art, functioning differently as symbols, cannot be absorbed into or derived from others. I cannot here go into the details of this explanation.

III

Reactions

6

Reflections on Goodman's *Ways of Worldmaking*

Hilary Putnam

One of the most important themes in Goodman's book *Ways of Worldmaking* (referred to below as *WoW*; parenthetical references in the text are to this book) is that there is no privileged basis. Reducing sense data to physical objects or events is an admissible research program for Goodman; it is no *more* (and no less) reasonable than reducing physical objects to sense data. As research programs, there is nothing wrong with either physicalism or phenomenalism; as dogmatic monisms there is everything wrong with both of them.

This is decidedly not the fashionable opinion today. Physicalism and "realism" are at the high tide of fashion; phenomenalism has sunk out of sight in a slough of philosophical disesteem and neglect. Goodman's assumption that physicalism and phenomenalism are *analogous* would be disputed by many philosophers.

It is this assumption that I wish to explain and defend before considering other aspects of *WoW*. Because it runs so counter to the fashion, it may be of great importance to see that it is correct. At the same time, the analogy leads directly to the heart of Goodman's book, which is its defense of pluralism.

In *WoW*, Goodman points out that the phenomenal itself has many equally valid descriptions. In his view, this arises from two causes. First of all, perception is itself notoriously influenced by interpretations provided by habit, culture, and theory. (Goodman's long and close acquaintance with actual psychological research shines through many sections of *WoW*.) We see toothbrushes and vacuum tubes *as* toothbrushes and vacuum tubes, not as arrangements of color patches. Secondly, there is, for

Goodman as for the late Wittgenstein, no sharp line to be drawn between the character of the experience and the description given by the subject. Thus, after reporting a finding by Kolers (92) that a disproportionate number of engineers and physicians are unable to see apparent motion at all, Goodman comments:

> Yet if an observer reports that he sees two distinct flashes, even at distances and intervals so short that most observers see one moving spot, perhaps he means that he sees the two as we might say we see a swarm of molecules when we look at a chair, or as we do when we say we see a round table top even when we look at it from an oblique angle. Since an observer can become adept at distinguishing apparent from real motion, he may take the appearance of motion as a sign that there are two flashes, as we take the oval appearance of the table top as a sign that it is round; and in both cases the signs may be or become so transparent that we look through them to physical events and objects. When the observer visually determines that what is before him is what we agree is before him, we can hardly charge him with an error in visual perception. Shall we say, rather, that he misunderstands the instruction, which is presumably just to tell what he sees? Then how, without prejudicing the outcome, can we so reframe the instruction as to prevent such a "misunderstanding"? Asking him to make no use of prior experience and to avoid all conceptualization will obviously leave him speechless; for to talk at all he must use words.

In the same way, there are different possible ways of reporting physical events and motions. And here too there is no sharp line to be drawn between the character of the object or motion and the description we give of it. As Goodman puts it (93):

> Did the sun set a while ago, or did the earth rise? Does the sun go around the earth or the earth go around the sun? Nowadays, we nonchalantly deal with what was once a life-and-death issue by saying that the answer depends on the framework. But here again, if we say that the geocentric and heliocentric systems are different versions of "the same facts," we must ask not what these facts are but rather how such phrases as "version of the same facts" or "descriptions of the same world" are to be understood. This varies from case to case; here, the geocentric and the heliocentric versions, while speaking of the same particular objects— the sun, moon, and planets—attribute very different motions to these objects. Still, we may say the two versions deal with the same facts if we mean by this that they not only speak of the same objects but are also routinely intertranslatable each into the other. As meanings vanish in favor of certain relationships among terms, so facts vanish in favor of certain relationships among versions. In the present case the relationship is comparatively obvious; sometimes it is much more elusive. For instance, the physical and perceptual versions of motion we were talking about do not evidently deal with the same objects, and the relationship if any

that constitutes license for saying that the two versions describe the same facts or the same world is no ready intertranslatability.

In the case of the subject who is being asked to describe apparent motion, Goodman says (92/3):

> The best we can do is to specify the sort of terms, the vocabulary, he is to use, telling him to describe what he sees in perceptual or phenomenal rather than physical terms. Whether or not this yields different responses, it casts an entirely different light on what is happening. That the instrument to be used in fashioning the facts must be specified makes pointless any identification of the physical with the real and of the perceptual with the merely apparent. The perceptual is no more a rather distorted version of the physical facts than the physical is a highly artificial version of the perceptual facts.

The examples are well selected, but they would not convince a die-hard physicalist. In the rest of this section I intend, therefore, to examine some standard physicalist rejoinders to the line Goodman takes.

6.1   The "We're Not Looking for Translations" Response

Phenomenalists were trying to find meaning-preserving translations from thing language into sense-datum language. Physicalists who hope that future science will vindicate them by finding a neural event or a functional state of the nervous system, or whatever, which can be identified with any given mental event are looking for empirical identities, not analytic ones. Thus Goodman's analogy between phenomenalism and physicalism fails.

Goodman, however, has never accepted the analytic-synthetic distinction, nor (as far back as *The Structure of Appearance*[1]) has he ever required that reductions must be meaning-preserving. If one could find what Goodman called an "extensional isomorphism" (in *SoA*) between thing language and (a part of) sense-datum language which enabled one to preserve truth value in "translating" from thing language into sense-datum language, then, even if the translation did not preserve "meaning," it could still be of great interest. If the physicalist is allowed to look for "reductions" in more than one sense, so is the phenomenalist. Indeed, one of Goodman's points is precisely that there are many senses of 'reduction'.

At this point the physicalist is likely to respond that physicalistic "translations" (of psychological talk into brain-state or functional-state talk) *will* eventually be found by neurology, or by cognitive psychology, but translations of thing talk into sense-datum talk will never be found for the simple reason that they don't exist. When one looks at an article like "Mental Representation" by Hartry Field,[2] however, it turns out that the translation will not be of psychological talk as it is but of a specially constructed substitute, and that even the translation of this substitute will depend on the successful carrying out of the program for translating "refers" (i.e., the two-place predicate "x refers to y," or, more generally, the relation of *satisfaction* in the sense of formal semantics) into physicalist language that Field proposed some years ago.[3] How to do this, Field gives no hint, and his discussion suggests that carrying out his program would require defining a physicalistic relation between signs (or sign uses) and things (or properties) which analyzes such things as the application of the Principle of Charity—i.e., on analyzing exhaustively scientific and interpretative rationality itself.[4]

At this point the analogy between physicalism and phenomenalism begins to emerge. Just as the phenomenalist runs into trouble when he tries to specify in phenomenal terms *all* the circumstances under which it would be true, or even warrantedly assertible, to say that there is a chair in a certain place, so the physicalist will run into trouble when he tries to specify in physical terms *all* the circumstances under which it would be true, or even warrantedly assertible, to say that some utterance-part refers to some thing or property. And the reasons are not unrelated. Just as an indefinite amount of theory (including theories that are not yet thought of) can intervene between the phenomenal data and the physical interpretation, so likewise an indefinite amount of theory can intervene between the physicalist data and the intentional interpretation. Both the physicalist and the phenomenalist leave their increasingly dubious clients with mere promissory notes for future translations, or else they say that the existence "in principle" of possibly infinite (and not effectively specifiable) translations is good enough.

6.2   The "Nobody Here but Us Ontologists" Response

Recently some sophisticated physicalists have begun to suggest that physicalism should never have been stated as a thesis concerning relations between languages, or a thesis concerning *syntactic* facts, at all. Donald Davidson in "Mental Events"[5] and Richard Boyd both defend the idea that one can say that mental events *are* physical events (Davidson), or even that mental properties are somehow physical properties or aspects (Boyd), without being committed to the existence of a finite open sentence in physicalist language with the same extension as a given term in "psychological" language. "We are talking about what mental events *are,* not about relations between open sentences" is the position of these ontologists.

There is something here with which I sympathize, and to which Goodman may not do full justice. Talk of "reduction" or "translation" invites the rejoinder "put up or shut up." But certainly one can sometimes know that an object or system of objects has a certain kind of description on the basis of a well-confirmed *theory;* and in such cases actually exhibiting the description may be beyond human powers, even beyond human powers *in principle,* and yet we do not doubt the existence of the sort of description in question.

For example, I may ask a physicist to explain why the engine fell off the DC10 that crashed in Chicago. The physicist will assume that the DC10 has a description as a system of molecules (he may have to go to an even deeper level if metallurgy enters), and he will approximate that description by estimating the relevant parameters. Now, if a philosopher should object that we cannot actually write down a necessary and sufficient condition for a system of molecules to be a DC10 wing *cum* engine *cum* pylon, and that such a description, if it exists at all, may be practically infinite and not actually able to be written down by human beings, we would say that he was missing the point.

The point is that we know that a DC10 wing consists of molecules in a certain arrangement; knowing this is not the same thing as actually being able to *say* which molecules in what arrangement. And the suggestion is that, in the same way, we might know that any given psychological event *consists* of neurological events without actually being able to say which events.

But none of this actually goes against what Goodman maintains. Combining versions and objects from versions so as to get a version that speaks of "airplane wings and molecules" (or "objects ranging from elementary particles through cells, trees, mountains, planets, stars, and whole galaxies," to give the sort of list one sometimes sees in a physics text) is one way of worldmaking, as is extending such relations as "part/whole," so that we can speak of the "molecules that are part of the wing." (Cf. *WoW*, chapter 1, especially section 4.) Composition, decomposition, and supplementation are all among the standard devices for making worlds. And that one could not speak of the airplane wing as consisting of molecules if one did not first have the notions of a wing and a molecule is also grist for Goodman's mill; for as he says, "facts are small theories, and true theories are big facts. This does not mean, I repeat, that right versions can be arrived at casually, or that worlds are built from scratch. We start, on any occasion, with some old version or world that we have on hand and that we are stuck with until we have the determination and skill to remake it into a new one. Some of the felt stubbornness of fact is the grip of habit: our firm foundation is indeed stolid. World making begins with one version and ends in another" (97). There is nothing in this, as far as I can see, that would preclude a version in which mental events consist of physical ones, as airplane wings consists of molecules.

But there is one important difference between the two cases which the *monistic* physicalist often fails to note. That airplane wings consists of molecules is uncontroversial; that the property of *being an airplane wing* can be identified with any property definable in physicalistic language is much more controversial. (Even if the number of structures that represent physically possible airplane wings is finite, if they are not graspable by human minds, there may not be a possible well-defined cut that we could actually make between those which are airplane wings and those which are not.) However, we do not feel that we need a general criterion for being an airplane wing to say that any particular wing consists of molecules, or even to say something significant about *which* molecules it contains. In the mind/body case one cannot decide that a particular mental event (say, a visual sensation of blue) "consisted of" particular neural events on a particular occasion without having some idea of a *general* necessary and sufficient condition. (This is a complication for Davidson's "anomalous monism.") For what it means to say that a particular mental event "consists of" certain neural events, or is "identical" with their union, is that this union has the "causal powers" of the mental event, or, in other words, that the neural event can adequately *explain* the actions (described in *human-action language*—otherwise every question is begged!) that the mental event explains. But one can say nothing about the "causal powers" of particulars apart from a *relevant theoretical description* of those particulars. The whole idea of saying that a *particular* brain event is a *sensation* without *any* "type-type" theory is a chimera.

To illustrate this point with an example, suppose that whenever I have a blue sense datum a particular event E takes place in the visual cortex. Was the event of my having a blue sense datum just now *identical* with the event E in my visual cortex just now? Or was it rather identical with the *larger* event of E *plus* signals to the speech center? If you say the *latter,* then very likely you will deny that patients with a split corpus collosum have blue sense data when blue is presented to the right lobe only; if you say the former, then very likely you will say they *do* (i.e., that there are two "loci" of consciousness in the split brain). In this way, even the decision about "token identity" in a particular case is inextricably bound up with what one wants to say about general issues, as fact is always bound up with theory.

The *special* trouble about the mind/body case is that it will never make an empirical difference whether we say the right lobe is conscious in the split-brain case or not. That the right lobe is only, so to speak, simulating consciousness and that it is "really" conscious are observationally indistinguishable theories as far as observers with unsplit brains are concerned. My own view is that there is an element of legislation or posit that enters here; the idea of a firm fact of the matter, not at all made by us, in the area of mind/brain relations is illusory.

If I am right, then this is another illustration of a theme to which Goodman constantly returns: that even where reduction is possible it is typically non-unique. Ontological identification is just another form of reduction and shares the non-uniqueness and the dependence upon legislation and posit which are characteristic of all reduction.

I wish now to make a different point about the physicalism-phenomenalism analogy. Those physicalists who say that such predicates as "is an airplane wing" refer to physical properties whose definition in the language of physics might be infinite—practically infinite for sure—often explain this in terms of what an "ideal theory" would say. I don't wish to say that talk of ideal theories is a bad thing (if we don't pretend that 'ideal' is better defined than it is); regulative ideals and research programs are important in science as in everything else, and speculation about what the specification of an airplane wing or a mental state might look like in some ideal limit could be important in focusing thinking and research in a particular area. But if the physicalist avails himself of "ideal limit" talk, he cannot consistently deny it to the phenomenalist. The phenomenalist can come back and tell the following sort of story about *his* "ideal limit":

> An ideally intelligent being could divide all the state descriptions in an ideal sense-datum language—that is, all the descriptions of possible total sets of experiences that observers might have (or of experiences that the *would* have if they did various things, if you are more tolerant than Nelson Goodman toward counterfactuals)—into three classes: those in which 'There is ivy growing on Emerson Hall on June 9, 1979' is true (or, not to beg questions, warrantedly assertible on the totality of all experiential evidence); those in which this sentence's negation is warrantedly assertible on total experiential evidence; and those in which it is undecided in the limit of total experiential evidence.
>
> Let S_1 be the infinite disjunction of all the state-descriptions of the first kind. These are themselves denumerably infinite sentences; so this is an infinite disjunction of infinite conjunctions. Let S_2 be the infinite disjunction of all the state descriptions of the second kind. Then I maintain that 'There is ivy growing on Emerson Hall on June 9, 1979' *does* have a *translation* into phenomenalist language—for the ordered pair $(S_1;S_2)$ is such a translation. The first member gives the cases in which the sentence is true, the second member gives the cases in which the sentence is false, and the remaining state descriptions are the truth-value gaps.

Of course, the physicalist can reject the translation as *really* (metaphysically) wrong. But the point is that if the technique the phenomenalist envisages is applied to the sentences of the physicalist's own "ideal scientific theory," then the result is a "translation" of that theory into phenomenalistic language which preserves truth value as far as we shall ever be able to tell. "Real metaphysical truth or falsity" is just what, insofar as it differs from ultimate warranted assertibility, we can never know.

What I have been saying is that, whether we talk of reduction or of ontological identification, Goodman's two big points still hold: all species of reduction and ontological identification involve posits, legislation, non-uniqueness; and there are both different kinds of reduction and different directions of reduction. If all versions can be reduced in one way to a physicalist version (in principle, in the ideal limit, as a regulative ideal), then they can all be reduced to a phenomenalist version in another way (in principle, in the ideal limit, as a regulative ideal).

One World or Many?

In his writings Goodman has consistently reminded us that there is no such thing as *comparing* any version with an "unconceptualized reality." We do check scientific theories against experiential data; but experiential data, as Goodman points out in his discussion of apparent motion, are themselves doubly the result of construction and interpretation: construction by the brain itself, and construal through the need of the subject to use language and public concepts to report and even grasp what he "sees." Comparison of theory with experience is *not* comparison with unconceptualized reality, even if some positivists once thought it was. It is comparison of one or another version with the version we take to be "experience" in the given context.

On the other hand, we can invert the comparison: we can take some physicalistic description of the environment as "the world" and analyze perceptual data (as construed) for salient correspondence or lack of salient correspondence to "the world" (as construed). This is not like comparing two versions of the morning newspaper, but more like comparing *Newsweek* with *U.S. News and World Report*. Such a comparison is legitimate and important; in his insistence on this Goodman is as much of an *empirical* realist as I am; but comparison of experience with physical theory is not comparison with unconceptualized reality, even if some of my friends in places like Princeton and Australia think it is. All we have is comparison of versions with versions.

If reduction to one version were possible, were unique, and were always in the preferred direction, then the philosophers I refer to would have an easy rejoinder to Goodman. "We don't *need* to suppose we can compare any version with an *unconceptualized* reality," they could say. "Since (to the extent that it is more than folk theory[6]) any version is embeddable in the physicalist version, we have, appearances to the contrary—in the ideal limit, some of them would add—*one* version. There is, as Goodman says, no point in talking about 'the world' apart from all versions, when there are incompatible true versions. But there *aren't* incompatible true versions; there is only one true version."

The problem of the non-uniqueness of reduction is the key difficulty with this stance. But Hartry Field has suggested an ingenious way for the metaphysical realist to meet it.[7] The idea (which is closely related to

Carnap's idea of "partial interpretation") is to regard some terms as *partially referring* to one property or magnitude or whatever and partially referring to another. The terms so treated do not have *both* of the properties in question in their extension; rather, in one admissible interpretation such a term has the one, and in another admissible interpretation it has the other in its extension. (I am speaking of singular terms denoting properties, but the idea may be extended to any kind of term.) The various multiply-referring terms are *linked* so that the choice of one admissible interpretation of one can force or restrict the choice of the admissible interpretation of another.

Thus, in the case of the split-brain problem I described above, a philosopher who agrees with me that there is no fact of the matter as to whether the occurrence of the neural event *E* in the right lobe of the split brain constitutes an occurrence of a visual sensation of blue could say that 'event of the occurrence of the visual sensation of blue' *partially refers* to the occurrence of neural events of kind *E* and partially refers to, say, the occurrence of *E* plus further processing in the speech center (which does not take place when the association paths between the right lobe and the speech center are cut). The element of posit I described is just the choice of an admissible interpretation. All versions *still* reduce to one—the physicalist version—but the ontological reducing function is a many-valued function and not a single-valued one.

The trouble with this move is that the version chosen as basic—the physicalist version—has *incompatible reductions to itself*. Goodman illustrates this problem with geometrical examples. For example, *points* can be identified with sets of concentric spheres or, alternatively, with intersections of three planes. Even if we were to bite the bullet and say, "Well, *point* partially refers to sets of concentric spheres and partially refers to triples of planes," we would have the problem that one of the things planes and spheres can be identified with is sets of points. When there are incompatible relative interpretations of a theory in itself, the Hartry Field idea of "partial reference" will not restore the kind of determinateness that the realist desires.

One can give similar examples from physics. In Newtonian physics fields can be reduced to particles acting at a distance, and particles exerting forces at a distance can be replaced by particles interacting locally with fields. Even general relativity, long thought to be inseparable from curved space-time, has an equivalent version due to Steven Weinberg which dispenses with warped space. Nor will it help to hope for an ideal limit in which uniqueness will finally appear; if there were an ideal limit, and some cognitive extensions of ourselves actually reached it, then they would have nothing left to do but construct equivalent incompatible versions of the ideal limit—and given ingenuity, I am sure they would succeed!

Another move that has been made to avoid Goodmanian pluralism, but one opposite in spirit to the Hartry Field move, is due to W. V. Quine. Quine holds that the failure of mentalistic psychology to reduce uniquely to physics shows that the sentences of mentalistic psychology and of all the discourses that employ mentalistic locutions have no truth value. These discourses are indispensable for daily life, but not truly cognitively significant. In *Word and Object,* Quine calls them "second class." Physical facts are all the facts there are, and to be underdetermined by all the facts there are is to lack truth value; so says Quine.

On the other hand, the existence of equivalent versions of physics which differ in ontology is now handled by Quine[8] by saying that such versions are mere notational variants. There is *one* Newtonian physics and *one* general relativity, notwithstanding the existence of the notational variants. The true physics, whatever it may be, is Quine's candidate for the true and ultimate description of the world. The world does have a true and ultimate description, on Quine's view, *even if it doesn't have a true and ultimate ontology.*

The deep differences between Quine and Goodman, notwithstanding certain commonalities, have recently burst out in the *New York Review of Books.*[9] In his review of *WoW* in that journal, Quine reaffirms that only *physical* versions describe worlds, and justifies this by saying "full coverage in this sense is the business of physics and only of physics." But all Quine has to say about *what* sense of "full coverage" physics aims at is that nothing happens without some redistribution of microphysical states. There clearly are missing premises between "nothing happens without some redistribution of microphysical states" and "full coverage."

What the missing premises are, I can only guess. The "full coverage" is only "the business" of physics; so once again we have physicalism defended on the basis of the achievements of the program *in the ideal limit.* Even assuming this ideal limit were at hand, in what does its "full coverage" *consist?*

If the "full coverage" consists in explaining all *physical* facts, then the argument is circular. A theory may predict all the motions of John's body without predicting that *John is angry;* and in what sense is such a theory "complete"? It may be true that "Nothing happens without some *gravitational* change," but that would not justify calling a theory that predicted all gravitational fields and nothing else "complete."

But there is a still more important objection. Imagine we belong to a community of art experts (it could be the entire species, if we all became art experts) for whom 'This painting has the characteristic Rembrandt paint quality' is an observation sentence, in Quine's sense (which requires that members of the language community have sufficiently high intersubjective agreement on when they assent and when they dissent). Even if the ideal physics explained the sensations we would have on viewing *The Polish Rider,* it would certainly not explain them *under this description.* And Goodman's point is that there is no reason to regard an explanation of which of our neurons fired as an explanation of our experience of the characteristic Rembrandt paint quality. From Goodman's perspective (as well as my own),[10] Quine's insistence that the physicalist description provides "full coverage" is a mere prejudice.

Goodman's attitudes are deeply connected with his attitudes toward an appreciation of the arts. In Chapter 4 ("When Is Art?"), Goodman makes points that are extremely relevant to what we have been discussing. Consider the experience of reading a novel like *Don Quixote.* One thing that happens to us is that our conceptual and perceptual repertoire becomes enlarged; we become able to "see" Don Quixote, not only in the book but in ourselves and in other people. This enlargement of our stock of predicates and of metaphors is *cognitive;* we now possess descriptive resources we did not have before. And these are immensely valuable for their own sake, and not only for the sake of the stimulations of nerve endings they allow us to anticipate.

Similarly, even an abstract work of art *exemplifies* patterns and formal properties which we have to learn to perceive *in* and *through* the work; and this too is an enlargement of perceptual and conceptual skills. Fundamentally, Quine sees cognition as having just two aims: guiding the anticipation of sensation, and, beyond that, satisfying methodological canons of simplicity, conservatism, etc. Goodman is a pluralist about the *purposes* as well as about the content of cognition; and these two pluralisms are intimately connected.

Goodman on Truth

It seems to me that Goodman's view is closely related to points recently made by Michael Dummett and by me,[11] notably the point that the metaphysical realist notion of truth cannot play any role in a theory of how we *understand* our various versions and languages. This is clear, on Goodman's view, since no actual psychological mechanism can play the required role of comparing our statements with unconceptualized reality. Donald Davidson has proposed to retain the verbal formula that to know the meaning of, say, 'Snow is white', is to know under what conditions that sentence is true; one can say that *whatever it takes to understand a sentence* is to be called implicit knowledge of the conditions under which the sentence is true. But if one plays the game *that* way, then it is a *tautology* that "If X understands the sentence *Snow is white,* then X knows (implicitly) the truth conditions of the sentence *Snow is white.*" If you make this a tautology, then you can't also claim it to be an *explanatory account of understanding.* But if the notion that truth is correspondence to reality cannot do any work for us, how are we to explain the notion of truth? The formal semantics of 'true' (especially the equivalence principle: that to say of any sentence that it is true is equivalent to asserting the sentence) enables us to decide as many sentences of the form *S is true* as there are sentences *S* we are willing to assert or deny. But how are we to account for what we are doing when we assert and deny statements? We can say, "when we assert statements we hope and intend that they should be true"; but this is almost empty, since there are not and cannot be independent tests for truth and for present warranted assertibility. In the first chapter of *WoW* Goodman writes, "A version is taken to be true when it offends no unyielding beliefs and none of its own precepts"; but evidently this is not meant as a *definition* of 'true'.

Goodman tells us that truth itself is only one aspect of a more general virtue he calls *rightness,* just as statement-making and referential use of language represent only one sort of symbolic functioning (*expression* and *exemplification* being cited as others). Truth and rightness may sometimes conflict, even in science, as when what we want is a perspicuous but only approximately true general law rather than a strictly true statement that is overburdened with unnecessary information. Truth applies only to versions that consist of statements; and in chapter 7 we are told that it depends on credibility and coherence, and are given as well some details about deductive and inductive rightness.

All this, however, occupies only a few pages in *WoW*. Perhaps Goodman has not yet worked out exactly what he wishes to say on this central issue. But the direction is clear.

The direction in which Goodman's thought takes him is the direction of verificationist or "nonrealist" semantics. That is, Goodman is saying, I think, that what we understand our languages in terms of is a grasp of conditions of warranted assertibility and "rightness"; not a grasp of "truth conditions" in the old realist sense. Truth is an idealization of warranted assertibility.

Perhaps I am reading too much in here; if so, the author will set us right. But my reading is supported, I think, by two passages in the book. The first is surely the most unfortunate sentence in the book for anyone to quote out of context: "Truth, like intelligence, is perhaps just what the tests test" (122). The meaning is not that Bridgmanian operationism is right (Goodman embraces coherence as a "test" on pages 124/5), but rather that we understand truth is a "verificationist" way. The second passage is the open question on page 124, "Shall we, then, identify unattainable total and permanent credibility with total truth?"—which, in the context, seems to say that "total truth" is an idealization of "credibility."

The discussion of truth, and of tests for truth, in *WoW* bothers me, however, by its descriptive stance.

Consider, for example, the position of a man who thinks that one must commit oneself to versions, precepts, unyielding beliefs, and who has so committed himself, all the while believing that there is nothing to be said in favor of his choice except that it is his existential choice. The position of such a man might be logically analyzed thus: it is as if he had decided that 'true' and 'right' are *indexical* words. 'True' (or rather, 'warrantedly assertible') means "true for me"—i.e., in keeping with *my* precepts and unyielding beliefs, and 'right' means "right for me"—i.e., in keeping with my standards and seat-of-the-pants feelings of rightness. I am sure Goodman would be horrified at such a position. But it could be the position of a culture (the young in California *do* say "true for me"), and the whole story Goodman tells about how we build versions from versions, about not starting *ex nihilo*, about precepts and unyielding beliefs, could be told about 'true for me'. Goodman says that not all versions are true; but imagine a voice saying "Not all versions are true for you, Professor Goodman, but so what?"

Goodman would, no doubt, reply that any superiority of our versions over other versions must be judged and claimed from *within* our collection of versions; there is no neutral place to stand. I heartily agree. But what I hope Goodman will say something about in the future is what makes our versions superior to others *by our lights,* not by some inconceivable neutral standard. "Our versions are true, or closer to the truth" is purely formal; even the relativist can say his versions are "truer for me"—truer for *him.*

For Quine there is no such problem. Quine does say from within his versions—the scientific versions he likes—what makes those versions better than nonscientific versions: it is simply that they better predict stimulations of nerve-endings. But Goodman does not agree that the be-all and end-all of versions is just to predict stimulations of nerve-endings (or to do so economically and in a way that accords with tradition). Goodman recognizes that we wish to build worlds because doing so enriches us in many ways. And this, it seems to me, requires him to recognize that the notions of truth and rightness subserve a vision of the good.

Consider, for example, the often-mentioned desiderata of simplicity and generality in scientific theory. The search for these is part of the search for what Goodman calls "rightness"; and if we refuse to accept versions that wilfully depart from this sort of rightness it is because having scientific versions that are simple and universal and exhibit internal coherence of a high order, as well as being technologically and predictively useful, is an end in itself for us; because it is part of our notion of human flourishing to have our scientific worlds be like that.

And if, as Goodman reminds us, art also serves cognitive functions, the reason for valuing the enlarged perception and conception that art provides is again the place of such perception and conception in our notion of human flourishing, of eudaemonia. The very term that Goodman chooses for the characteristic of the versions that meet our desiderata—*rightness*—is a term that bears its normative character on its face.

Goodman himself toys with the idea of extending what he has to say to the moral domain in a footnote on the first page of his concluding chapter. He writes, "Any treatment of rightness may, of course, give rise to speculation concerning an application to moral rightness; but I willingly leave that to others. One point might be pondered, though: in the present context at least, relativity of rightness and the admissibility of conflicting right renderings in no way precludes rigorous standards for distinguishing right from wrong." The direction that this footnote points out, however hesitantly, is the direction I think philosophers sympathetic to the general story Goodman tells should pursue.

Notes

1. New York: Bobbs-Merrill, 1966; hereafter *SoA*.

2. *Erkenntnis*, XIII, 1 (July 1978): 9–61.

3. Cf. Field's "Tarski's Theory of Truth," *The Journal of Philosophy*, LXIX, 13 (July 13, 1972): 347–375.

4. For a detailed criticism of Field's program and of the idea that reference is a "physicalistic" relation, see my *Meaning and the Moral Sciences* (London: Routledge & Kegan Paul, 1978). That his "physicalistic definition" of reference would incorporate such principles of interpretation as charity was stated by Field in a discussion of my "Reference and Understanding" (op. cit., part III) at a Chapel Hill conference some years ago.

5. In Lawrence Foster and J. W. Swanson, *Experience & Theory* (Amherst: Univ. of Massachusetts Press, 1970).

6. The use of the notion of "folk theory" by *scientistic* philosophers turns on a confusion that should be noted: a confusion between *false* theories (e.g., astrology) and theories whose terms are not "scientifically precise" by the standards of physics and other *exact* sciences. 'Brown' and 'angry' might be said to belong to "folk color theory" and "folk psychology," respectively; but it doesn't follow (*pace* "eliminative materialism") that there aren't brown objects or angry people.

7. Cf. Field's "Theory Change and the Indeterminacy of Reference," *The Journal of Philosophy*, LXIX, 13 (July 13, 1972): 347–375, and "Quine and the Correspondence Theory," *Philosophical Review*, LXXXIII, 2 (April 1974): 200–228.

8. Cf. "On Empirically Equivalent Systems of the World," *Erkenntnis*, IX, 2 (1975): 313–328.

9. Quine's review of *WoW* appeared in NYR on November 25, 1978 (p. 25). Exchanges of letters by Quine and Goodman and others appeared in *NYR* on January 25 and May 17, 1979.

10. Cf. "Philosophy and Our Mental Life," ch. 14 of my *Mind, Language, and Reality* (New York: Cambridge, 1975).

11. Dummett's views were most completely stated in his William James Lectures at Harvard in the Spring of 1976, published as *The Logical Basis of Metaphysics* (Cambridge, MA: Harvard University Press, 1991); mine are stated in "Realism and Reason" (Presidential Address to the Eastern Division of the American Philosophical Association, 29 December 1976; reprinted in *Meaning and the Moral Sciences*). See also Part Three of my book, and my "Models and Reality" (*Journal of Symbolic Logic,* 45 (1980), 464–482.

7

Comments on Goodman's *Ways of Worldmaking*

Carl G. Hempel

7.1

Nelson Goodman's book and Hilary Putnam's observations on it evoked in me vivid memories of the conception of empirical knowledge that was propounded by Otto Neurath of the Vienna Circle about 1930, and which contrasted sharply with the views held by other members of the Circle at that time.

Neurath certainly cannot be claimed to have anticipated Goodman's ideas with their very wide scope; moreover, there are also important differences in fundamentals.

But there are striking similarities between some of the basic ideas informing the two conceptions, and it may be of interest to begin with a brief consideration of those similarities; this will illuminate some of the virtues of Goodman's ideas, but it will also afford me an opportunity to suggest the desirability of a certain supplementation of the account given in *Ways of Worldmaking*.

7.2

The central idea in Goodman's book that has a strong kinship with one of Neurath's theses is to the effect that the rightness of a version cannot be characterized as its applicability to the world. "We cannot test a version by comparing it with a world undescribed," ". . . all we learn about the world is contained in right versions of it; and while the underlying world, bereft of these, need not be denied to those who love it, it is perhaps on the whole a world well lost."[1] Putnam agrees: "Comparison of theory with experience . . . is comparison of one or another version with the version we take to be 'experience' in the given context"; "it is *not* comparison with unconceptualized reality, even if some positivists once thought it was."[2]

Neurath was one positivist who decidedly did not think that. Concerning the testing of empirical claims, he says this:

It is always science as a system of statements which is at issue. *Statements are compared with statements,* not with 'experience', 'the world', or anything else. All these meaningless *duplications* belong to a more or less refined metaphysics and are, for that reason, to be rejected. Each new statement is compared with the totality of existing statements previously coordinated. To say that a statement is correct, therefore, means that it can be incorporated in this totality.[3]

He adds that if a statement cannot be incorporated, it is rejected as incorrect or else—but only with reluctance—the entire accepted system is modified so as to permit incorporation of the new statement. Thus, he stresses, his characterization of "correct" and "incorrect" limits itself to the linguistic sphere. These pronouncements seem to me to accord well with Goodman's insistence that versions are always compared with versions, and that new versions are always made from earlier ones.

7.3

What *reasons* did Neurath have for advocating this conception? His philosophical style was not very explicit or precise, and often did not take the form of well-articulated argumentation. But there are three or four considerations that can reasonably be said to underlie his views.

(3a) As shown by the passage just quoted, Neurath rejected all talk of "reality," "the facts," "the world" as metaphysical and a potential source of meaningless and misleading disputation; indeed, he relegated the very words 'reality', 'fact', and so forth to his famous *index verborum prohibitorum*. Goodman, in less doctrinaire language, says, in effect, that nothing hangs on the assumption of a world to which our versions refer; that it is, on the whole, a world well lost.

(3b) Neurath combined his claims with the doctrine that all empirical statements can be expressed in the language of physics. His physicalism was no doubt informed by his materialist and strongly anti-idealist leanings: all branches of empirical science, including psychology and the social sciences, were concerned, in his view, with conglomerations of material or physical systems whose behavior is fully describable in physical terms.

This marks a point of sharp disagreement with Goodman, who rejects conceptions of this kind as monopolistic materialism or physicalism and advocates a rich pluralism instead. Neurath's background conception is akin, I think, to what Putnam calls the "nobody here but us ontologists" response, and his rejection of the latter seems compelling to me.

I would add that the physicalistic claim that the language of physics can serve as a unitary language of science is inherently obscure: the language of *what* physics is meant? Surely not that of, say, eighteenth-century physics; for it contains terms like "caloric fluid," whose use is governed by theoretical assumptions now thought false. Nor can the language of contemporary physics claim the role of unitary language, since it will no doubt undergo further changes, too. The thesis of physicalism would seem to require a language in which a *true* theory of all physical phenomena can be formulated. But it is quite unclear what is to be understood here by a physical phenomenon, especially in the context of a doctrine that has taken a determinedly linguistic turn.

(3c) As for the rejection of the notion that statements can be tested by a comparison with facts, Goodman's view is informed by considerations that are not, to my knowledge, explicit in Neurath, though they certainly accord with his views. As noted earlier, Goodman insists that we cannot test a version by comparing it with a world *undescribed*. This might be put more positively by saying that what we call experimental findings can serve to test a given hypothesis only if they are expressed in *sentences* that sustain relations of confirmation or disconfirmation to the hypothesis. Evidential findings permit a critical confrontation with a given hypothesis only under appropriate sentential descriptions.

(3d) There is still one further consideration, strongly emphasized by Neurath and now very widely accepted, which fits in with the rejection of the idea of comparing statements with facts.

Logical empiricists assumed that the empirical data serving to test scientific hypotheses were ultimately expressible in sentences of some characteristic form, for example, as observation sentences, as basic sentences, or as protocal sentences of the sort envisaged by Neurath. And some of the early logical empiricists temporarily entertained the notion that such evidence sentences might be established with finality by means of direct observation, without any need of further test. If this were the case, then such observation sentences might plausibly be viewed as describing the immutable facts with which, in a test, a hypothesis is confronted or compared.

Neurath sharply rejected this notion;

the transformation of the sciences is effected by the discarding of sentences utilized in a previous historical period. . . . *Every . . . sentence of unified-science . . . is subject to such change. And the same holds for protocol sentences.*[4]

Neurath expressed his disavowal of the idea that all scientific knowledge claims rest on an immutable foundation of observed facts in a metaphor that was to become a motto of Quine's *Word and Object:* in our search for knowledge, we are like seafarers condemned to repair and rebuild their ship forever on the open ocean, without any possibility of taking it into a dry-dock and rebuilding it there on a firm basis.[5]

7.4

This conception is in good accord with Goodman's views. But Neurath's formulations—and I think to some extent Goodman's—give rise to the uneasy feeling that we are being offered a coherence theory of knowledge, in which simplicity, scope, and coherence are the dominant requirements for acceptable theories; and one wonders how the empirical character of scientific claims or versions is accommodated in this conception of making versions from versions and adjudicating proposed hypotheses by their fit with the accepted system.

The issue was interestingly addressed by Popper who, like Neurath, rejected the notion of a rock-bottom observational basis for the system of scientific hypotheses. Popper emphasizes that any observational report we use in testing a hypothesis is itself amenable to further test. But each test, "must stop at some basic statement or other which we *decide to accept.*"[6] Of these he says:

The basic statements at which we stop, which we decide to accept as satisfactory
. . . have admittedly the character of *dogmas,* but only in so far as we may desist
from justifying them by . . . further tests.[7]

Basic statements are accepted as the result of a decision. . . , and to that extent
they are conventions.[8]

This characterization is to indicate that the sentences in question are, at
the time, accepted without support or justification: by hypothesis, they
are not supported by other, already accepted, sentences; and they cannot
be justified by our observational experiences, for experiences are not the
kind of thing that can justify an empirical statement. But, Popper adds,
"the decision to accept a basic statement . . . is causally connected with
our experiences."[9]

One way, therefore, of exhibiting the *empirical* character of scientific
versions of the world might be to supplement the account of how versions
are made and changed by a causal theory of observation or, more generally perhaps, of acceptance. Such an account could provide a tenable construal of the realistic intuition that there is a world, that there are facts,
some of whose features our theories account for. But this still may not be
very satisfactory to a realist, considering that the causal theory of observation would be an extension of a particular version that is to be characterized as empirical: we would still be confined to a version.

7.5

This would be especially discouraging if different but competing versions
were totally incomparable or incommensurable, as has been claimed for
competing paradigms in the sense of Kuhn, which are, I think, a species
of versions in Goodman's more comprehensive understanding.

If indeed two competing paradigms are incommensurable, then there is
no possibility of a common account—even a partial one—of the causal
factors involved in their acceptance. In this case, as Kuhn has said, proponents of different paradigms would live in different worlds.

But surely this is didactic exaggeration. If adherents of different paradigms did inhabit totally separate worlds, I feel tempted to ask, how can
they ever have lunch together and discuss each other's views? Surely, there
is a passageway connecting their worlds; indeed it seems that their worlds

overlap to a considerable extent. The fact that proponents of such conflicting paradigms as Newtonian and relativistic physics pit their theories against each other in an effort to explain certain phenomena shows that they agree on the relevant features of those phenomena—e.g., the rotation of the perihelion of Mercury—in one common description; and indeed, they agree on a good deal more. There is an overlap of versions, of empirical assertions shared by conflicting paradigms; otherwise, it is not clear how they could be said to offer conflicting accounts of the same phenomenon. This seems to me to suggest another way of explicating, and at least partially justifying, the conception that the versions made by empirical science offer accounts of certain facts that are not determined by the versions themselves.

7.6

Goodman, to be sure, does take account of what I have called the empirical character of scientific versions by including certain pertinent features in his characterization of what he calls truth, but what had perhaps better be referred to as acceptability, in contradistinction to truth. "A version is taken to be true," he says, "when it offends no unyielding beliefs and none of its own precepts," and among the potential candidates for the status of unyielding beliefs he mentions "short-lived reflections of recent observations,"[10] i.e., in effect, sentences whose acceptance has been prompted by observational experiences, but which remain open to possible revision.

What would seem very desirable to me is a fuller account of the empirical character of scientific versions, and of the "stubbornness of facts," which surely is one of the roots of the idea of facts that are independent of our version-making. Goodman says at one point "Some of the felt stubbornness of fact is the grip of habit";[11] but that remark seems to me too dismissive and, at any rate, not a sufficiently full response to what puzzles philosophers of a more realist bent.

Let me give a final example. Speaking of the criteria we use to determine the temporal order and the duration of events, Goodman remarks: "these modes of organization . . . are not 'found in the world' but *built into a world.*"[12] To be sure, this is so: but in the search for scientifically right versions, the stubbornness of facts shows itself in the realization that we cannot well use just any criteria we please. If, for example, we were to measure the duration of an event by the number of pulse beats of the Dalai Lama during that event, we would obtain a world version in which the rate of change of all processes would depend on the Dalai Lama's state of health; thus, during periods of what is usually called increased pulse rate, the axial rotation of the earth would be slower, the period of every pendulum would be longer, etc. than during periods of a normal pulse. In addition to containing these curious causal connections, the version in question would have the grave flaw of not permitting the formulation of any general and reasonably simple laws of nature. Therefore, when Goodman declares that "the uniformity of nature we marvel at . . . belongs to a world of our own making,"[13] I think he does not do full justice to the stubbornness of facts.

Goodman does, in fact, comment on the realistic uneasiness which I have suggested though certainly not formulated very sharply. He says,

The realist will resist the conclusion that there is no world; the idealist will resist the conclusion that all conflicting versions describe different worlds. As for me, I find these views equally delightful and equally deplorable—for after all, the difference between them is purely conventional![14]

But how can this verdict be reconciled with Goodman's view[15] that there is no clear distinction between truth by convention and truth by content any more than between analytic and synthetic truth?

Notes

1. Nelson Goodman, *Ways of Worldmaking*, Hackett Press, Indianapolis, 1978, p. 4.

2. Hilary Putnam, "Reflections on Goodman's *Ways of Worldmaking*," *The Journal of Philosophy* 76 (1979), p. 611. Italics cited.

3. Otto Neurath, "Sociology and Physicalism," in *Logical Positivism* (ed. by A. J. Ayer), The Free Press, New York, 1959, p. 291. Translated from the German original, which appeared in *Erkenntnis* 2 (1931–32). Italics quoted.

4. Otto Neurath, "Protocol Sentences," in A. J. Ayer (ed.), *op. cit.*, p. 203. Translated from the German original in *Erkenntnis* 2 (1931–32). Italics quoted.

5. Neurath, "Protocol Sentences," p. 201.

6. Karl R. Popper, *The Logic of Scientific Discovery.* Hutchinson Press, (1959) London, p. 104.

7. Popper, *op. cit.*, p. 105.
8. Popper, *op. cit.*, p. 106.
9. Popper, *op. cit.*, p. 105.
10. Goodman, *op. cit.*, p. 17.
11. Goodman, *op. cit.*, p. 97.
12. Goodman, *op. cit.*, p. 14.
13. Goodman, *op. cit.*, p. 10.
14. Goodman, *op. cit.*, p. 119.
15. Cf. pp. 124–25 of his book.

8

The Wonderful Worlds of Goodman

Israel Scheffler

8.1   What Are Worlds?

"Worldmaking," Goodman tells us, "begins with one version and ends with another."[1] Is worldmaking, then, simply the making of versions, that is, descriptions, depictions or other representations, and are worlds to be construed just as versions? The answer does not lie on the surface. The term 'world' is nowhere defined in the book and an examination of the passages in which the term appears yields two conflicting interpretations: On the first, or *versional*, interpretation, a world is a true (or right) world-version and the pluralism defended simply reflects, and extends to versions generally, the *Structure of Appearance* doctrine that conflicting systematizations can be found for any prephilosophical subject matter. On the second, or *objectual* interpretation, a world is a realm of things (versions or non-versions) referred to or described by (119) a right world-version. Pluralistic talk of worlds is here not simply talk of conflicting versions; "multiple actual worlds" is Goodman's watchword and he cautions us that it should not "be passed over as purely rhetorical" (110).[2]

8.2   Worlds as Versions

Each of these two interpretations of "worlds" can call upon implicit as well as explicit statements in support. Take first the versional interpretation. After suggesting that sometimes a cluster of versions rather than a single version may constitute a world (itself a non-objectual view), Goodman says, "but for many purposes, right world-descriptions and world-depictions and world-perceptions, the ways-the-world-is, or just versions, can be treated as our worlds" (4). "In what non-trivial sense," he goes on to ask, "are there . . . many worlds?" And he answers, "Just this, I think: that many different world-versions are of independent interest and importance, without any requirement or presumption of reducibility to a single base" (4). Worlds are here right world-versions, and the multiplicity of worlds is the multiplicity of such world-versions. Clinching this interpretation, Goodman then introduces his treatment of "ways of worldmaking" as follows: "With false hope of a firm foundation gone, *with the world displaced by worlds that are but versions* . . . we face the questions how *worlds* are made, tested, and known" (7, my italics). The basic discussion that follows of "processes that go into worldmaking" (7) is, then, to be understood as concerned with *versions* rather than with *things, objects, or realms* described by them, and the testing and making of *worlds* is to be construed as the testing and making of *versions*.

That it is versions that are at stake is implicit throughout this discussion, where the individuation of worlds is said at times to hinge on the concepts and distinctions available to relevant groups of persons (9), on emphasis and accent (11), on relevant kinds (11), on ordering (12), and on modes of organization "*built into a world*" (14, italics in the original). "Worlds not differing in entities . . . may differ in ordering" (12), says Goodman, thus distinguishing worlds where there is no difference whatever in the things denoted. He allows indeed that ". . . a green emerald and a grue one, *even if the same emerald* . . . belong to worlds organized into different kinds" (11, my italics, see also 101). Now since Goodman explicitly upholds the nominalistic principle "no difference without a difference of individuals" (95), when he here differentiates worlds simply by the order or emphasis of versions or the kinds indicated by them, he must be referring neither to the realms of individuals described, nor, surely, to various abstract entities associated with them, but rather to the versions themselves.

The point is strikingly illustrated by two contrasting discussions of the question of variant histories—one in Goodman's early paper "A World of Individuals,"[3] and the other in the present book. In the first of these discussions, he writes, "We do not take the varied histories of the Battle of Bull Run as recounting different occurrences. In daily life a multiplicity of descriptions is no evidence for a corresponding multiplicity of things described." [4] On the other hand, in *Ways of Worldmaking*, he says of "two histories in the Renaissance: one that, without excluding the battles, stresses the arts; and another that, without excluding the arts, stresses the battles" that "This difference in style is a difference in weighting that gives us *two different Renaissance worlds* (101–2, my italics). Consistency with the nominalist principle demands that the worlds mentioned in this last quotation not be construed as comprising the described occurrences, but that they be taken rather as versional.

8.3 Worlds as Objects

Let us now turn to the objectual interpretation of worlds. Goodman speaks of "the many stuffs—matter, energy, waves, phenomena—that worlds are made of" (6), and the presumption of the passage is that he is not simply referring to the inscriptions constituting versions. He uses the adjective "actual" to modify "worlds," characterizing the "multiple worlds" he countenances as "just the actual worlds . . . *answering to* true or right versions" (94, my italics), the natural reading of "answering to" being: "denoted by," "referred to," "compliant with," or "described by." Goodman indeed expressly distinguishes between "versions that do and those that do not refer," and he insists that we want "to talk about the things and *worlds*, if any, *referred* to . . ." (96, my italics). Furthermore, he introduces the notion of truth "in a given actual world," holding that a statement is true in such a world if "true insofar as that world alone is taken into consideration" (110). Here, "world" presumably cannot be intended as "world-version," as is further implicit in the following consideration: he remarks that conflicting statements cannot be taken as "true in the same world without admitting all statements whatsoever . . . as true in the same world, and that world itself as impossible." (110) Were "world" to be taken in this passage as "world-version," there would here be no impossibility whatever—only inconsistency.

   Goodman explains both truth and rightness in terms of *fitting a world:* ". . . a statement is true, and a description or representation right, for a world it fits" (132), he declares. Like the notion of "answering to," that of "fit" appears also to be a semantic idea, and the related use of "world" clearly objectual rather than versional.

The objectual interpretation is necessitated, finally, by those passages in which Goodman explicitly treats worlds as comprised of *ranges of application* of predicates, or as consisting of the *realms* of different versions. In this vein, he writes,

the statements that the Parthenon is intact and that it is ruined are both true—for different temporal parts of the building; and the statement that the apple is white and that it is red are both true—for different spatial parts of the apple. . . . In each of these cases, the two *ranges of application* combine readily into a recognized kind or object; and the two statements are true in different parts or subclasses of the same *world*. (111, my italics)

Clearly, the reference here is not to different parts of subclasses of the same version.

This example concerned ranges of application; consider now the reference to worlds as *realms*. Discussing two geometrical systems with rival accounts of points, Goodman asserts that if they are both true they are so in different realms—the first "in our sample space taken as consisting solely of lines," and the second "in that space taken as consisting solely of points." For more comprehensive versions that conflict similarly, he says that "their *realms* are thus less aptly regarded as within one world than as *two different worlds* . . . " (116, my italics). The reference of "worlds" in this passage is not to versions but to things to which versions apply; the interpretation here, in short, is objectual.

8.4   Are Worlds Made?

Now the versional and the objectual interpretations of worlds do not mix; they are in conflict. As we have seen, the idea of *different Renaissance worlds* emerging from variant histories cannot be objectual, since their realms of application are assumed identical. Conversely, the versional interpretation is precluded by the notion of actual worlds *referred to* by true versions, since such versions in fact refer to all sorts of things, nonversions as well as versions.

Goodman seems to hold, indeed, that these conflicting interpretations of "worlds" reflect the vacillations of antecedent theoretical practice. The line drawn by such practice between "versionizing" and "objectifying" is, he believes, not a hard but a variable line, motivated by convenience and convention. "In practice," he writes, "we draw the line wherever we like, and change it as often as suits our purposes. On the level of theory, we flit back and forth between extremes as blithely as a physicist between particle and field theories. When the verbiage view threatens to dissolve everything into nothing, we insist that all true versions describe worlds. When the right-to-life sentiment threatens an overpopulation of worlds, we call it all talk" (119). Yet, the availability of these two interpretations—however the line may be drawn—makes it important to examine closely Goodman's thesis that worlds are made. I can accept this thesis with "worlds" taken versionally, but I find it impossible to accept otherwise.

8.5   Worldmaking: Versional Yes, Objectual No

That Goodman himself intends worldmaking to be taken both ways is shown in a variety of passages. In a summary statement toward the end of the book, he says,

Briefly, then, truth of statements and rightness of descriptions, representations, exemplifications . . . is primarily a matter of fit: fit to what is *referred to* in one way or another, or *to other renderings*, or to modes and manners of organization. The differences between *fitting a version to a world, a world to a version, and a version together or to other versions* fade when the role of versions in *making the worlds they fit* is recognized. (138, my italics)

Moreover, Goodman specifically speaks of worlds, taken objectually, as made. In a crucial passage, he writes, ". . . we make worlds by making versions. . . . The multiple worlds I countenance are just the actual worlds made by and answering to true or right versions" (94). That this passage requires the objectual interpretation is shown by the mention of worlds as *answering to* true versions. Thus, in saying we make worlds by making versions, Goodman is not uttering the triviality that we make versions by making them. Can he then be asserting rather that in making right versions we make what they refer to—that is, in making true descriptions we make what they describe, in making applicable words we make what they denote?

Apparently, the answer is yes. "Of course," he writes, "we want to distinguish between versions that do and those that do not refer, and to talk about the things and worlds, if any, referred to: but these things and worlds and even the stuff they are made of—matter, anti-matter, mind, energy, or what not—are fashioned along with the versions themselves" (96). Here he clearly says that we make not only versions but also the things they refer to and even the material of which these things are made.

Now the claim that it is we who made the stars by making the word "star" I consider absurd, taking this claim in its plain and literal sense. It mistakes a feature of discourse for a feature of the subject of discourse— a mistake Goodman himself has warned against in an earlier paper,[5] and it seems to conflict with his own insistence on the difference between a version and what it refers to. Goodman himself emphasizes (94) that his "willingness to accept countless alternative true or right world-versions does not mean that everything goes . . . that truths are no longer distinguished from falsehoods . . ." Since, as I believe, the claim that we made the stars is false if anything is, his version of versions is itself false if it implies this claim. Nor is it helpful to say that we made the stars *as* stars— that before the word 'star' existed, stars did not exist *qua* stars. For, in the first place, that stars did not exist *qua* stars does not imply that they did not exist, or that we made them. And, in the second place, the existence of stars *qua* stars is just their existence plus their being called 'stars'. No one disputes that before we had the word 'stars', stars weren't called 'stars', but that doesn't mean they didn't exist. It would be altogether misleading on this basis alone to say we *made* them.[6]

But a deeper philosophical motivation underlies Goodman's notion of worldmaking. A pervasive theme in his work is the rejection both of the given and the notion of a "ready-made world" that "lies waiting to be described" (132). He urges again and again that the organization of our concepts and categories is not unique, that such "modes of organization . . . are not 'found in the world' but *built into a world*" (12–14, esp. 14, italics in original). The supposition is perhaps that unless we take our star-versions to have made the stars, we will be driven to accept either a neutral given without concepts altogether or else the pre-existence of our conceptual scheme to the exclusion of all others. While agreeing with the underlying philosophical motivation, I cannot, however, see that the latter supposition is sound. That stars existed before people implies nothing about concepts, their uniqueness or pre-existence. Star-concepts did not, but stars did, antedate the emergence of living creatures. Star-concepts were surely not ready-made, waiting to be used; they were indeed made by us. It doesn't follow the stars were therefore made by us rather than in fact (but in a metaphorical sense) waiting to be described. To reject the given and to allow a multiplicity of conceptual schemes does not require objectual worldmaking.

The objectual version of worldmaking may, however, perhaps have another philosophical source in Goodman's view of *facts*—more particularly his recognition of how vocabulary constrains and shapes our factual descriptions. The topic arises in his discussion of the phenomenon of apparent motion, that is, the seeing of a moving light where there are, physically, just two distinct flashes, the one following the other a short distance away. Discussing the case of certain subjects who report not seeing the apparent motion, Goodman asks whether they are not perhaps indeed aware of it, but taking it as a *sign* of the physical sequence of light flashes—that is, *looking through* the phenomenal to the physical state "as we take the oval appearance of the table top as a sign that it is round" (92). Can this possibility be tested? Can such subjects be brought to report directly on their actual perceptual experience? To ask them "to avoid all conceptualization" would be useless, since it would leave them "speechless." Rather, as Goodman suggests, "the best we can do is to specify the sort of terms, the vocabulary" to be used, instructing the subjects to describe what they see "in perceptual or phenomenal rather than physical terms." And this, says Goodman,

casts an entirely different light on what is happening. That the instruments to be used in fashioning the facts must be specified makes pointless any identification of the physical with the real and of the perceptual with the merely apparent. (92)

He concludes, further, that we must not say "both are versions of the same facts" in any sense that implies "there are independent facts of which both are versions" (93).

There are then, for Goodman, no independent facts, construed as entities discrete from versions and their objects. What then does his talk of "fashioning the facts" (92) come to? Presumably this: that the true reports of observations giving descriptions of such objects are constrained by the vocabularies employed; these vocabularies are thus instruments for creating factual descriptions. Since all our knowledge of objects is, moreover, embodied in such descriptions, our knowledge is, itself, in the same way, shaped by our vocabularies. But what are objects themselves? We have no access to objects aside from our knowledge of them; they are therefore themselves shaped by our vocabularies. It is thus we can say that in making our versions we make their objects. Possibly some such line of reasoning motivates Goodman's objectual worldmaking.

Whether it does or not, I do not myself find it convincing. Even were it true that we have no access to objects aside from our knowledge of them, it would not follow that objects are made by our knowledge. Moreover, to say we have no access to, or contact with objects aside from our knowledge of them is true only if by "access" we intend such things as understanding and awareness, that is, "cognitive access." Thus the statement is trivial; it assures us that we can have knowledge of objects only in having knowledge of them. And to say that our knowledge of objects is shaped by our vocabularies boils down to saying that the descriptions we compose are made up of the words we have. From this triviality it clearly does not follow that we create or shape the things to which our words refer, or determine that our descriptions shall be true. In making the true statement that there were stars before men, we do not also make the stars that were there then.

Now Goodman himself insists on the separation of truth from falsehood; as we have seen, he denies "that everything goes" (94). There are, he asserts, false as well as true versions; he rules out the idea that any version can be made true at will. And his discussion of fiction indeed offers concrete examples of such constraints. "Some depictions and descriptions," he writes, do not literally denote anything. Painted or written portrayals of Don Quixote, for example, do not denote Don Quixote— who is *simply not there* to be denoted" (103, my italics). The creation of a Don Quixote version evidently does not automatically create an object for it. The mere making of the word does not guarantee it will be nonnull. Whether there is or is not an object satisfying a version of our making is thus not, in general, up to us. Whether a world answers to a version is, in general, independent of what we may wish or will. How then can Goodman describe his "actual worlds" as both "made by" and "answering to true or right versions"? How can he say "we make worlds by making versions" (94)? I conclude that he cannot and that, despite his disclaimer (110), objectual talk of worldmaking had *better* be taken as "purely rhetorical."

Notes

This paper was presented at a symposium sponsored by the American Philosophical Association on Goodman's *Ways of Worldmaking*, on December 28, 1979. (Footnote 6 is added here for the first time.) I am grateful to Samuel Scheffler for discussion and criticism.

1. Nelson Goodman, *Ways of Worldmaking* (Indianapolis: Hackett Publishing Company, 1978), p. 97. From here on, all page references to this book will be given in parentheses following their respective citations in the text.

2. For the *versional* but not the *objectual* interpretation, 'world' is always, strictly speaking, short for 'world-version', a compound in which the constituent 'world' is syncategorematic and non-referential, its position inaccessible to variables of quantification.

3. N. Goodman, "A World of Individuals," *The Problem of Universals* (Notre Dame, Indiana: University of Notre Dame Press, 1956), pp. 13–31, now reprinted in Goodman, *Problems and Projects* (Indianapolis: Bobbs-Merrill, 1972), pp. 155–72.

4. *Problems and Projects*, p. 164.

5. "Philosophers sometimes mistake features of discourse for features of the subject of discourse. We seldom conclude that the world consists of words just because a true description of it does, but we sometimes suppose that the structure of the world is the same as the structure of the description." *Problems and Projects*, op. cit., p. 24.

6. In his *Languages of Art* (Indianapolis: Hackett Publishing Company, 1968, 1976), p. 88, Goodman defends himself against the charge that he makes what a picture expresses depend upon what is said about it, thus "crediting the expression achieved not to the artist but to the commentator." He writes: " 'Sad' may apply to a picture even though no one ever happens to use the term in describing the picture; and calling a picture sad by no means *makes* it so" (my italics). Exactly. 'Star' may apply to something even though no one ever happens to use the term in describing it; and calling something a star by no means makes it one.

9

On Starmaking

Nelson Goodman

To most of what Hilary Putnam writes about *Ways of Worldmaking*,[1] I can only say "Bravo!" And while I might want to modify some passages in his paper, finding fault while saying "Bravo!" is rather awkward. More appropriate here, perhaps, is a rather general discussion of some questions commonly raised about the radical relativism with rigorous restraints and the irrealism outlined in my book.

I maintain that many world versions—some conflicting with each other, some so disparate that conflict or compatibility among them is indeterminable—are equally right. Nevertheless, right versions are different from wrong versions: relativism is restrained by considerations of rightness. Rightness, however, is neither constituted nor tested by correspondence with a world independent of all versions.

But then the objection is raised "Are the criteria of rightness themselves relative? And if so, are we not again lost in complete subjectivity?" First, note that my suggestion that permanent credibility might be taken, within certain bounds, as a sufficient condition for truth is itself credible only if credibility is no more to be equated with belief than being red is to be equated with looking red. We often believe what is not credible and disbelieve what is credible. Standards of credibility do not vary with individual opinion, over the worlds in the world of worlds sketched in *Ways of Worldmaking*. But neither are they absolute; they may vary from one world of worlds to another. Relativity goes all the way up.

"How then," comes the question, "can we ever establish anything finally and completely and for sure, even the most obvious truism and the most cherished credos?" And the answer is, of course, that we can't, and that that is no fault of mine. Neither by logic nor any other means can we prove something from nothing. We have to start with some premises and principles; and there are no absolute and incontrovertible certainties available. But that does not mean that we must start from careless guesses. We follow our confidence and convictions, which are subject to strengthening or weakening or even reversal as we strive to build right versions or worlds on the basis of these. No starting points or ending points or points along the way *are either absolute or arbitrary*. None of this is peculiar to me. But I am repeatedly forced to insist that my relativism is equidistant from intransigent absolutism and unlimited license.

Scheffler says I am ambiguous[2]—and Scheffler is an honorable man. He says I also say that worlds are other than, and answer to, right versions; and he takes the words from my own pen. And so? Do I stand guilty, then, and come before you now to bury not defend myself?

Not so. Instead, borrowing the tactics of modern diplomacy, I brazenly declare that *I am not sorry* for what I have written. Somewhat like the physicist with his field theory and his particle theory, we can have it both ways. To say that every right version is a world and to say that every right version has a world answering to it may be equally right even if they are at odds with each other. Moreover, talk of worlds and talk of right versions are often interchangeable.

Let's begin by acknowledging that a right version and its world are different. A version saying that there is a star up there is not itself bright or far off, and the star is not made up of letters. On the other hand, saying that there is a star up there and saying that the statement "There is a star up there" is true amount, trivially, to much the same thing, even though the one seems to talk about a star and the other to talk about a statement. What is more important, we cannot find any world-feature independent of all versions. Whatever can be said truly of a world is dependent on the saying—not that whatever we say is true but that whatever we say truly (or otherwise present rightly) is nevertheless informed by and relative to the language or other symbol system we use. No firm line can be drawn between world-features that are discourse-dependent and those that are not. As I have said, "In practice, of course, we draw the line wherever we like, and change it as often as suits our purposes." If I take advantage of the privilege to speak sometimes as if there are only versions and other times as if there are worlds for all right versions, I often do it just to emphasize that point.

Scheffler also objects to the idea that we make worlds, and he is not alone in this. Much of the usual resistance can be attributed to one of two complexes. The first is the-world-is-so-wonderful-I-couldn't-do-that-well complex, otherwise known as the only-God-can-make-a-tree complex. The other is the-world-is-so-terrible-I-don't-want-to-be-blamed-for-it complex. Both rest on the fallacy that whatever we make we can make any way we like. The source of the fallacy is hard to perceive. We make chairs, computers, books, planes; and making any of these right takes skill, care, and hard work. A chair I make is likely to wobble; a book takes endless pains; I can't make a computer at all; and no one has been able to make a plane that flies far on batteries. Making right world-versions—or making worlds—is harder than making chairs or planes, and failure is common largely because all we have available is scrap material recycled from old and stubborn worlds. Our having done no better or worse is no evidence that chairs or planes or worlds are found rather than made.

Scheffler contends that we cannot have made the stars. I ask him which features of the stars we did not make, and challenge him to state how these differ from features clearly dependent on discourse. Does he ask how we can have made anything older than we are? Plainly, by making a space and time that contains those stars. By means of science, that world (and many another) was made with great difficulty and is, like the several worlds of phenomena that also contain stars, a more or less right or real world. We can make the sun stand still, not in the manner of Joshua but in the manner of Bruno. We make a star as we make a constellation, by putting its parts together and marking off its boundaries.

In short, we do not make stars as we make bricks; not all making is a matter of molding mud. The worldmaking mainly in question here is making not with hands but with minds, or rather with languages or other symbol systems. Yet when I say that worlds are made, I mean it literally; and what I mean should be clear from what I have already said. Surely we make versions, and right versions make worlds. And however distinct worlds may be from right versions, making right versions is making worlds. This is a conspicuous case of how talk of worlds and talk of versions coalesce.

C. G. Hempel,[3] after carefully comparing my views with Otto Neurath's, urges the point that although I say that modes of organization are built into rather than found in a world, we cannot use "just any criteria we please." I agree. But his argument here is curious. He suggests an example where the measurement of the duration of an event is by the number of pulse beats of the Dalai Lama during that event. This recalls my own example of a frame of reference such that the motion of the earth matches the dance of Petrouchka. But whereas my example is given to stress the wide variety of conflicting right versions, his is cited against my contention that "the uniformity of nature we marvel at . . . belongs to a world of our own making"; for, Hempel says, the Dalai Lama version would not permit "the formulation of any general and reasonably simple laws of nature." Now simplicity is indeed one major criterion used in choosing among theories and thus in seeking truth; for simplification is systematization, and systematization is virtually the soul of science. But I cannot see that this in any way implies that nature apart from every version of it is simple, whatever that might mean.

Discussion of a book like *Ways of Worldmaking* often tends to focus on matters of sweeping general doctrine and venerable issues, but what I say on such matters is a by-product rather than the primary concern of the book. The main undertaking, as in *The Structure of Appearance,* is examination and comparison of the ways we make what we make—call them versions or worlds as you like—and of the criteria we use in judging what we make. Rather than argue over broad metaphysical issues, I am inclined to say "Have it your way; it matters not" (or, quoting from *Ways of Worldmaking,* "Never mind mind, essence is not essential, and matter doesn't matter"). Let's look at the ways we work, the instruments we use, and the varied and fascinating results. At the beginning of the book realism and idealism, empiricism and rationalism, and many another doctrine are dismissed in favor of what I call irrealism, which is not one more doctrine—does not say that everything or even anything is unreal—but is rather an attitude of unconcern with most issues between such doctrines. And toward the end of the book I argue that the issue between realism and idealism is undermined by the recognition that the line between convention and content is arbitrary and variable. By moving the line to one extreme or the other we get idealism or realism. I wrote:

The realist will resist the conclusion that there is no world; the idealist will resist the conclusion that all conflicting versions describe different worlds. As for me, I find these views equally delightful and equally deplorable—for, after all, the difference between them is purely conventional!

Hempel protests, asking how I can, having just rejected the distinction between content and convention, now so calmly use the term "conventional" as if it were not suspect. I do become more forgetful as time goes on, but I did not here forget from one paragraph to the next. I had hoped the reader might be stopped short by this blatant use of a term just disparaged, and be moved to ask himself how to interpret my statement. Many different interpretations of it may reflect facets of the philosophical attitude of the book. Perhaps the most straightforward way of putting it is that as the distinction between what is due to discourse and what is not flickers out, so does the significance of the issue between realism and idealism; and perhaps I should have put it that simply. But after a time, one wearies of writing flatfooted philosophy.

This brings me to one final philosophical reflection. Readers often find in my work—to their delight or disgust—many quips and cracks, puns and paradoxes, alliterations and allegories, metaphors and metonymies, synecdoches and other sins. If there are as many routes of reference as I think, perhaps some of these devices are not mere decoration or unsuccessful attempts to keep the reader awake but part and parcel of the philosophy presented and the worlds made.

While I do not know what is meant by saying that *the* world is simple or complex, I have some idea what is meant by saying that among the many worlds there are, if there are any, some are simple and some complex, some ingenuous and some ingenious, and even by saying that some are prosaic and some poetic.

Notes

1. In "Reflections on Goodman's *Ways of Worldmaking*," *Journal of Philosophy* 76 (1979) 603–618.

2. In Israel Scheffler's "The Wonderful Worlds of Goodman," *Synthese* 45 (1980) 201–209.

3. In "Comments on Goodman's *Ways of Worldmaking*," *Synthese* 45 (1980) 193–199.

IV

Elaborations

10
Notes on the Well-Made World

Nelson Goodman

Since it seems obvious that words are usually different from what they refer to, that we cannot in general make anything by merely describing or picturing it, and that not all descriptions or pictures are right, how can I talk of worldmaking, find facts fluid, acknowledge conflicting truths, and suggest that the distinction between world and version is elusive? Here I want to review and clarify some themes of *Ways of Worldmaking,* discuss some common objections to it, and reaffirm some of its paradoxes.

10.1   Monism, Pluralism, Nihilism

Some truths conflict. The earth stands still, revolves about the sun, and runs many another course all at the same time. Yet nothing moves while at rest. We flinch at recognition of conflicting truths; for since all statements follow from a contradiction, acceptance of a statement and its negate erases the difference between truth and falsity.

Usually we seek refuge in simple-minded relativization: according to a geocentric system the earth stands still, while according to a heliocentric system it moves. But there is no solid comfort here. Merely that a given version says something does not make what it says true; after all, some versions say the earth is flat or that it rests on the back of a tortoise. That the earth is at rest according to one system and moves according to another says nothing about how the earth behaves but only something about what these versions say. What must be added is that these versions are true. But then the contradiction reappears, and our escape is blocked.

Should we rather consider "The earth is at rest" and "The earth moves" as incomplete fragments of statements, true or false only when

completed in some such way as in "The earth moves relative to the sun"
or "The earth is at rest relative to Mount Everest"? This does not work
either; for what can these statements mean? Perhaps, in the former case,
"If the sun is at rest, then the earth moves." But then the antecedent and
consequent are themselves fragments of statements, without truth-value
until completed; and so on ad infinitum. Or should we translate to "If the
sun's position is plotted as a point, the earth's positions will be plotted as
a path"? Then, since the diagrams are simply (nonverbal) versions, we are
back to simple-minded relativization.

How, then, are we to accommodate conflicting truths without sacrific-
ing the difference between truth and falsity? Perhaps by treating these
versions as true in different worlds. Versions not applying in the same
world no longer conflict; contradiction is avoided by segregation. A true
version is true in some worlds, a false version in none. Thus the multiple
worlds of conflicting true versions are actual worlds, not the merely possible worlds or nonworlds of false versions.

So if there is any actual world, there are many. For there are conflicting
true versions and they cannot be true in the same world. If the notion of
a multiplicity of actual worlds is odd and unpalatable, we nevertheless
seem forced to it by the intolerable alternative of a world in which contra-
dictory and therefore all versions are true.

But where are these many actual worlds? How are they related to one
another? Are there many earths all going along different routes at the
same time and risking collision? Of course not; in any world there is only
one Earth; and the several worlds are not distributed in any space-time.
Space-time is an ordering within a world; the space-times of different
worlds are not embraced within some greater space-time. Worlds are distinguished by the conflict or irreconcilability of their versions; and any
ordering among them is other than spatio-temporal.

Yet however intricately and plausibly this idea may be developed, how
can there really be many worlds? There may be many stars, many planets,
many chairs, many things, many events; and truths about them may conflict and contrast in all sorts of ways. But "world" is all-inclusive, covers
all there is. A world is a totality; there can be no multiplicity of totalities,
no more than one all-inclusive whole. By assigning conflicting versions
to different worlds, we preclude composition of these totalities into one.
Whatever we may mean by saying that the motion of the Earth, or of

different earths, differs in different worlds, we rule out any more comprehensive whole comprised of these. For a totality cannot be partial; a world cannot be a piece of something bigger.

So if there is any world, there are many, and if many, none. And if none, what becomes of truth and the relationship of a version to what it describes? Parmenides ran into this trouble long ago: because truths conflict, we cannot describe the world. Even when he said "It is" he went too far. "It is" gives way to "They are"; and "They are" to "None is." Monism, pluralism, nihilism coalesce.

Part of the trouble comes, as in the Kantian antinomies, from stretching some terms or notions beyond their reach. So long as we keep within a version, "world" or "totality" is clear enough, but when we consider conflicting true versions and their several worlds, paradox enters. This sometimes leads to utter resignation, sometimes to an irresponsible relativism that takes all statements as equally true. Neither attitude is very productive. More serviceable is a policy common in daily life and impressively endorsed by modern science: namely, judicious vacillation. After all, we shift point of view and frame of reference for motion frequently from sun to earth to train to plane, and so on. The physicist flits back and forth between a world of waves and a world of particles as suits his purpose. We usually think and work within one world-version at a time—hence Hilary Putnam's term "internal realism"[1]—but we shift from one to another often. When we undertake to relate different versions, we introduce multiple worlds. When that becomes awkward, we drop the worlds for the time being and consider only the versions. We are monists, pluralists, or nihilists not quite as the wind blows but as befits the context.

According to one variety of solipsism, only I exist but this holds for each of the many people in the world. Somewhat analogously, one might say that there is only one world but this holds for each of the many worlds. In both cases the equivocation is stark—yet perhaps negotiable.

10.2   Ontology Evanescent

Or have we gone too far too fast? May the conflicts we encounter among truths turn out on closer examination to amount less to genuine differences in what is said than to differences in manner of saying? Rather than disagreements on objective fact, are these merely superficial differences, chargeable to the varying perspectives and languages of our versions, with the real world to be sought beneath such surface disturbances?

Consider again, for example, the true statements that the earth is at rest, that it revolves around the sun, that it dances a jig, and so on. The suggestion is that the conflicts between these have no more to do with the earth, sun, or other heavenly bodies than do the different orders in which these objects may be described, but arise from the differing biases of the several versions; and that statements concerning the direction, speed, and acceleration of motion are different ways of describing the neutral facts of variation in distance between objects at different times. If all features responsible for disagreements among versions are thus dismissed as artificial, truths will no longer conflict in a way that calls for different worlds.

But once we recognize that some supposed features of the world derive from—are made and imposed by—versions, 'the world' rapidly evaporates. For there is no version-independent feature, no true version compatible with all true versions. Our so-called neutral version of motion is as prejudiced as any other; for if direction and speed and acceleration are relative to observer and frame of reference, so also is distance between objects. And, as I shall argue below, the objects themselves and the time and space they occupy are version-dependent. No organization into units is unique or mandatory, nor is there any featureless raw material underlying different organizations. Any raw stuff is as much the creature of a version as is what is made out of that stuff.

Yet if all features of a world are creatures of a version, are generated and imposed by the version, what can they be imposed upon? The question is pertinent but slightly awry. The world of a true version is a construct; the features are not conferred upon something independent of the version but combined with one another to make the world of that version. The world is not the version itself; the version may have features—such as being in English or consisting of words—that its world does not. But the world depends upon the version.

Some inkling of what I mean by saying we make worlds may begin to glimmer here: we make versions, and true versions make worlds. This calls for further explanation on more than one score. How can we be said to make worlds by making versions, when making a true description of a chair, for example, falls far short of making a chair? And while we make versions, and we hope some true versions, we can hardly make versions true. Moreover, if there is no independent world to match a version against, what constitutes truth and what are the tests for it?

10.3   How to Make Things with Words[2]

That we can make the stars dance, as Galileo and Bruno made the earth move and the sun stop, not by physical force but by verbal invention, is plain enough. That we by like means also make things what they are in respects other than motion has now begun to be clear. From here a short step leads to the conclusion that we make the things themselves. But that, on the face of it, seems silly. Downright refutations are ready at hand in the form of challenges to produce forthwith, by means of a potent description, an extra planet, a chair to sit in, or a tender beefsteak. Inevitable failure is taken to prove the point.

But I have not said that we can make a steak or a chair or a world at will and as we like by making a version. Only if true does description make things; and making a true version can be hard work. But isn't that begging the question? Doesn't that amount to saying that versions can make only what is already there? And how can that properly be said to be making at all? If versions can make neither what is nor what is not already there, that seems a closed case against their making anything at all.

Yet I am not ready to give up; 'being already there' needs further examination, and finding what is already there may turn out to be very much a matter of making.

I sit in a cluttered waiting room, unaware of any stereo system. Gradually I make out two speakers built into the bookcase, a receiver and turntable in a corner cabinet, and a remote control switch on the mantel. I find a system that was already there. But see what this finding involves: distinguishing the several components from the surroundings, categorizing them by function, and uniting them into a single whole. A good deal of making, with complex conceptual equipment, has gone into finding what is already there. Another visitor, fresh from a lifetime in the deepest jungle, will not find, because he has not the means of making, any stereo system in that room. Nor will he find books there; but in the books and plants I find he may find fuel and food that I do not. Not only does he not know that the stereo set is one; he does not recognize as a thing at all that which I know to be a stereo system—that is, he does not make out or make any such object.

Now you may complain that all I am doing is applying a different term to a familiar process to bring out the constructive aspect of cognition. And you may ask, as Israel Scheffler has, how we can reasonably say that we, or versions, make the stars, which existed long before us and all versions.[3] Let me defer that question for a moment to look at a slightly different case.

Has a constellation been there as long as the stars that compose it, or did it come into being only when selected and designated? In the latter case, the constellation was created by a version. And what could be meant by saying that the constellation was always there, before any version? Does this mean that all configurations of stars whatever are always constellations whether or not picked out and designated as such? I suggest that to say that all configurations are constellations is in effect to say that none are: that a constellation becomes such only through being chosen from among all configurations, much as a class becomes a kind[4] only through being distinguished, according to some principle, from other classes.

Now as we thus make constellations by picking out and putting together certain stars rather than others, so we make stars by drawing certain boundaries rather than others. Nothing dictates whether the skies shall be marked off into constellations or other objects. We have to make what we find, be it the Great Dipper, Sirius, food, fuel, or a stereo system.[5]

Still, if stars like constellations are made by versions, how can the stars have been there eons before all versions? Plainly, through being made by a version that puts the stars much earlier than itself in its own space-time. As the physicist J. R. Wheeler writes:

The universe does not exist "out there" independent of us. We are inescapably involved in bringing about that which appears to be happening. We are not only observers. We are participators . . . in making [the] past as well as the present and the future.[6]

10.4 Truthmaking

Yet our making by means of versions is subject to severe constraints; and if nothing stands apart from all versions, what can be the basis and nature of these constraints? How can a version be wrong about a world it makes? We must obviously look for truth not in the relation of a version to something outside that it refers to but in characteristics of the version itself and its relationships to other versions. Could a version perhaps be false somewhat in the way a jigsaw puzzle can be wrongly put together, or a motor fail to run, a poster to attract attention, or a camouflage to conceal?

When the world is lost and correspondence along with it, the first thought is usually coherence. But the answer cannot lie in coherence alone; for a false or otherwise wrong version can hold together as well as a right one. Nor do we have any self-evident truths, absolute axioms, unlimited warranties, to serve as touchstones in distinguishing right from among coherent versions; other considerations must enter into that choice. Let us begin by looking at some of these that have to do with varieties of rightness other than truth.

Validity of inductive inference, though a property of a relation among statements, requires truth neither of premises nor of conclusion; a valid inductive argument may even yield a false conclusion from true premises. What, then, is required for inductive validity? Certain formal relationships among the sentences in question *plus* what I shall call right categorization. Now a category or system of categories—a way of sorting—is not sentential, is not true or false; but use of wrong categories will make an induction invalid no matter how true the conclusion. For example, if an emerald is said to be grue just in case it is either examined before a given time and determined to be green or is not so examined and is blue, then the same formal rules that lead from evidence statements about green emeralds to the hypothesis "All emeralds are green" will also lead from evidence-statements about "grue emeralds" to the hypothesis "All emeralds are grue"; but the former inference is valid, the latter not. For although the evidence-statements are true in both cases, and the truth of both hypotheses is as yet undetermined, "grue" picks out a category wrong in this context, a nonrelevant kind. Valid induction runs within—

is constrained by—right categories; and only through distinguishing right categories from among classes in general can we distinguish valid from invalid induction. But what makes a category right? Very briefly, and oversimply, its adoption in inductive practice, its entrenchment, resulting from inertia modified by invention.[7] Why some categories rather than others have become entrenched—a subject of avid philosophical debate—does not matter here; the entrenchment, however achieved, provides the required distinction. Rightness of categorization, in my view, derives from rather than underlies entrenchment.

Inductive validity is not only an example of rightness other than truth but is also one of the criteria applied in the search for truth: a hypothesis validly inferred is favored over an alternative invalidly inferred from the same evidence. Yet how is acceptability as determined by such considerations related to truth, and does this help us answer the question what constitutes truth? Obviously we cannot equate truth with acceptability; for we take truth to be constant while acceptability is transient. Even what is maximally acceptable at one moment may become inacceptable later. But *ultimate* acceptability—acceptability that is not subsequently lost—is of course as steadfast as truth. Such ultimate acceptability, although we may seldom if ever know when or whether it has been or will be achieved, serves as a sufficient condition for truth.[8] And since acceptability involves inductive validity, which involves right categorization, which involves entrenchment, habit must be recognized as an integral ingredient of truth. Though that may give pause, it follows as the day the night. For if we make worlds, the meaning of truth lies not in these worlds but in ourselves—or better, in our versions and what we do with them.

So far, for simplicity, I have been speaking as if all versions consisted of statements, but actually many versions are in symbols of other kinds and in nonverbal media. Since any version may be right or wrong, though only statements are true or false, truth as rightness of what is said is a narrow species of rightness. Moreover, it is a species of but one aspect of rightness; for symbols, verbal or not, may refer not only by denotation but by exemplification or expression or by complex chains made up of homogeneous or heterogeneous referential steps, or in two or more of these ways. And a version may be right or wrong in any of these respects. A nonrepresentational painting, for instance, may exemplify certain forms and patterns, many show a way of seeing that is tested in further seeing somewhat as a proposed hypothesis is tested in further cases. The painting does not say anything, cannot be true or false, yet may be right or wrong. I cannot go into all this here, but I am convinced that philosophy must take into account all the ways and means of worldmaking.

Notes

1. See, for example, his *Meaning and the Moral Sciences* (London: Routledge and Kegan Paul, 1978), pp. 123–140.

2. With apologies to J. L. Austin, who did not explicitly include making things in what we do with words.

3. See his "The Wonderful Worlds of Goodman," *Synthese* 45 (1980) 201–209, and my reply, pp. 211–215.

4. That is, a *relevant*—sometimes miscalled *natural*—kind.

5. And this, as I have mentioned earlier, goes all the way down. Not all differences between true versions can be thought of as differences in grouping or marking off within something common to all. For there are no absolute elements, no space-time or other stuff common to all, no entity that is under all guises or under none.

6. In *Science 81* (June) p. 67.

7. The matter is more complex than can be made clear here. Some outlines are offered in *Fact, Fiction, and Forecast* (FFF), IV.

8. Pending a broadening of scope in the next paragraph, I speak here only of versions comprised of statements and only of the acceptability of what they say, without regard to other ways they symbolize or to such other considerations as relevance. Even within these limitations I am not, despite some passages in *Ways of Worldmaking* (WW) that suggest the contrary, proposing to *define* truth as ultimate acceptability.

11
Reply to Goodman

Israel Scheffler

I offer now some further comments on my controversy with Nelson Goodman regarding world-making. Let me begin with a preliminary remark: I don't much like the elastic term "world" and do not want to be taken as defending some doctrine about the world—arguing that there really is one world, or that the world is the touchstone of truth, or independent of mind, or the like. I should not wish to express any of my philosophical convictions by using this term in a primitive, literal, and essential way. My references employing the term are wholly addressed, in critical vein, to Goodman's uses, or else are to be cashed out by terms denoting more limited and more comprehensible entities. For this reason, I introduced reference to stars, about which sensible and scientifically sound things can be said, for example, that in any case stars were not made by men.

Another preliminary point is this: I do not dispute the sort of relativism, or pluralism, propounded in Goodman's *The Structure of Appearance*,[1] for which, given any pre-philosophical subject matter, there are likely to be conflicting though adequate systematizations for it, the points of conflict falling in the region of "don't cares." The existence of such systematizations underlies Goodman's espousal of extensional isomorphism rather than identity as a criterion of adequacy for what he calls "constructional systems." Thus, a systematic definition of points as certain classes of lines does not establish that points are identical with such classes but only that, relative to our purpose to preserve certain pre-philosophical "cares," they do not need to be construed as nonidentical with them. We can, indeed, compatibly say something similar concerning a conflicting systematic definition of points as certain classes of volumes. There is, in this sort of account in *The Structure of Appearance,* no talk of worlds at all and certainly no talk of world-making, although the same form of relativism shines through.

What I criticize in my paper is not such relativism, but the later, accreted talk of worlds and their making, construed "objectually" and not simply "versionally." I find no difficulty in taking worlds to be made, *if* by "worlds" one means versions. But I cannot see how one can suppose worlds to be made, if by "worlds" one means things "answering to true versions"—including, as Goodman says, "matter, anti-matter, mind, energy, or what not . . . fashioned along with the versions themselves."[2] Now Goodman does not define "world" in his book, and he uses it ambiguously, drawing what I can only consider cold comfort from the alleged fact that physicists' talk is also ambiguous. But when he insists that worlds are literally made, in *both* of the interpretations he gives to this claim, I conclude that he can avoid outright falsity only by such an unnatural construal of "made" as to cause high philosophical mischief. My paper offers a variety of considerations in support of my argument, to which Goodman offers five main replies, as follows:

First, he admits to the ambiguity in his use of the term "world," arguing that, though conflicting, the versional and objectual interpretations are equally right and often interchangeable.[3] But I do not object to mere ambiguity, which can as a rule be cleared up with sufficient care and the refinement of terminology.

Second, he says, "We cannot find any world feature independent of all versions. Whatever can be said truly of a world is dependent on the saying—not that whatever we say is true but that whatever we say truly . . . is nevertheless informed by and relative to the language or other symbol system we use. No firm line can be drawn between world-features that are discourse-dependent and those that are not."

The trouble with this reply is that it appeals to the notion of a feature. But what *is* a feature? I presume that, for a nominalist such as Goodman, features will not be properties or classes but terms or predicates, construed as, or constituted by, tokens of one or another sort. Then of course features will obviously be dependent on the saying—that is, brought forth by the process of token production. Indeed, whatever we say, whether truly *or* falsely, will in this sense be dependent on the saying, informed by and relative to our language or symbolism. However, whether a feature or predicate of our making is *null or not* is not in the same way dependent on the saying; whether a statement is true or not is, as Goodman agrees, independent of our saying. Thus if by a *world*-feature, Goodman means a feature that is not null in fact, then that any given feature *is* a world-feature is indeed independent of our version. Its status *as* a world-feature is *not* discourse dependent.

Third, Goodman suggests that it is fallacious to assume "that whatever we make we can make any way we like." I agree in rejecting this assumption. I certainly do not deny the difficulty of making a true or right version. What I deny is that by making a true version we make that to which it refers.

In his book, Goodman speaks of "actual worlds made by and answering to true or right versions." Now, whether a world answers to a version of our making is, in general, not up to us. Thus, if an "actual world" answers to a version of our making, we can hardly be supposed to have made it do so. Moreover, if a version of our making turns out to be true, it hardly follows that we have made its object. Neither Pasteur nor his version of the germ theory made the bacteria he postulated, nor was Neptune created either by Adams and Leverrier or by their prescient computations.

Fourth, Goodman asks me "which features of the stars we did not make" and challenges me "to state how these differ from features clearly dependent on discourse." Surely we made the words by which we describe stars; that these words are discourse-dependent is trivially true. But the fact that the word "star" is non-null is not therefore of our making; its discourse-dependence does not imply our making it happen that there *are* stars, or in short, our making the stars: It doesn't imply that the *stars* are *themselves* discourse dependent. Goodman writes, in *Languages of Art,* " 'Sad' may apply to a picture even though no one ever happens to use the term in describing the picture; and calling a picture sad by no means makes it so." Analogously, "star" may apply to something even though no one ever happens to use the term in describing it; and calling something a star by no means makes it one.

Finally, Goodman tries to dispel the absurdity of supposing that we made the stars by arguing that we made "a space and time that contains those stars. . . . We make a star as we make a constellation, by putting its parts together and marking off its boundaries." I find this singularly unconvincing. We have surely made the scientific schemes by which we formulate temporal and spatial descriptions, but to say that we have therefore made space and time can be no less absurd than to say we made the stars. Nor did we make the Big Dipper or Orion merely by defining their respective boundaries.

Goodman concludes by saying, "We do not make stars as we make bricks; not all making is a matter of molding mud. The worldmaking mainly in question here is making not with hands but with minds, or rather with languages or other symbol systems. Yet when I say that worlds are made, I mean it literally. . . . Surely we make versions, and right versions make worlds." The suggestion here is that my critique of worldmaking construes it as a physical rather than a symbolic process.

But my argument is altogether independent of this contrast. My claim is that in any normal understanding of the words, we did not make the stars, whether by hand, mind, or symbol. Certainly, we make things with minds; we thus make words, symbols, versions. The issue is whether in thus making star-descriptions, we also make stars. To propose, as Goodman does, that we may be said to make something whenever we devise a true description for it is certainly possible, even if wildly unnatural; we can certainly make language mean anything we want it to mean. But such a proposal seems to me unusually mischievous in inviting confusions, paradoxes, and misunderstandings—and encouraging an overblown voluntarism. And it blurs the ordinary distinction between making an omelet and writing a recipe for one. Rather than Goodman's "We make versions, and right versions make worlds," I would rather adopt the slogan "we make versions, and things (made by others, by us, or by no one) make them right."

Notes

1. Goodman, *The Structure of Appearance,* 3d ed. (Dordrecht: Reidel, 1977).

2. Goodman, *Ways of Worldmaking* (Indianapolis: Hackett Publishing, 1978).

3. This and the following passages quoted from Goodman are taken from *Of Mind and Other Matters.*

12

On Some Worldly Worries

Nelson Goodman

12.1 Questions and Answers

Israel Scheffler has several complaints against what I have written about worldmaking. Some of these I have discussed earlier,[1] but in his subsequent book[2] he adds further questions and arguments.

He asks how my inclusion of ordering among ways of worldmaking can be reconciled with my nominalistic prohibition of generating more than $2^n - 1$ entities out of n atomic individuals. I have indeed said that the composition of individuals is unique; that taking individuals in different orders does not yield different wholes. How then can reordering the same individuals make anything new? Given five square cards, surely different arrangements of them may yield wholes of different shapes; and if the cards bear certain letter inscriptions, a reordering may turn "cause" into "sauce." But what we speak of here as a difference in arrangement of the (enduring) cards amounts to a difference in arrangement between *different temporal parts* of the cards. The time slices of the cards at t_1 are different from the time slices at t_2; and the sum of the t_1 slices is different from the sum of the t_2 slices. Nothing here violates the nominalistic principle. The enduring cards have but one sum; but sums of different temporal parts of the cards can differ in shape or spelling as well as time. Confusion arises from an ellipsis in ordinary speech; what we speak of as a difference in arrangement of cards amounts, more explicitly, to a difference in arrangement between different temporal parts of the cards.

A second complaint of Scheffler's is that although I say that varied histories of the Battle of Bull Run are no evidence for a multiplicity of things described, I also say that two histories of the Renaissance may give us two different Renaissance worlds. There is no inconsistency here; the principle is not "different right versions, different worlds," but "*disagreeing* right versions, different worlds (if any)." In the first case, I was remarking that right versions may differ without being of different worlds. In the second, I was pointing out that right versions may be of different worlds through disagreement in what they say. This calls for, of course, a broadened notion of disagreement, not confined to statements or even to the verbal.[3]

Again, Scheffler is disturbed by my saying both that a term or picture or other version is ordinarily different from what it denotes and yet also that talk of worlds tends to be interchangeable with talk of right versions. But although what denotes is usually different from what is denoted, what is denoted may itself be a version; some words denote others. And although "table" is different from tables, and "constellation" different from constellations, still tables and constellations and all other things are version dependent.

12.2   Dialogue

Scheffler, though, will have none of this making of worlds by versions or of worlds dissolving into right versions. Elsewhere I have tried to explain what I mean by this, and I cannot go over it all again here. But consider briefly the question whether a constellation, say the Great Dipper, has been there for millions of years or was made by a version made by a human being? Imagine a fragmentary dialogue:

"The Great Dipper was made by an adopted world version."

"No, it was made by Nature."

"Did Nature make it the Great Dipper?"

"Well, no; it was made the Great Dipper by being picked out and so called by a version."

"What is the *it* that was made by Nature and was there to be picked out and named?"

"A particular constellation."

"Was it made a constellation by Nature?"

"Well, no; it was made a constellation by a version that distinguished certain configurations of stars from others under the general term 'constellations.'"[4]

"But did Nature make the stars?"

"Certainly."

"Did it make them stars?"

"Again, no; they were made stars by a version that distinguished certain conglomerations of particles, or objects in the sky, from others under the general term 'star.'"

"Did Nature make the—."

"This could go on and on; but your arguments seem at most to show that without versions stars, for example, do not exist *qua* stars, not that they do not exist at all."

"But do stars-not-*qua*-stars, stars-not-*qua*-moving and not-*qua*-fixed, move or not? Without a version, they are neither moving nor fixed. And whatever neither moves nor is fixed, is neither *qua* so-and-so nor *qua* not so-and-so, comes to nothing."

12.3   Time Troubles

Yet we may still be plagued with recurrent worry over the simple question of how a star that existed before all versions could be made by a version. Indeed, according to any of our trusted familiar world-versions, a star came much earlier than any version. Such a version, call it W, politely puts its own origin much later than the origin of the star—that is, much earlier *in this version's own time-ordering*. Yet according to a quite different version, call it V, (perhaps a version at a different level or metaversion) the star and everything else come into being only *via* a version. As we have seen, there is no ready-made world waiting to be labeled. There is no absolute time. In the time of W, the star comes first; in the time of V, the version comes first.[5] Which is right? The answer is "*both*."

At bottom, I think, what bothers Scheffler is that he cannot reconcile common sense with talk of multiple worlds or conflicting right versions or worldmaking. What bothers me, on the other hand, is that I cannot make any sense whatever, common or uncommon, of a notion of *the* world independent of all versions yet such that all right versions, however much they disagree, correspond to it. Thinking should go straight when it can but sometimes has to find its way around corners.

Notes

1. See Nelson Goodman *Of Mind and Other Matters* (Harvard University Press, Cambridge, Mass., 1984), pp. 40–42.

2. *Inquiries* (Hackett Publishing Co., Indianapolis, 1986), pp. 271–278.

3. See Nelson Goodman and Catherine Elgin, *Reconceptions* (Hackett, 1988), p. 6.

4. Making something a so-and-so does not require that it be individually baptized a so-and-so but only that it fall under a general label used by a version to distinguish so-and-so's from other things. Herein lies the answer to Scheffler's question (his note 6, p. 278) how I can say that a picture may be sad without ever being called "sad."

5. In explaining a related point in *Nietzsche,* Alexander Nehamas writes: "Yet it is not easy to say what *the* past is in the first place. The events of the past are necessarily located through and within a narrative, and different narratives can generate quite different events" (*Nietzsche* [Harvard, 1985], p. 160).

V

Responses

13

Worldmaking: Why Worry

Israel Scheffler

13.1 Introduction

I have learned so much from Nelson Goodman over the years, and I have
so much respect for his work, that our disagreement about worldmaking
comes as something of a surprise to us both. Yet this disagreement has
survived our various exchanges of the last fourteen years and so must, I
suspect, indicate some deep-seated misunderstanding or conflict of visions. I shall here respond to his most recent paper on the issue[1] and say
why worldmaking does indeed cause me to worry: here we have perhaps
a conflict of visions. I hope, however, to pinpoint certain misunderstandings as well, which underlie at least some of our differences and
mask our substantial agreements.

13.2 The Question of Order

In my paper, "The Wonderful Worlds of Goodman"[2] I offer some ancillary considerations to illustrate Goodman's treatment of "worlds" as
sometimes versional, sometimes objectual. Since this variable treatment
is explicitly affirmed by Goodman,[3] the disposition of my ancillary illustrations does not bear on the main point, that is, the variable treatment,
which is not in contention. Nevertheless, let us consider the two particular illustrations I offered, both related to the individuation of worlds by
ordering.

Goodman writes, "Worlds not differing in entities . . . may differ in
ordering."[4] On this, I commented that worlds differentiated by their ordering alone must be versions if his nominalistic principle ("no difference

without a difference of individuals") is to be upheld. He now replies by distinguishing enduring entities from their time-slices, arguing that "confusion arises from an ellipsis in ordinary speech; what we speak of as a difference in arrangement of cards amounts, more explicitly, to a difference in arrangement between different temporal parts of the cards."[5]

But it is Goodman himself, after all, who spoke of worlds not differing in *entities* yet differing in ordering. Can he then be claiming now himself to have traded on the confusion he mentions, by taking the word "entities" to refer to the selfsame individuals whose time-slice sums (but not they themselves) may yet differ in ordering from one another? Goodman says, "Nothing here violates the nominalistic principle."[6] My intent was not to show a violation but to argue that if worlds not differing in entities differ in ordering, they must be construed as versions. And the main point, that is, that Goodman at times takes "worlds" as "world-versions," is not here at issue.

Much of the same can be said of my argument that, in allowing varied histories to determine different worlds, Goodman was apparently interpreting worlds as versional. This argument was not, as Goodman terms it, a "complaint";[7] it was not intended, as he apparently thinks, to show an inconsistency. The point was rather, to illustrate his versional use of "worlds."

He now replies that although "varied histories of the battle of Bull Run are no evidence for a multiplicity of things described," two histories of the Renaissance may indeed "give us two different Renaissance worlds." This is so, he says, because his operative principle is not "different right versions, different worlds" but rather "*disagreeing* right versions, different worlds (if any)."[8]

Does this reply then imply that the two histories of the Renaissance yielding different worlds disagree in the occurrences they denote, so that "worlds" in his usage here is to be understood as objectual after all? This seems to run counter to his description of the variance between the histories, which he terms a "difference in style . . . a difference in weighting," where one history, *without excluding the battles,* stresses the arts," while the other, "*without excluding the arts,* stresses the battles."[9] I conclude from this passage not that he is inconsistent but that he is here treating "worlds" with versional rather than objectual reference. I am, however, in any case content to leave the last word on this and the previous example to Goodman. However he decides them, no disagreement remains over the main point that he sometimes takes "worlds" as "world-versions."

13.3 What Disturbs Me

Goodman says I am "disturbed" by his saying "that a term or picture or other version is ordinarily different from what it denotes and yet also that talk of worlds tends to be interchangeable with talk of right versions."[10] I am in fact not at all disturbed by this sort of statement, the flavor of which has become widely familiar through Alfred Tarski's semantic criterion of truth. Thus Goodman writes, "A version saying that there is a star up there is not itself bright or far off, and the star is not made up of letters. On the other hand, saying that there is a star up there and saying that the statement 'There is a star up there' is true amount, trivially, to much the same thing, even though the one seems to talk about a star and the other to talk about a statement."[11]

Rather, what disturbs me is what Goodman has himself criticized, namely, "philosophers [who] sometimes mistake features of discourse for features of the subject of discourse." As he continues, "We seldom conclude that the world consists of words just because a true description of it does."[12] And here I would add, "We seldom conclude that the world is made by us just because a true description of it is."

I can understand the making of words but not the making thereby of the worlds they refer to. I can accept that versions are made but not that the "things and worlds and even the stuff they are made of—matter, antimatter, mind, energy, or whatnot—are fashioned along with the versions themselves."[13]

13.4 Multiplicity Yes, Worldmaking No

Goodman thinks that what "bothers" me is "talk of multiple worlds or conflicting right versions or worldmaking."[14] He is right about the third item but not about the first two. Here I believe that he just misunderstands me.

I remarked favorably on the "multiplicity of conceptual schemes" in my original paper,[15] and affirmed its consistency with a rejection of objectual worldmaking. I certainly have no quarrel with the sort of relativism propounded in Goodman's *The Structure of Appearance*[16] and agree completely with his statement "that many different world-versions are of independent interest and importance, without any requirement or presumption of reducibility to a single base."[17]

I am as opposed as he is to any such requirement or presumption; my argument is not with his pluralism or relativism but with his voluntarism. More particularly, what I criticize is his affirmation of the making of worlds, objectually construed, whether one or many. "We make versions," says Goodman, "and right versions make worlds."[18] But I say: "We make versions but it is not we who make them right."

13.5   Time

To the question of "how a star that existed before all versions could be made by a version," Goodman responds by appealing to the relativity of time. He imagines a version for which "the star and everything else come into being only *via* a version."[19]

Now, the mere possibility of such an imagined version is radically weaker than Goodman's categorical claim that right versions make worlds. The latter claim already presumes a version that places versions before stars and does not merely assert its possibility. But nowhere are the details of such a fantastic version, which would require fundamental alterations in "any of our trusted world-versions," spelled out. Nor is an argument forthcoming to show that the effort to produce a workable version along these lines could in fact be carried through. Finally, Goodman asks whether this hypothetical version or one of our familiar versions is right, and he answers "Both."[20] He is thus apparently prepared to relinquish his categorical claim altogether.

13.6   Goodman's Dialogue

Goodman hopes to clinch his case for worldmaking by offering "a fragmentary dialogue." The critical conclusion of the dialogue has Goodman's protagonist saying, "But do stars-not-*qua*-stars, stars-not-*qua*-moving and not-*qua*-fixed move or not? Without a version, they are neither moving nor fixed. And whatever neither moves nor is fixed, is neither *qua* so-and-so nor *qua* not so-and-so, comes to nothing."[21]

Of course, whoever writes an imaginary dialogue determines the outcome. I should myself rephrase the concluding passage as follows:

> But do stars not yet called 'stars', stars not yet describable as "moving" or as "fixed," move or not? Without a language capable of describing anything as a star we cannot call a star "a star"; without the language to describe anything as moving or as fixed, we cannot describe a star as "moving" or as "fixed."

Given the language to do so, we may, however, of course decide to describe a star as moving, even as having moved before we acquired our language. But acquiring such language does not automatically ensure its applicability to any given instance. Acquiring the word "moving" does not in itself determine that it is non-null. We certainly do not claim that the later origination of our language caused the star to move then. Nevertheless, we may truly describe it as having moved then.

13.7   Counter-Dialogue

As an alternative to Goodman's dialogue, I offer the following counter-dialogue, to bring out my main point:

"The Big Dipper was made by our adopted world version."

"You mean, I suppose, that this version contains the applicable term, 'Big Dipper.'"

"Yes."

"And does the containing of that term imply that our version actually made the Big Dipper itself?"

"Exactly. As Goodman has said, 'We make worlds by making versions.'"[22]

"Does the containing of the term 'Don Quixote' in an adopted version similarly imply that the version actually made Don Quixote?"

"Of course not. As Goodman has written, 'Painted or written portrayals of Don Quixote . . . do not denote Don Quixote—who is simply not there to be denoted.'"[23]

"Then a version may contain terms that are null as well as terms that are non-null—whose objects are either there or not there?"

"I have just said as much. The Don Quixote version is after all false, while the Big Dipper version is true."

"Then the non-null character of 'Big Dipper' (i.e., the truth of its containing version) is not determined by the fact that our version contains the term."

"Correct."

"That the term is non-null is therefore not version dependent?"

"That seems undeniable."

"And the Big Dipper itself, as distinct from the Big Dipper version is thus also not version dependent?"

"I suppose so."

"Then our Big Dipper version did not make it happen that the Big Dipper in fact exists—that it is *there* to be denoted. Our version did not, after all, make the Big Dipper."

13.8   Conclusion

Goodman concludes his paper by saying that "thinking should go straight when it can but sometimes has to find its way around corners." [24]

I should add that, in doing so, it needs to keep alert for hidden pitfalls around the bend. Can't we maneuver the corner safely by agreeing on pluralism and on version making, while avoiding the creation of parallel worlds?

Notes

1. Nelson Goodman, "On Some Worldly Worries," published by the author at Emerson Hall, Harvard University, Cambridge, MA, September 1, 1988. See also *Synthese* 95 (1993), 9–12. See chapter 12, this volume.

2. Israel Scheffler, "The Wonderful Worlds of Goodman," *Synthese* 45 (1980): 201–209. Reprinted in my *Inquiries* (Hackett: Indianapolis, 1986), 271–278. See also chapter 8, this volume.

   Goodman, incidentally, begins his paper by saying he is going to consider arguments raised in *Inquiries* that I had not raised in my paper. There are indeed such additional arguments in my book, on pp. 82–86, but I regret to say that Goodman does not address these, considering only points found in my earlier paper. Had he addressed the additional arguments, might he have found them persuasive?

3. See, for example, his *Of Minds and Other Matters* (Harvard: Cambridge, MA,

1984), 41: "we can have it both ways. To say that every right version is a world and to say that every right version has a world answering to it may be equally right even if they are at odds with each other."

4. Goodman, *Ways of Worldmaking* (Hackett: Indianapolis, 1978), 12.

5. "On Some Worldly Worries," p. 1. See also Goodman's "A World of Individuals" in his *Problems and Projects* (Indianapolis: Hackett, 1972), especially pp. 163–164.

6. Ibid.

7. Ibid.

8. Ibid., 2.

9. Goodman, *Ways of Worldmaking*, 101–102.

10. Goodman, "On Some Worldly Worries," 2.

11. Goodman, *Of Mind and Other Matters*, 41.

12. Nelson Goodman, *Problems and Projects* (Bobbs-Merrill: Indianapolis, 1972), 24.

13. Goodman, *Ways of Worldmaking*, 96.

14. Goodman, "On Some Worldly Worries," 4.

15. See Scheffler, *Inquiries*, 276.

16. See Scheffler, *Inquiries*, 271 and 83.

17. Goodman, *Ways of Worldmaking*, 4.

18. Goodman, *Of Mind and Other Matters*, 42.

19. Goodman, "On Some Worldly Worries," 3–4.

20. Ibid., 4.

21. Ibid., 2–3.

22. *Ways of Worldmaking*, 94.

23. Ibid., 103.

24. "On Some Worldly Worries," 4.

14

Irrealism and Deconstruction

Hilary Putnam

14.1 Nelson Goodman's "Irrealism"

Nelson Goodman first announced his "irrealism" in a challenging and unquestionably path-breaking little book provocatively titled *Ways of Worldmaking*. The title captures two of the most important claims of the book: that we inhabit not one world, but many simultaneously; and that these worlds are worlds of our own making.

The idea of a plurality of worlds is connected with an idea I shall look at shortly, the idea that there is not one unique "right version" of the world, but rather a number of different "right versions" of it. This is an idea that I agree with. An example—mine, not Goodman's—is that there is no unique right version of the relation between ordinary objects (tables and trees and animals) and scientific objects. We can speak as if such ordinary objects were identical with scientific objects, or as if they were distinct from the physical systems which constitute their matter,[1] or we can say that which physical system a given common sense object is identical with is to some degree vague (as I would urge) but that there are some physical systems that this chair, or whatever the example may be, is definitely *not* identical with. Moreover, there are many possible choices as to what we should take the physical system to be, if we want to identify chairs and trees with physical systems: space-time regions (or the gravitational, electromagnetic, and other fields that occupy those regions), or aggregates of portions of the histories of various molecules. Each of these ways of speaking can be formalized, and each of the resulting formalisms[2] represents a perfectly admissible way of speaking; but Goodman would say (and I would agree) none of them can claim to be "the way things are independent of experience." There is no one uniquely true description of reality.

The idea that the facts admit of more than one picture has been around for over a century, however. It is anticipated by Herz's talk of equally good "world pictures" in the introduction to his *Principles of Mechanics,* and it is referred to by William James.[3] Goodman's innovation is to attack the claim that our conceptual schemes *are* just different "descriptions" of what are in some sense "the same facts." Goodman regards this idea as empty. For him it is immaterial whether we speak of versions as descriptions of worlds or say that there are no worlds and only versions. What Goodman is adamant about, however, is that if we do choose to speak of worlds as distinct from versions, then we must say that incompatible versions refer to different worlds. It cannot be true of one and the same world that the space-time points are individual things and that they are abstractions. Thus we ought to say—if we keep the concept of a world at all—not that we describe the world (as philosophers) sometimes using a language in which tables and chairs are talked of as aggregates of "time-slices" of molecules and sometimes using a language in which those aggregates of "time-slices" of molecules are regarded as the *matter* of the tables and chairs (and the matter is spoken of as something distinct from the table or chair); but rather that we *sometimes choose to make a world in which tables and chair are aggregates of "time-slices" of molecules and sometimes choose to make a world in which tables and chairs are distinct from those aggregates of "time-slices" of molecules.* Goodman confronts us with a choice between saying that there are many worlds or that world-talk is nonsense.[4] True to his own pluralism, Goodman sometimes speaks as if there were no world(s) at all, and sometimes speaks as if there were many.

But if we choose to speak of worlds, where do these worlds come from? Goodman's answer is unequivocal: they are made by us. They are not made *ex nihilo,* but out of previous worlds—or out of previous versions, since the distinction between a world and a version is of no moment. Springing full-blown within contemporary analytic philosophy, a form of idealism as extreme as Hegel's or Fichte's!

In addition to Goodman's more technical arguments, there is a more accessible argument that he first used in commenting on the papers in a symposium on *Ways of Worldmaking* at the December meeting of the American Philosophical Association in 1979.[5] Goodman discussed the question, raised by Israel Scheffler, "Is it a consequence of Goodman's philosophy that *we made the stars?*" Goodman answered that while there is a sense in which we did not make the stars (we don't make stars in the way in which a brickmaker makes a brick), there is indeed a sense in which we did make the stars. Goodman illustrated this by asking us to consider a constellation, say the Big Dipper. Did we make the Big Dipper? There is an obvious sense in which the answer is no. All right, we didn't make it in the way in which a carpenter makes a table, but *did we make it a constellation?* Did we make it the Big Dipper? At this point, perhaps many of us might say yes, there is a sense in which we made "it" the Big Dipper. After all, it is hard to think of the fact that a group of stars is a "dipper" as one which is mind independent or language independent. Perhaps we should give Goodman this much, that we didn't "make" the Big Dipper as a carpenter makes a table, but we did make it by constructing a version in which that group of stars is seen as exhibiting a dipper shape, and by giving it a name, thus, as it were, institutionalizing the fact that that group of stars is metaphorically a big dipper. Nowadays, there is a Big Dipper up there in the sky, and we, so to speak, "put" a Big Dipper up there in the sky by constructing that version. But—and Goodman is, of course, waiting for this objection—we didn't make the stars of which that constellation consists. Stars are a "natural kind," whereas constellations are an "artificial kind." [6]

But let us take a look at this so-called natural kind. Natural kinds, when we examine them, almost always turn out to have boundaries which are to some degree arbitrary, even if the degree of arbitrariness is much less than in the case of a completely conventional kind like "constellation." [7] Stars are clouds of glowing gas, glowing because of thermonuclear reactions which are caused by the gravitational field of the star itself, but not every cloud of glowing gas is considered a star; some such clouds fall into other astronomical categories, and some stars do not glow at all. Is it not *we* who group together all these different objects into a single category "star" with our inclusions and exclusions? It is true that we did not make the stars as a carpenter makes a table, but didn't we, after all, *make them stars?*

Now Goodman makes a daring extrapolation. He proposes that in the sense illustrated by these examples, the sense in which we "make" certain things the Big Dipper and make certain things stars, there is nothing that we did not make to be what it is. (Theologically, one might say that Goodman makes man the Creator.) If, for example, you say that we didn't make the elementary particles, Goodman can point to the present situation in quantum mechanics and ask whether you really want to view elementary particles as a mind-independent reality.[8] It is clear that if we try to beat Goodman at his own game, by trying to name some "mind-independent stuff," we shall be in deep trouble.

In spite of its elegance, it seems to me that this little argument of Goodman's is easily defused. There *is* a fundamental difference between the terms "constellation" and "Big Dipper," on the one hand, and a term like "star" on the other. The extension of the term "Big Dipper" is fixed by linguistic convention. The term applies to a finite group of stars, and one learns which stars are in the group and how they are arranged when one learns the meaning of the term. In this respect, "Big Dipper" is a typical *proper name.*

We know which stars belong to the Big Dipper by knowing what it is we call "the Big Dipper." I would not say that it is "analytic" that the Big Dipper contains *all* of those stars, because if one of those stars "went out" or was totally removed by aliens with vast superscientific powers we would undoubtedly go on speaking of the Big Dipper and just say that the Big Dipper didn't have as many stars as it used to have. In the same way, we will continue to refer to John Smith as "John Smith" even if he loses his hair. (If a new star appeared "in" the Big Dipper, however, it would not automatically count as a part of the Big Dipper. Whether it came to count as a part of the Big Dipper would depend entirely on subsequent linguistic practice; which stars are part of the Big Dipper is a question for an anthropologist or a linguist, not a question for an astrophysicist.)

In contrast to the term "Big Dipper," the term "star" has an extension that cannot be fixed by giving a list. And no particular object is in the extension of "star" simply by virtue of being *called* a star; it might be crazy to doubt that Sirius is really a star, but someone who thought that Sirius is really a giant light bulb or a glowing spaceship wouldn't thereby show an inability to use "star" in the way in which someone who doubted that that constellation is really the Big Dipper would show an inability to use "Big Dipper."

In these respects, the term "constellation" lies somewhere in between "Big Dipper" and "star." If we discovered that all the stars in the Big Dipper are really giant fakes installed to fool us by those superscientific aliens (giant light bulbs in the sky, so to speak), we would say "they aren't really stars," but we wouldn't say "that isn't really the Big Dipper." Would we cease to regard the Big Dipper as a constellation? Perhaps we would, but I am completely unsure.

The upshot is very simple. One perfectly good answer to Goodman's rhetorical question "Can you tell me something that we didn't make?" is that we didn't make Sirius a star. Not only didn't we make Sirius a star in the sense in which a carpenter makes a table, *we didn't make it a star.* Our ancestors and our contemporaries (including astrophysicists), in shaping and creating our language, created the concept *star,* with its partly conventional boundaries, with its partly indeterminate boundaries, and so on. And that concept *applies* to Sirius. The fact that the concept *star* has conventional elements doesn't mean that *we* make it the case that that concept applies to any particular thing, in the way in which we made it the case that the concept "Big Dipper" applies to a particular group of stars. The concept *bachelor* is far more strongly conventional than the concept *star,* and that concept applies to Joseph Ullian, but our linguistic practices didn't make Joe a bachelor. (They did make him "Joe Ullian".)[9] General names like "star" and "bachelor" are very different from proper names like "the Big Dipper" and "Joe Ullian," and Goodman's argument depends upon our not noticing the difference.

14.2 Irrealism and Conceptual Relativity

Goodman has far more serious arguments for his theses, and these arguments contain many real insights (even if they lead to wrong conclusions). We have to discuss them with some delicacy. Those arguments depend on a phenomenon I have called "conceptual relativity."[10] Here is an example. Points in space (or nowadays one often refers instead to points in space-time) can be regarded as concrete[11] particulars of which space consists (the ultimate parts of space) or, alternatively, as "mere limits." [12] Geometrical discourse can be adequately formalized from either point of view;[13] so can all of physics. And whether formalized or left unformalized, both ways of speaking will do perfectly well for all the purposes of geometry and physics.

Goodman regards these two versions of space-time theory as "incompatible." At the same time, he regards them as both right. And since incompatible versions cannot be true of the same world, he concludes that they are true of different worlds "if true of any."

One well-known objection to views like Goodman's has been advanced by Donald Davidson[14] (and Quine has recently been converted to it as well). Davidson's argument is as quick and dirty as Goodman's: Davidson simply accepts Goodman's view that the two versions are incompatible, points out that according to standard logic incompatible statements cannot both be true, and concludes that it is unintelligible to maintain that both versions are true. Even if both versions are equally good for practical purposes, I cannot say that they are both true, according to Davidson and Quine. Quine does say[15] that I may pick one of these versions some of the time (say Mondays, Wednesdays, and Fridays?) and the other one at other times, but at any given time I must say that the version I am using then is true and the version I am not using then is false, on pain of self-contradiction.

Goodman's view, as we have seen, is to say that logic does indeed tell us that incompatible statements cannot both be true *of the same world,* but, in his view, the equal "rightness" of both of these incompatible versions shows that they are true *of different worlds.* Davidson does not explicitly discuss this move, but Quine rejects it on the ground that to split reality into a number of different worlds is to violate the principle of parsimony. (The possibility of saying that there are no worlds at all, that is, no extralinguistic reality, is one that Quine apparently does not deem worthy of discussion.)

Goodman and Davidson seem to me to be making the same mistake—although, as often happens in philosophy, it leads them into opposite camps. Davidson and Goodman both accept without question the idea that statements which appear to be incompatible, taken according to their surface grammar, really are incompatible, even in cases like these. If the sentence "points are mere limits" is a contrary of the sentence "points are not limits but parts of space," even when the first sentence occurs in a systematic scheme for describing physical reality and the second occurs in another systematic scheme for describing physical reality *even though the two schemes are in practice thoroughly equivalent,*[16] then we are in trouble indeed. But the whole point of saying that the two schemes are in practice thoroughly equivalent is that, far from leading us to incompatible predictions or incompatible actions, it makes no difference to our predictions or actions which of the two schemes we use. Nor are the two schemes "equivalent" only in the weak sense of what is sometimes called "empirical equivalence" (that is, leading to the same predictions); rather, each sentence in one of them, say the scheme in which points are concrete particulars, can be correlated in an effective way with a "translation" in the other scheme, and the sentence and its translation will be used to describe the same states of affairs.

In saying that they are used to describe the same states of affairs, I am not introducing a transcendent ontology of states of affairs. By a "state of affairs" I mean something like a particle's being at a point, or a place X's being between a place Y and a place Z; in short, I assume a familiar language to be already in place. I am not saying that Noumenal Reality consists of states of affairs. (I could have spoken of "situations," or "physical events," or in many other ways. The relation of language to the world is also something that can be described in more than one way.) Nor am I assuming a one-to-one correspondence between sentences and states of affairs, thus populating the world with "sentence-shaped objects," in a phrase taken from Richard Rorty. The whole point of what I just said is that very *different* sentences can describe the very same state of affairs. In short, what I meant by a "state of affairs" when I said that a sentence in one formalization of physical geometry and its "translation" in the alternative formalization will be used to describe the same "states of affairs" is just what anyone would mean by that phrase who was *not* giving it a metaphysical emphasis.

That the sentence in one such scheme that we use in practice can be correlated with the sentences in another such scheme was pointed out long ago by Goodman himself. The nature of such correlations was studied by Goodman,[17] who referred to this kind of correlation as "extensional isomorphism." Am I saying, then, that the sentence "points are mere limits" and the sentence "points are not mere limits but parts of space" actually have the same meaning? Not at all. Some sentences function virtually as tautologies within their own "version." If we identify points with limits by definition, then, in our version, "points are mere limits" will be a conventional truth. And we do not generally translate such conventional truths in one version into the other version (although we could; we could, for example, translate every quasi-logical truth in the one version by any fixed tautology in the other). But the more interesting, less conventional, truths in the one version—say, theorems of ordinary Euclidean geometry, or the statement that there is a particle with a certain mass at a certain place—can be "translated" from one version into another version; these are the statements for which we provide correlates.

Should we say that any such statement in the version in which points are treated as concrete particulars—say, the statement that between any two points on a line there is a third point—has exactly the same *meaning* as its "translation" into the version in which points are identified with limits (say, with convergent sets of concentric spheres)? I would say that in the context of real-life physics and real-life mathematics it makes no difference which of these two ways one talks and thinks. I am saying that if a sentence in one version is true in that version, then its correlate in the other version is true in the other version. But to ask if these two sentences have the same meaning is to try to force the ordinary-language notion of meaning to do a job for which it was never designed.

The phenomenon of conceptual relativity is a mind-boggling one. To suppose that questions like "Do S_1 and S_2 have the same meaning or a different meaning?" make any sense in *this* case seems to me precisely the assumption that we should not make. The sentence "Between any two points on a line there is a third point" and its "translation" into the version in which points are identified with convergent sets of concentric spheres have the same truth conditions in the sense that they are mathematically equivalent. The answer to the question "Do the two sentences have the same meaning?" is that the ordinary notion of meaning simply crumbles in the face of such a question. It was never meant to do *that* job.[18]

Now to the question of "incompatibility," which exercises both Goodman and Davidson so: "point," "line," "limit," and so on are used in different ways in the two versions. To say that the sentence "points are convergent sets of concentric spheres,"[19] as used in the one version, is incompatible with "points are not sets but individuals," as used in the other version, is much too simple. Rather than conclude with Goodman that either there is no world at all or else we live in more than one world, or to conclude with Davidson that the phenomenon of equivalent descriptions, which we have recognized in science since the end of the nineteenth century, somehow involves a logical contradiction, we should simply give up the idea that the sentences we have been discussing preserve something called their "meaning" when we go from one such version into another such version.

Am I not, then, saying that the sentence has a *different* meaning in the two versions? (If a sentence doesn't preserve its meaning, it must change it, right?) I repeat that the answer is that the notion of "meaning," and the ordinary practices of translation and paraphrase to which it is linked, crumble when confronted with such cases. We can say that the words "point," "limit," and so forth have different "uses" in these two versions, if we like. In view of that difference in use, one should not treat a sentence in one version as though it contradicted what the same physicists or the same mathematicians might say on another day when they are employing the other version. But whether such a change of use is or is not a change of "meaning" is not a question that need have an answer.

14.3   The Significance of Conceptual Relativity

The significance of conceptual relativity might come out more clearly if we consider a somewhat different case. In *The Many Faces of Realism* I described in detail a case in which the same situation, in a perfectly commonsensical sense of "the same situation," can be described as involving entirely different numbers and kinds of objects (colored "atoms" alone, versus colored atoms plus "aggregates" of atoms). If you have a world in which there are two black "atoms" and one red one, you can either say that there are three objects (the atoms), or that there are seven objects (the atoms and the various aggregates of two or more atoms). How many objects are there "really" in such a world? I suggest that *either way of describing it is equally "true."* The idea that "object" has some sense which is independent of how we are counting objects and what we are counting as an "object" in a given situation is an illusion. I do not mean by this that there "really" are "aggregates," and there really are atoms and there really are sets and there really are numbers, and so on, and it is just that *sometimes* "object" does not refer to "all objects." I mean that the metaphysical notion of "all objects" has no sense.

Again, in quantum mechanics, any two states of a system can be in a "superposition"; that is to say, any particular state of a system, involving having a particular number of particles or a particular energy or a particular momentum, can be represented by a kind of "vector" in an abstract space, and the superposition of any two such states can be represented by forming a vector sum. These vector sums are sometimes classically very difficult to interpret: what do we make of a state in which the answer to the question "How many electrons are there in this box?" is "Well, there is a superposition of there being three electrons in the box and there being seventeen"? But we can represent such unthinkable states mathematically, and we know how to derive predictions and formulate explanations using them. This principle of superposition applies to field theory as well as to particle theory; the "field states" of the quantum field theorist are not the field states of the classical field theorist; they are typically *superpositions* of the field states of the classical theory. We may say, then (and here I leave out entirely the puzzling role of the observer in quantum mechanics), that from the point of view of quantum mechanics, the world consists of fields in "funny" states. But—and this was the discovery of Richard Feynman—it is also possible to think in a very different way. We can think of the world as consisting of particles (although we have to vastly increase the number of particles we postulate in order to carry this through) and we can think of any situation that we describe in field physics as a superposition of an infinite number of different *particle* situations. In short, there are two different ways of thinking in quantum field theory. In one way of thinking, the way the physicist thinks when performing the usual field calculations, the system is in a superposition of field states. In the other way of thinking, the way of thinking when drawing "Feynman diagrams," the system is in a superposition of particle states. In short, the system may be thought of as consisting either of fields or of particles, but it cannot be thought of as consisting of either classical fields or classical particles.

Consider a given physical system which the physicist represents twice over, once in the language of fields and once in the language of particles (say, by drawing Feynman diagrams). What I am saying is that this is a real system, and that these are two legitimate ways of talking about that real system. The fact that the real system allows itself to be talked about in these two very different ways does not mean either that there is no real physical system being talked about, or that there are two different physical systems in two different Goodmanian worlds being talked about.

The point is even clearer in the case of the first example, the example in which "the same situation" was described as involving entirely different numbers and kinds of objects. It is absolutely clear, it seems to me, that the two descriptions are descriptions of *one and the same world*, not two different worlds.

Part of Goodman's challenge—as it was part of the challenge of German idealists like Hegel and Fichte in the beginning of the nineteenth century—is to say, "Well, if you say that these two ways of talking are both descriptions of the same reality, then *describe that reality as it is apart from those ways of talking.*" But why should one suppose that reality can be described independent of our descriptions? And why should the fact that reality cannot be described independent of our descriptions lead us to suppose that there are only the descriptions? After all, according to our descriptions themselves, the word "quark" is one thing and a quark is quite a different thing.

Nevertheless, the phenomenon of conceptual relativity does have real philosophical importance. As long as we think of the world as consisting of objects and properties in some one, philosophically preferred sense of "object" and "property"—as long as we think that reality itself, if viewed with enough metaphysical seriousness, will *determine* for us how we are to use the words "object" and "property"—then we will not see how the number and kind of objects and their properties can vary from one correct description of a situation[20] to another correct description of that same situation. Although our sentences do "correspond to reality" in the sense of describing it, they are not simply copies of reality. To revert for a second to Bernard Williams's book, the idea that some descriptions are "descriptions of reality as it is independent of perspective" is a chimera. Our language cannot be divided up into two parts, a part that describes the world "as it is anyway" and a part that describes our conceptual contribution. This does not mean that reality is hidden or noumenal; it simply means that you can't describe the world without describing it.

14.4   Irrealism and Deconstruction

We may now begin to appraise the frequently heard claim that "the problematique of representation has collapsed."[21] What people who talk like this mean is that the notion of reference to an objective world has collapsed. Goodman's work has the virtue of setting forth an *argument* for this position which is much clearer than any that one can extract from the work of Derrida. Goodman's argument does, I have claimed, destroy one traditional version of "realism," the version I like to call metaphysical realism.[22] According to that version, the notions of an object and a property each have just one philosophically serious "meaning," and the world divides itself up into objects and properties in one definite unique way. This is the myth of the ready-made world. (This is also one form of what Derrida would call the "metaphysics of presence.")

The myth of the ready-made world is a myth which has become linked with a number of other ideas. For example, there is the expectation, which we have already encountered, that the objects and properties of which the world ("in itself") consists are the objects and properties of "finished science," and there is the tendency—it is much more than a tendency in fact—to forget that the principle of bivalence of classical logic is simply a useful idealization, which is not conformed to fully and cannot be conformed to fully by any actual language, natural or artificial, that human beings could possibly use.

But the collapse of a certain picture of the world, and of the conceptions of representation and truth that went with that picture of the world, is very far from being a collapse of the notions of representation and truth. To identify the collapse of one philosophical picture of representation with the collapse of the idea that we represent things that we did not bring into existence is, quite simply, dotty. Deconstructionists are right in claiming that a certain philosophical tradition is bankrupt; but to identify that metaphysical tradition with our lives and our language is to give metaphysics an altogether exaggerated importance. For deconstructionists, metaphysics was the *basis* of our entire culture, the pedestal on which it all rested; if the pedestal has broken, the entire culture must have collapsed—indeed, our whole language must lie in ruins. But of course we can and do make sense of the idea of a reality we did not make, even though we cannot make sense of the idea of a reality that is "present" in the metaphysical sense of dictating its own unique description. As we saw, seemingly incompatible words may actually describe the same situation or event or the same physical system.

At this point we run into another source of contemporary philosophical scepticism. This source is the doctrine of incommensurability. Although that doctrine has been associated in recent years with the writings of Thomas Kuhn, it appeared in French thought decades before Kuhn's work. A version of it appeared in Ferdinand Saussure's *Cours de linguistique generale,*[23] a work whose influence on both structuralist and poststructuralist French philosophy is unquestionable. Saussure's route to incommensurability was the following: along with other linguists of his time (for example, the Prague school) Saussure learned that the basic phonetic units of language, the phonemes, were not themselves identifiable in terms of their physical features. One can characterize a phoneme in a language only by contrast with the other phonemes in the language. It is the whole system of contrasts that determines what the phonemes of a given language are. Phonemes are not "sounds" in the physicist's sense of sound. One cannot say that the English phoneme *p* is the "same" as the German phoneme *p;* they simply belong to different systems of contrasts. Saussure assumed that something similar would have to be true of the semantic units of the language; that is, he assumed that the meanings expressible in a language could be characterized only by the ways in which they contrasted or failed to contrast with other meanings available in the same language. The idea of describing the language as a system of differences (a system of available contrasts) was to be extended from phonemics to semantics.

But different languages do not, in fact, provide the same semantical contrasts. A language which recognizes only four fundamental colors provides a different system of contrasts from one which provides seven fundamental colors, for example. The line of thinking that Saussure had embarked on leads fairly quickly to the conclusion that meanings are parochial to languages (and from here it is not far to the thought that they may be parochial to individual "texts"). No two languages ever express the same meanings; no meaning can ever be expressed in more than one language (or even text). The very notion of a sign's meaning, as something separable from the sign, collapses.

In an interview with Kristeva,[24] Derrida makes clear his wholehearted acceptance of this line of thinking; he criticizes Saussure only for not going further and abandoning talk of "signs" altogether (since the notion of a "signified" independent of the system of signs has collapsed):

> To take only one example, one should show that a semiology of the Saussurean type has had a double role. *On the one hand*, an absolutely decisive role:
> 1. It has marked, against the tradition, that the signified is inseparable from the signifier, that the signified and the signifier are two sides of one and the same coin. Saussure even purposefully refused to have this opposition or this "two-sided unity" conform to the relationship between soul and body, as had always been done. "This two-sided unity has often been compared to the unity of the human person, composed of a body and a soul. The comparison is hardly satisfactory."[25]
> 2. By emphasizing the *differential* and *formal* characteristics of semiological functioning, by showing that it is "impossible for sound, the material element, itself to belong to language," and that "in its essence it [the linguistic signifier] is not at all phonic";[26] by desubstantializing both the signified content and the "expressive substance"—which therefore is no longer in a privileged or exclusive way phonic—by making linguistics a division of general semiology—Saussure powerfully contributed to turning against the metaphysical tradition the concept of the sign that he borrowed from it.

Derrida fails to notice that a Utopian project lay behind Saussure's way of thinking. The hope was for a strictly scientific account of meaning, one that would exactly parallel the structure of the newly emergent phonemics. Since that hope has collapsed (it was hardly coherent to begin with), we are not forced to the bizarre view that no one can understand any language but his or her own ideolect. Nor does Derrida himself go so far; like Quine, after having denounced the notion of meaning-preserving translation, he recognizes the indispensability of translation in practice, although in a very guarded way:

> In the limits to which it is possible, or at least *appears* possible, translation practices the difference between signified and signifier.[27] But if this difference is never

pure, no more so is translation, and for the notion of translation we would have to substitute the notion of *transformation:* a regulated transformation of one language by another, of one text by another. We will never have, and in fact never had, to do with some "transport" of pure signifieds from one language to another, or within one and the same language, that the signifying instrument would leave virgin and untouched. (*Positions*, p. 20; emphasis in the original)

The alternative to Saussure's view is to keep the notion of "sameness of meaning" while recognizing that it is not to be interpreted as the self-identity of objects called "meanings" or "signifieds." When two uses of words may be regarded as "the same" and when they may be regarded as "not the same" is not a matter of some clean mathematical relation of equivalence or non-equivalence between two systems of contrasts. If people inquire about the meaning of something that someone says, we generally have some idea as to why they are asking and what they are going to do with the answer. Given the context and the interests of the people involved, we can usually come up with a pretty good answer. Can it be that in Derrida's use of Saussure we see some of the same mistakes that are made by American analytic philosophers like Jerry Fodor? Fodor would, of course, reject the idea, which is implicit in the argument I have cited, that sameness of meaning makes strict sense only in the impossible case in which the two languages or texts in question are *isomorphic*. But the fact that Derrida takes this idea seriously, while not even considering the possibility that the kind of "sameness of meaning" we seek in translation might be an interest-relative (but still quite real) relation, one which involves a normative judgment, a judgment as to what is *reasonable* in the particular case, does remind me of Fodor's scientism.

I don't want to claim that the two factors that I have discussed—the way in which metaphysical realism has gotten itself into trouble in the twentieth century, and the way in which the doctrine of incommensurability of different languages and even different texts has come to seem coercive to Derrida—are the sole reasons which shape Derrida's eventual deconstructionist position. Certainly there are many other influences, including Heidegger, Marx, Freud, and Nietzsche. But when one looks for *arguments* in and around Derrida's writings to support the radical claims that he repeats over and over, I think one finds that they are related to, on the one hand, Goodman's irrealism[28] and, on the other hand, Saussure's form of the doctrine of incommensurability. While those doctrines are well worth reflecting on—they do show much that is of interest—they do not justify the extreme philosophical radicalisms of either Goodman or Derrida.

14.5   Differences between Goodman and Derrida

Although Goodman and Derrida might both be described as "irrealists," the philosophical morals that they draw from their respective irrealisms are quite different. Although Goodman sees difficulties with the notion of truth, he never proposes that we should give it up. Instead, he proposes that we should widen the range of philosophical discussion. Instead of talking exclusively or primarily about language, about versions that consist of statements, we should also consider other "versions" of the world, such as paintings, musical compositions, and so on. (According to Goodman, all works of art function semantically and constitute versions/ worlds.) Truth is a predicate which we apply only to statements, and statements occur only in verbal versions of the world, but non-verbal versions can also contribute to understanding and can be right or wrong. Goodman is fully aware that there are no necessary and sufficient conditions that we are at present able to state for either rightness or truth— there is certainly no "algorithm" for either rightness or truth. Moreover, he is aware that any even partial and vague standards that a philosopher might propose will always be controversial. But neither the lack of an algorithm nor the controversial character of such general statements as we are able to make should occasion dismay. Even if we do not have a general characterization of rightness, we have partial characterizations of certain kinds of rightness, as Goodman points out. For deductive validity, we have long had such a partial characterization. (That it is only partial is shown by the Gödel incompleteness theorem.) For inductive validity, Goodman has himself proposed the beginnings of an account, although he is well aware that that account does not constitute a formal inductive logic, in the sense of Rudolf Carnap. Generally Goodman's attitude towards the lack of "standards" for rightness or truth is that it is the job of the philosopher to try to devise standards, if not for truth *simpliciter* or for rightness *simpliciter,* then for rightness and truth in various areas. If those standards are not an algorithm, they can at least be the beginnings of an account. If we don't yet have even the beginnings of an account in many areas, then that shows that there is a great deal of work for philosophers to do. Goodman describes himself as a "constructionalist"; he constantly stresses the idea that the lack of pre-existing standards is a challenge to philosophers, rather than a reason for dismay.

How should philosophers go about constructing standards for different kinds of rightness? They should look at what we already believe about various cases, and try to formulate standards that agree with those beliefs. But they should not be the slaves of their beliefs. As we try to develop standards, we often find that the very activity of trying to formulate principles leads us to change our view about particular cases. We have thus to aim at "delicate mutual adjustment" of standards and individual cases to one another, hoping for something like a Rawlsian "reflective equilibrium" at the end. But what if our own reflective equilibrium is not regarded as a reflective equilibrium by others? Then, Goodman says, we must simply try to "sell" what seems right to us. The criterion of rightness (in philosophy or anywhere else) cannot be universal consent.[29] Goodman is not afraid of incompleteness, and he is not afraid of making normative judgments.

Derrida's attitudes are much harder to make out. Although this is certainly a misinterpretation,[30] his attacks on the "logocentricism" of Western culture have been interpreted by some of his more left-wing followers as licensing an all-out rejection of the very idea of rational justification. These followers interpret Derrida as teaching that logic and standards of rightness are themselves repressive. Freeing ourselves from capitalism is seen as requiring that we free ourselves from notions like rightness and truth. Goodman would be seen as a hopeless reactionary by these people.

In certain ways, one can understand the reasons for this interpretation. Traditional beliefs include much that is repressive (think of traditional beliefs about various races, about women, about workers, about gays). Our "standards" require not only rational reconstruction but criticism. But criticism requires argument, not the abandonment of argument. The view that all the left has to do is tear down what is, and not discuss what might replace it, is the most dangerous politics of all, and one that could easily be borrowed by the extreme right.

Derrida himself is not guilty of this kind of thinking. He has movingly replied to the charge of nihilism: "We can easily see on which side obscurantism and nihilism are lurking when on occasion great professors or representatives of prestigious institutions lose all sense of proportion and control; on such occasions they forget the principles that they claim to defend in their work and suddenly begin to heap insults, to say whatever comes into their heads on the subject of texts that they obviously have never opened, or that they have encountered through mediocre journalism that in other circumstances they would pretend to scorn." [31]

Yet the fact remains that the thrust of Derrida's work is so negative, so lacking in any sense of what and how we should construct, politically or otherwise, that it is difficult to exonerate him complete from responsibility for the effect of his teaching. He himself does not exonerate Nietzsche completely:

> I do not wish to "clear" its author and neutralize or defuse either what might be troublesome in it for democratic pedagogy or "leftist" politics, or what served as "language" for the most sinister rallying cries of National Socialism. On the contrary, the greatest indecency is *de rigueur* in this place. One may even wonder why it is not enough to say: "Nietzsche did not think that," "he did not want that," or "he would have vomited this," that there is falsification of the legacy and interpretative mystification going on here. One may wonder how and why what is so naively called a falsification was possible (one can't falsify just anything), how and why the "same" words and the "same" statements—if they are indeed the same— might several times be made to serve certain meanings and certain contexts that are said to be different, even incompatible. [32]

Commenting on this passage, Richard Bernstein has written:

> I am not suggesting that Derrida's texts are the occasion for "the most sinister rallying cries." It is difficult to imagine any texts which are more anti-authoritarian and subversive for any (and all) "true believers". But I am asking whether the signatory of these texts bears some responsibility for their reception. If the desire to write "is the desire to perfect a program or a matrix having the greatest potential variability, undecidability, plurivocality, et cetera, so that each time something returns it will be as different as possible," then doesn't the signatory bear some "responsibility" for the divergent and incompatible ways in which the texts are read and heard. One may wonder "how and why" the texts signed by J. D. can be read (or heard) as being nihilistic, obscurantist, self-indulgent logorrhea and (and I have argued) passionate, political, subversive, committed to opening the spaces of differánce and respecting what is irreducibly other. What is it about the texts of Derrida that allows for, indeed invites, this double reading? After all, "one can't falsify just anything." [33]

I would suggest that the bind Derrida is in is the bind those will find themselves in who do not want to be "irresponsible," but who "problematize" the notions of reason and truth themselves, by teaching that, even if they are indispensable, nevertheless they "retain us in the logocentric circle," they have "collapsed," and so forth.

The problem is that notwithstanding certain moments of argument, the thrust of Derrida's writing is that the notions of "justification," "good reason," "warrant," and the like are primarily repressive gestures. And *that* view is dangerous because it provides aid and comfort for extremists (especially extremists of a romantic bent) of all kinds, both left and right. The twentieth century has witnessed horrible events, and the extreme left and the extreme right are both responsible for its horrors. Today, as we face the twenty-first century, our task is not to repeat the mistakes of the twentieth century. Thinking of reason as just a repressive notion is certainly not going to help us to do that.

Derrida, I repeat, is not an extremist. His own political pronouncements are, in my view, generally admirable. But the philosophical irresponsibility of one decade can become the real-world political tragedy of a few decades later. And deconstruction without reconstruction is irresponsibility.

Notes

1. This has been urged by Saul Kripke, in *Naming and Necessity* (Cambridge, Mass.: Harvard University Press, 1980).

2. I should emphasize that, for Goodman, versions do not have to be formalized, although the differences between versions tend to come out more sharply if we do formalize them to some extent.

3. "So many rival formulations are proposed in all the branches of science that investigators have become accustomed to the notion that no theory is absolutely a transcript of reality . . . They are only a man-made language, a conceptual shorthand, as someone calls them, in which we write our reports of nature; and languages, as is well known, tolerate much choice of expression and many dialects." *Pragmatism and the Meaning of Truth* (Cambridge, Mass.: Harvard University Press, 1978), with introduction by A. J. Ayer, p. 33.

4. See "Works, Words, Worlds," The first chapter in Nelson Goodman, *Ways of Worldmaking* (Indianapolis: Hackett, 1979).

5. Goodman's reply to talks by myself and Scheffler is reprinted, titled "Starmaking," in his *On Mind and Other Matters* (Cambridge, Mass.: Harvard University Press, 1984), pp. 39–44. Unfortunately, the printed version leaves out the Big Dipper example. My talk, "Reflections on Goodman's *Ways of Worldmaking*," is

reprinted in my *Realism with a Human Face* (Cambridge, Mass.: Harvard University Press, 1990); Scheffler's talk appears in *Synthese* 45 (1980):201–209, with a reply by Goodman, pp. 211–215.

6. This form of the objection is from Avishai Margalit (in conversation).

7. Water, for example, is not really just H_2O: real water always contains H_4O_2, H_6O_3 ... as well as D_2O, D_4O_2, D_6O_3 ... as well as superpositions (in the quantum mechanical sense) of all of the foregoing. Suppose one had a bowl full of H_4O_2; would it be a bowl of *water*?

8. Indeed, elementary particles may not even be *relativistically invariant*. On this, see P. C. W. Davies, "Elementary Particles Do Not Exist," in *Quantum Theory of Gravitation*, ed. Steven M. Christensen (London: Adam Helger Ltd., 1984).

9. Note to fans of possible-worlds semantics: when I say that our linguistic practices made him Joe Ullian, I am using "Joe Ullian" non-rigidly (it is to indicate this that I put quotation marks around "Joe Ullian" in the text). The "rigid" use is not relevant here; speaking in terms of rigid designation, one cannot even say that our linguistic practices made the Big Dipper the Big Dipper.

10. See "Lecture One: Is There Still Anything to Say About Reality and Truth," in *The Many Faces of Realism* (LaSalle, Ind.: Open Court, 1985); "A Defense of Internal Realism" and "Truth and Convention," in *Realism with a Human Face*.

11. I say "concrete" because those who take this view sometimes refer to space-time as the "matter" of which everything is made, and think of the space-time points as the ultimate "atoms" of which this matter consists.

12. That points in space are "mere limits" was the view of Kant in the *Critique of Pure Reason* (see the Second Antinomy).

13. The idea that points in space are mere limits can be formalized by identifying points with *equivalence classes of convergent series of spheres*. A series of spheres is convergent if (1) each sphere (except the first) is contained in the preceding sphere; and (2) the radius of the i-th sphere approaches 0 as *i* increases without limit. Two series are *equivalent* if any sphere in either series contains all the spheres after the i-th, for some *i*, in the other. This way of formalizing Kant's intuitive idea is due to Whitehead, in Whitehead and Russell's *Principia Mathematica*.

14. Davidson, "The Very Idea of a Conceptual Scheme," in his *Inquiries into Truth and Interpretation* (Oxford: Oxford University Press, 1985). This does not mention Goodman by name, but Quine's review of Goodman's *Fact, Fiction and Forecast*, in *Theories and Things*, (Cambridge, Mass.: Harvard University Press, 1981) takes a similar line. See also Quine's reference to Davidson in his rejection of conceptual relativism (which he refers to as "the ecumenical point of view") in "Reply to Roger F. Gibson, Jr.," in *The Philosophy of W. V. Quine*, ed. L. Hahn and P. A. Schilpp (LaSalle, Ind.: Open Court, 1986), pp. 155–157.

15. See Quine, "Things and Their Place in Theories," in *Theories and Things*, esp. pp. 21–22.

16. For an analysis of the notion of equivalence involved, see "Equivalence" in my *Philosophical Papers*, vol. 3; *Realism and Reason* (Cambridge: Cambridge University Press, 1983).

17. See Goodman, *The Structure of Appearance* (Dordrecht: Reidel, 1977), first published in 1951.

18. The fact that we cannot say that a sentence in the one version has the same "meaning" as either (1) its "translation" into the other version, or (2) the sentence with the very same spelling in the other version, does not mean we are stuck with just saying that the two versions are *incommensurable*. Rather it is that we *treat* a sentence and its "translation" as if they had the same meaning, even though ordinary translation practice does not sanction doing so.

19. Taking points to be sets of *concentric* spheres is still another way of formalizing the idea that points are "mere limits." If one adopts this way, then "identity" of points has to be reinterpreted as *equivalence* in the sense proposed in note 13.

20. Speaking in this way about "correct descriptions of a situation" does not commit me to thinking of situations as having precise boundaries ("he stood roughly there" can be a perfectly good description of a situation), or to treating situations as the ultimate metaphysical realities. Situation-language is just one *more* way of talking that it is sometimes convenient to employ.

21. Derrida goes on to say "the word 'signifier' leads us back to or retains us in the logocentric circle . . . I have already told you what I think about the notion of the signifier. The same holds for the notions of *representation* and *subject*." *Positions,* ed. and annotated by Alan Bass (Chicago: University of Chicago Press, 1981), pp. 82–83.

22. See my "A Defense of Internal Realism," in *Realism with a Human Face*.

23. *A Course in General Linguistics* (first published in 1916), translated and annotated by Roy Harris (LaSalle, Ind.: Open Court, 1986), with the original pagination indicated in the margins.

24. In *Positions*, pp. 15–36.

25. Derrida is here quoting from Saussure's *Cours de linguistique generale,* p. 145.

26. Derrida is quoting from ibid., p. 164.

27. Note that in French semiology the "signified" is the sense, or intension of the signifier, not its extension. Derrida is saying that in translation we speak as if there were a "meaning" that two different signs could share.

28. I don't, of course, mean to suggest any causal influence here. Derrida's position was worked out long before Goodman turned "irrealist."

29. *Ways of Worldmaking*, pp. 139–140.

30. One reason this is a misinterpretation is that Derrida himself stresses that the logocentric predicament is not a "pathology" for which he is offering us a cure; it is rather, a predicament we are fated to be in. See *De la grammatologie* (Paris:

Editions de Minuit, 1967). At the same time, however, notions that "retain us in" the logocentric predicament are spoken of as having "collapsed," as we saw above.

31. Derrida, "The Principle of Reason: The University in the Eyes of Its Pupils," *Diacritics* 13 (1983):44.

32. *The Ear of the Other,* trans. Christie V. McDonald (New York: Schocken Books, 1985), pp. 23–24.

33. "Serious Play: The Ethical-Political Horizon of Jacques Derrida," *The Journal of Speculative Philosophy* 1:2 (1987):93–117. The quotation is from p. 111.

VI

Beyond Realism and Anti-Realism

15

Comments

Nelson Goodman

Peter McCormick's pointed selection of papers by some of the writers most attentive to my work focuses on irrealism. I first introduced the term "irrealism" into my work rather diffidently in the foreword to *Ways of Worldmaking* (Hackett, 1978):[1]

Few familiar philosophical labels fit comfortably a book that is at odds with rationalism and empiricism alike, with materialism and idealism and dualism, with essentialism and existentialism, with mechanism and vitalism, with mysticism and scientism, and with most other ardent doctrines. What emerges can perhaps be described as a radical relativism under rigorous restraints, that eventuates in something akin to irrealism.

In *Of Mind and Other Matters* (Harvard, 1984) I add that "I am a relativist who nevertheless maintains that there is a distinction between right and wrong among theories, interpretations, and works of art," and that I am an anti-realist and an anti-idealist—hence an irrealist.

15.1   On Putnam's Papers (chaps. 2, 6, and 14)

Realism and idealism disagree over what is admissible in the foundation of the unique correct description of the world. Irrealism dismisses the issue, denying that there can be any such unique version. When Hilary Putnam writes (in chap. 6 above):

Goodman's two big points still hold: all species of reduction and ontological identification involve posits, legislation, non-uniqueness; and there are both different kinds of reduction and different directions of reduction. If all versions can be reduced in one way to a physicalist version . . . in principle. . . , then they can all be reduced to a phenomenalist version in another way . . . in principle, he seems clearly to understand and go along with irrealism. And this is confirmed by much else he writes in this volume examining irrealism and defending it against mistaken objections. But then in the midst of all this, we are suddenly taken aback when Putnam describes my philosophy (in chap. 14 above) as "springing full-blown within contemporary analytic philosophy, a form of idealism as extreme as Hegel's or Fichte's!"[2] apparently forgetting that my irrealism rejects idealism as decisively as it rejects realism. According to my usage of these terms, "realism" shuns all idealistic systems; "idealism" shuns all realistic systems; "irrealism" does not discriminate either way.

What has happened here is that Putnam, without warning or adequate explanation, has shifted to a usage of "idealism" different from mine. This altered usage does not distinguish idealism on the basis of what is admitted in the foundation of a constructional system; and no considered new criterion is supplied. Rather, the characterization of my philosophy as extreme idealism seems to be a negative reaction against some of what I write about the relationship between versions and worlds. After all, statements like "there is no unique right version or world"; "versions make worlds"; and "conflicting right versions are of different worlds if any"; are likely to strike the realistically minded thinker as hostile, and to provoke in return an indictment of my philosophy as "extreme idealism". But on two scores, I plead "not guilty". In the first place, I have not said that there are no worlds, but only that conflicting right versions are of different worlds if any. My nihilism and my pluralism are complementarily conditional; and that, I submit, has more the flavor of irrealism than of idealism. In the second place, I do not see why even saying that there are no worlds but only versions would be idealistic, for I do not think of versions, verbal or pictorial, as mental or as being or in general referring to ideas or Ideas, but as objects functioning as symbols.

Putnam's three-chapter contribution to this book, based on years of study of most of my writings, is friendly, searching and informed. It is also rather cruelly complex, touching on a profusion of topics, including some troublesome basic philosophical problems, using some new technical terminology, and exploring works of other philosophers for comparison with mine. Moreover, the difficulties for a commentator on Putnam's text are aggravated by a pervasive ambivalence, already noticed above and not unexpected from a long-devoted realistically minded thinker who finds himself attracted and threatened by irrealism.

This ambivalence flickers through the text and eventually erupts into a desperate struggle toward a resolution. Early and frequent talk of two kinds of realism plays a prominent role, sometimes clarifying, sometimes confusing. He writes:

> The key to working out the program of preserving commonsense realism while avoiding the absurdities and antinomies of metaphysical realism in all its familiar varieties (Brand X: Materialism; Brand Y: Subjective Idealism; Brand Z: Dualism. . . . . . .) is something I have called *internal realism* (I should have called it pragmatic realism!) Internal realism is . . . a view that takes our familiar commonsense scheme, as well as our scientific and artistic and other schemes, at face value, without helping itself to the notion of the thing 'in itself'.

A little later, he characterizes *metaphysical* realism as arguing over senseless questions about which among correct conflicting versions describe the world in itself independent of all versions.

Internal realism does have a link with irrealism: both look askance at talk of 'the unique world'. But the two are still far apart, for irrealism can by no means brook any acceptance of commonsense at face value but at most as only presystematic[3] discourse urgently requiring critical examination and organization into well-made versions. Whether for this or other good reasons, Putnam seems not wholly satisfied with commonsense realism. Without finally dropping it, he sets forth on a different tortuous and devious search for a sturdier and more resounding realism.

His first thought toward this is a bold one: a frontal attack on the tattered, ill-conceived, and insoluble, but still much-agitated, problem of distinguishing natural from conventional (or genuine from artificial, or discovered from contrived, or . . .) kinds. But he soon defaults on this task, writing: "Natural kinds, when we examine them, almost always turn out to have boundaries which are to some degree arbitrary"; and then, forgoing any attempt to draw a categorical distinction, confines himself to some rather vague talk of kinds that are more or less strongly natural or conventional than others. Passing thought of a somewhat related hope for access to the unique real world is quickly rejected as a chimera: "Our language cannot be divided up into two parts, a part that describes the world 'as it is anyway' and a part that describes our conceptual contribution" (chap. 14).

I shall have to leave the reader to trace a way through the rest of these involuted, close-packed pages. They range from some emphatic realistic thoughts, such as "very *different* sentences can describe the very same state of affairs"; and

"Consider a given physical system which the physicist represents twice over, once in the language of fields and once in the language of particles. . . . that the real system allows itself to be talked about in these two very different ways does not mean either that there is no real physical system being talked about, or that there are two . . . in different Goodmanian worlds . . . It is absolutely clear, it seems to me, that the two descriptions are descriptions of *one and the same world*";

to side studies and digressions (on meaning, apparent and actual conflict, linguistics), and comparisons with other authors (Rorty, Derrida, Carnap, B. Williams, Saussure, Kuhn, Fodor, Feynman). All this serves as basis for Putnam's appraisal of the argument for my views. My argument does, he says, destroy one traditional version of "realism", the version he calls metaphysical realism—the myth of the ready-made world.

And his final sentence here is a hearty endorsement of irrealism: "And deconstruction without reconstruction is irresponsibility."

Notes (for Putnam)

1. Although the principles and attitude of irrealism were already evident in my earliest philosophical writing, not only in *The Structure of Appearance* (1951) but even in *A Study of Qualities* (1940, but not published until 1990), and in unpublished studies during the preceding decade. Lately, I have more often called the same complex of views "constructionalism".

2. This is not a momentary aberration but is almost verbatim Putnam's first reaction when I told him of proposed theses in my then forthcoming *Ways of Worldmaking* (1978).

3. On "presystematic discourse" as a background for construction of systems, see *A Study of Qualities*. I do not share Putnam's affection for common sense. It has no sharp or stable boundaries, and is often at odds with itself. In such cases, does "common sense" call for "taking it at face-value" or for demanding consistency?

15.2 On Hempel's Paper (chap. 7)

Carl Hempel's clear and authoritative account of Neurath's ideas in comparison with mine is a valuable document. It was through Hempel that I first heard of Neurath's work, but I have not had before such an explicit critical and comparative statement.

Hempel points out that Neurath and I share some views central to my philosophy: that we cannot test a version by directly comparing it with a world undescribed, that versions are never confronted with unconceptualized experience or anything but other versions, and that new versions are made from old ones. And along with Popper, we regard all versions as subject to revision or rejection. Nothing is given, mandatory; there are no fixed foundations, no privileged sacrosanct 'protocol' versions. Neurath and I both shy away from metaphysical talk of Reality, The World, The Facts. On the other hand, his ruling out as nonempirical all versions not in the language of physics has no counterpart in my impartial irrealism.

If we stop here, the most prominent feature common to Neurath's views and mine seems to be what they lack. If we cannot establish any version by access to something beyond versions, and if no version by itself stands supreme over all competitors, what decides between alternative versions, especially conflicting ones? Hempel focuses his own critical remarks on this question. He wants either some firm anchor for proof or, for choice among versions, a criterion that carries some guarantee or grounded expectation that applying it will yield decisions in accord with the way the world is. Neurath, so far as I know (and this is an important difference between us) has concerned himself very little with the question, while I have devoted a good deal of study to rightness of choice among alternative versions. This has involved considering nonverbal versions, rightness of categories, the fitting and working together of items other than beliefs, and much more. What is sought is not a simple overall definition of rightness, but a pluralistic treatment that allows rightness to have species, to vary with context, and sometimes to be graded or comparative. Entrenchment, simplicity, convenience are often highly relevant. This study will not now or ever satisfy Hempel's demands. It provides no warrants or assurance, no starting points or hitching posts. It will tell us no more than how worlds are made.

One minor point. Hempel suggests that taking the pulse beat of the Dalai Lama to determine the temporal order and duration of events is blocked by being out of whack with the way the world runs. Actually it is a good example of how some proposals fail to fit and work easily and well with our familiar versions of time.

15.3   On Scheffler's Papers (chaps. 3, 8, 11, and 13)

Here, after some preliminary clarification, I want to review briefly what most needs to be remembered about versions and worlds and the relations between them, and then examine what Israel Scheffler stresses as the main issue between us.

Order

My selection of an example to illustrate ordering as a way of worldmaking was inapt; for rearranging a pack of cards is a case of physical reordering, while the question under consideration was rather of reordering by version. Let me take instead the case of two or more orderings of the cards (with no physical movement required) according to their point values in different games. Such disagreeing versions are of different worlds, if any.

By way of contrast, consider two versions of the Battle of Bull Run: one, a day-to-day log by a staff clerk; the other, a later story of the battle, reciting the same events and as occurring in the same order but telling the story in the reverse order, working from the end to the beginning. The same story is told in the two versions, but the tellings are in opposite order. There is no conflict here. The tellings are different; what is told is the same.

Time

When I first read Scheffler's "Time" (13.5) I was shocked, for he seemed to be denying the relativity of time and challenging me to give details of some 'fantastic' version temporally disagreeing with *the* absolute fixed order of time. But after another reading of my own text (see section 12.3 above) I realized that the fault was partly mine. As the result of trying to deal with two matters at once, my exposition was compressed and tangled enough to confuse many a reader. The best course now is to consider section 12.3 eliminated. The first of the jobs it was supposed to do— to illustrate temporal relativity—is easily accomplished: Consider three past stellar explosions at different distances from the earth, and two correct versions of their temporal order. In version K, the three are ordered according to precedence of their occurrence in astronomical time; in version L, they are ordered according to precedence of their appearance or perception on earth. Depending on the particular events chosen and details of K and L, if the ordering by K is a, b, c, the ordering of L may be the reverse or the same or any other including simultaneity. Since K and L are by specification both true, they are of different worlds if they conflict. And neither is the universally elect version. They provide different information and are right under different circumstances. To such a question, "When was the latest of the three explosions?," K may say "One million years ago," while L says "Yesterday." Even if both are speaking of the same explosion a, their answers respond to different interests and needs.

The second job that was to have been done by the now-cancelled section 12.3 was to deal with questions like "How can a version be said to make what existed only long before the version itself?" I shall leave this until later.

The Main Issue

Scheffler goes much further than most of my critics in accepting key and unpopular principles of constructionalism. He does not object to my conditional pluralism or to my recognition that there are conflicting right versions, but he draws the line at my saying that right versions make worlds or are worldmakers.

First, we should be clear that I do not say that a version makes a world out of nothing, or entirely by itself under all circumstances. The making is mostly remaking and may involve the participation of other means and the presence of other conditions.[4] None of this makes calling versions "worldmakers" inappropriate any more than parallel reservations disqualify such terms as "shoemaker", "cabinetmaker", "coffee-maker", or, for that matter, "homemaker" or "peacemaker". Nevertheless, Scheffler persists in his objection; argument for it incorporates an imaginary dialogue (section 13.7) proposed to replace mine in section 12.2.

I take serious exception to most of the responses in the dialogue that are implicitly or explicitly charged to me. I number the extracts below for easy reference:

i.   "The Big Dipper was made by our adopted world version."

ii.   "You mean, I suppose, that this version contains the applicable term, 'Big Dipper'."

iii.   "Yes."

iv.   "And does the containing of that term imply that our version actually made the Big Dipper itself?"

v.   "Exactly. As Goodman has said, 'We make worlds by making versions'."

In (i)–(v), I am supposed to be assenting to the absurd proposition that if a statement contains in any way a term that normally denotes so-and-so's, that statement is about so-and-so's. But obviously many a locution is such that a statement containing the term only in that way is not about so-and-so's.

Moreover, by no means all the predicates in a version participate in worldmaking. We must carefully distinguish from all the rest those that the version attributes, or ascribes, or imputes[5] to what it is about (from, for example, predicates belonging to the version itself). While in general these two classes will be disjoint, we may note in passing that in some cases a feature (say *shortness*) of a version may also be imputed to something in the world of that version, and also that if a version imputes a feature to its world, the version itself has the feature of so imputing that feature. But what matters most concerning versions is picking out the features it imputes.

vi.   "Does the containing of the term 'Don Quixote' in an adopted version similarly imply that the version actually made Don Quixote?"

vii.   "Of course not. As Goodman has written, 'Painted or written portrayals of Don Quixote . . . do not denote Don Quixote—who is simply not there to be denoted'."

In (vi) and (vii) I am being reminded needlessly that some versions make no world because they are false. The sentence quoted in (vii) does come from *Ways of Worldmaking,* but is used here for a purpose totally different from that in the book. Here it is used to give an example showing that not all versions make actual worlds. In *Ways of Worldmaking,* the sentence is used to set a problem: how to reconcile confident and important fictional discourse with its falsity? That problem is a major topic not only in the section of *Ways of Worldmaking* (vi, 5), where the Don Quixote sentence appears, but in the whole book. Treatment of the problem is based on the recognition that what is literally false may be metaphorically true. Although *Hamlet* is fiction, Hamlet is as plainly Danish and not Egyptian as Churchill is English and not Eskimo. Judgments of rightness of fictional and factual statements have much in common with each other. Moreover, the distinction between imputed and nonimputed features is unaffected by whether a version is fictional or factual; the imputation is an open one, to whatever if anything actual or fictive the version may be about.

Versions and What Else?

We can skip now to the end of the imaginary dialogue:

> Then our Big Dipper version did not make it happen that the Big Dipper in fact exists—that it is *there* to be denoted. Our version did not, after all, make the Big Dipper.

Briefly and more generally, Scheffler is arguing that we should not say that versions make worlds, since we cannot, merely by producing a version, bring into being something that answers to it. *What* a world is but not *that* it is may be dependent on versions. Scheffler wisely stops short of asking: on what?, then?, where from?, and how? He does not appeal to Nature or a Deity, or offer any other account. His view seems to come to this: "A version cannot make a world; something else is needed. The needed auxiliary, quite independent of all versions, must be bare facts ('states of affairs', 'situations', etc.); that is, belong to the world itself." So what is needed to make a world is a version plus its world. This, of course, is utterly unsatisfactory. And the argument for it has gone astray in several ways.

On Some Confusions

The first mistake has been too quick and broad generalization from too few and insufficiently varied examples. I have never held that every version makes a world, only that some do. Thus, to cite some versions that make no commitment to the existence of anything is no counterargument; other more crucial cases have to be looked at. Take the case of conflicting versions of the motion of a certain body *B* in space. According to one, *B* rotates continuously; according to another, *B* never moves (and there are many other versions, all of them equally true and all conflicting with each other). Choice among them has to be on grounds other than truth—that is, on relevant rightness. In a very clear sense, the motion or rest is made by the version chosen on each occasion. No two can be true of *B* at once; the conjunction, being inconsistent, applies to nothing; separate applications replace *B* by two objects from different worlds.

Frequent further trouble in the argument that led us astray arises from misidentification of the versions involved in cases under consideration and from some inattention to logical principles. When we are comparing versions, we focus on differences between them and ignore their common part. For two versions of object *B*:

(V) "*B* always rotates."
(V′) "*B* never moves."

we sometimes for convenience use the abbreviations: "always rotates" and "never moves" as temporary stand-ins for *V* and *V′*. But we must guard against identifying these extractions with versions, for that would beg the whole question we have been debating. These extracted predicates are not statements,[6] not true or false, do not by themselves conflict, and carry no existential commitment. The conflict is between *V* and *V′*, that impute both predicates to *B*. The mention of *B* in these versions is by no means a negligible matter, for such mention, excluded from the extracts, is just what carries existential commitment; *V* for example, expanded according to the familiar logic of description, becomes

"There is something such that it is (or is identical with) *B*, and that always rotates."
or
in symbols, "$(\exists x.Bx \text{ (or } X=B). Rx$"

Scheffler's contention can thus be definitely dismissed. Worlds are version dependent (that is, vary with different versions) with respect not only to *what* they are but also to *that* they are. The answer to the question, "Versions and What Else?" is "Nothing." The nonversional auxiliary, thought to be needed, is all encompassed within the versions.

Such version dependence does not imply that versions make their worlds but only that they have worlds answering to them. The question I have postponed so often will now be pressed again: "How can a version make something that existed only long before the version itself?" Often declaimed as if it were plainly unanswerable and devastating, the question raises no special difficulty. Notice first that parallel questions such as "How can a version make something far away from it?" seem to give us no concern, and so also for simpler commonplaces such as a flat version of a solid object, a black-and-white version of a multicolored object; we do not insist that a version of a green lawn be green, or that a drawing of moving hockey players must move. No principle requires that features imputed to a world be features of the version. Why be disturbed, then, by a present version imputing a past temporal location to an event?

Take one more example. On a clear night in Cambridge in April, look at the section of the sky where body *B* shines in the center, and write a description of the lights showing there. Call that version *D*. Now take from a recent astronomical textbook a description of *B*; call that version *T*. It tells the size, distance, motion, temperature, and composition of *B*, and says that *B* was formed one million years ago and was destroyed some centuries later, but that light from it will continue to reach earth until after the year 2000. So version *T*, not available until the present century, puts the life of *B* in the far past; while for *D*, *B* still sparkles. *T* is typical of versions that distribute things over time and space, and in doing so make the time and space. This is done in all historical and much other discourse without disquieting the philosopher.

Notes (for Scheffler)

4. See further below.

5. Words like "ascribes", "describes", and "attributes" seem suitable only for versions that are statements, as are all the versions used and cited in this chapter. But I am concerned with the development of a general theory of symbols, covering also versions that are not statements, and even not verbal. To keep this in mind, I often adopt for technical use the less familiar term "imputes".

6. What I say here applies to the versions involved in the discussion above, but not to all versions under the general theory of symbols; some of these are not statements or even verbal.

Index

Physicalism, 107, 109–110, 113, 126–127
Picasso, Pablo, 7, 72
Pictures, 6
Picturing, 8, 9
Piero della Francesca, 68
Pluralism, xvi, 5, 117, 151–153, 180
Polish Rider, The, 118
Popper, Karl, 128–129
Predicates
  entrenched, 93
  projectible, 91–93
Projectibility, 92, 98, 99
Properties, xviii, 65
  analytic and synthetic, 4
  dispositional, 13, 15
  intrinsic, 15, 16, 18
  non-dispositional, 13
  "real," 13
Propositional attitudes, 20, 22, 26

Qualities, xviii, 4
Quine, Willard, 26, 53, 55, 117, 121, 128, 184, 192

Raphael, 101
"Real," xviii
Realism, 11, 204–205
  commonsense realism, 12
  degrees of, 6
  internal, 23, 205
  metaphysical, 22, 24, 206
  pragmatic, 23
  scientific, xvii, xix, 12
Realist, xii, xvii, xviii
Reality
  as relative, 74–75
  as unconceptualized, 115
"Reduction," 109–110, 115
Reference, xiv, xv, 55
  vs. acceptance, 33
  extra-linguistic, 50
  frames of, 62
  partial, 116
  of statements, 33
Relativism, xvi, 23, 143, 161

Relativity, conceptual, 23, 24
  significance of, 187–190
Rembrandt, 68, 118
Rendering, 79
Repetition, 67
Representation, 94–96
"Right," 120–121
Rightness, xv, 74, 79, 100–102, 119–122
  of abstract works, 96
  of categorization, 92, 100, 157–158
  criteria of, 88
  deductive, 91
  inductive, 91
  moral, 122
  of samples, 97
  systems, 95
Rouault, Georges, 68
Rorty, Richard, 22, 185
Russell, Bertrand, 50, 55

Samples, 96–100
Saussure, Ferdinand, 191–193
Schlick, Moritz, xvii, 30, 38–49
Science, xviii, 4
Seeing, 8
Sellars, Wilfrid, 11, 20
Sense data, xviii, 14, 109
Seurat, Georges, 101
Sharaku, 7
Soutine, Chaim, 95–96
Standards, 194–195
"Star," 163
Stars, 138–139, 144–145
  and constellations, 156, 163–164, 166–167, 175–176, 181–184, 210
State of affairs, 185
Statements, factual and fictional, 210
Sturgis, Katharine, 70
"Substance," 20, 21
Symbols, 61, 64
  theory of, 94

Tarski, Alfred, 8, 55, 72
Things, 155–157, 164
Time, 165, 167, 174, 208–209